The Canada–US Border

Critical Insights in American Studies
Series editors: Martin Halliwell and Joe Street

Recent books in the series:
American Imperialism: The Territorial Expansion of the United States, 1783–2013
Adam Burns

The Open Door Era: United States Foreign Policy in the Twentieth Century
Michael Patrick Cullinane and Alex Goodall

Black Nationalism in American History: From the Nineteenth Century to the Million Man March
Mark Newman

The American Photo-Text, 1930–1960
Caroline Blinder

The Beats: Authorships, Legacies
A. Robert Lee

The Classical Tradition and Modern American Fiction
Tessa Roynon

The US Graphic Novel
Paul Williams

The Canada–US Border: Culture and Theory
David Stirrup and Jeffrey Orr

Forthcoming
American Detective Fiction
Ruth Hawthorn

Staging Transatlantic Relations, 1776–1917
Theresa Saxon

American Poetry since 1900
Nick Selby

The Culture and Politics of Contemporary US Prison Narratives
Josephine Metcalf

The Modern Black Press in America
James West

The Canada–US Border

Culture and Theory

Edited by
DAVID STIRRUP AND JEFFREY ORR

EDINBURGH
University Press

Edinburgh University Press is one of the leading university presses in the UK. We publish academic books and journals in our selected subject areas across the humanities and social sciences, combining cutting-edge scholarship with high editorial and production values to produce academic works of lasting importance. For more information visit our website: edinburghuniversitypress.com

© editorial matter and organisation David Stirrup and Jeffrey Orr 2024
© the chapters their several authors 2024

Published with the support of the University of Edinburgh Scholarly Publishing Initiatives Fund.

Edinburgh University Press Ltd
The Tun – Holyrood Road
12(2f) Jackson's Entry
Edinburgh EH8 8PJ

Typeset in 10/12pt Adobe Sabon Pro
by Cheshire Typesetting Ltd, Cuddington, Cheshire

A CIP record for this book is available from the British Library

ISBN 978 1 4744 5328 8 (hardback)
ISBN 978 1 4744 5329 5 (paperback)
ISBN 978 1 4744 5330 1 (webready PDF)
ISBN 978 1 4744 5331 8 (epub)

The right of David Stirrup and Jeffrey Orr to be identified as the editor of this work has been asserted in accordance with the Copyright, Designs and Patents Act 1988, and the Copyright and Related Rights Regulations 2003 (SI No. 2498).

Contents

List of Illustrations vii
Acknowledgements viii
Series Editors' Preface ix

Introduction: Borderline Considerations, Conditions, Constructions and Contradictions 1
Jeffrey Orr and David Stirrup

1. Getting Played: Confession, Identity and *Border Security* 29
   Jeffrey Orr

2. Border Media: Contributions to a Non-Linear History of the Detroit River 52
   Vincent Manzerolle

3. Comparing Twin Towns along the US Southern and Northern Borders: A Historical Review 83
   Pierre-Alexandre Beylier

4. Continental Liberty, Natural Reason, *Survivance*: Gerald Vizenor's Sojourning in the Borderlands 114
   Chris LaLonde

5. The Logics of Border Theory: Negotiating Sovereignties at the Impasse 131
   David Stirrup

6. Grit and Grief: Wayde Compton's *49th Parallel Psalm* as borderblur elegy 158
   Tanis MacDonald

7. Border Hypotheses: Speculations on Territory and Sovereignty in Wayde Compton's *The Outer Harbour* 174
   Gillian Roberts

8. Afterword: Naming, Knowing and Negotiating Third
   Spaces of the Border 195
   Victor Konrad

   Chronology of the Canada–US Border 216
   Author Biographies 241
   Index 244

Illustrations

Figures

2.1	Map of Essex County *c.* 1930	55
2.2	Map and plan of Fort Pontchartrain in 1764	58
2.3	Postcard of CPR rail car ferry and dock, Windsor, Canada, *c.* 1916	68
2.4	Postcard of Detroit River Tunnel, Detroit, *c.* 1915	70
2.5	Postcard of the 'New' Michigan Central Station *c.* 1936	70
2.6	Ambassador Bridge looking north towards Detroit, January 2016. Photo by James Pineau	71
2.7	Michigan Central Station, February 2016. Photo by James Pineau	72
2.8	Conceptual design for the proposed Gordie Howe International Bridge and customs plaza. Image courtesy of the Windsor-Detroit Bridge Authority	73
3.1	The major twin cities along the Mexico–US border	98
3.2	Selected twin cities along the Canada–US border	101

Tables

1.1	Possible outcomes of border encounters on *Border Security: Canada's Front Line*	40
3.1	Twin cities with over 10,000 inhabitants along the Mexico–US border	99
3.2	Population of twin cities with over 10,000 people along the Canada–US border	102

Acknowledgements

This book has been a very long time in the making. Particular thanks are due to the principal investigators of the Culture and the Canada–US Border (CCUSB) network, David Stirrup and Gillian Roberts, whose perspective, depth and intellectual insight have redefined the approach to a previously overlooked aspect of border studies. That work would not have been possible without the generous support of the Leverhulme Trust. Thanks too are due to the steering committee of the CCUSB project, Jeffrey Orr, Munroe Eagles, Kelly Hewson, Lee Easton and Jan Clarke, and to the contributors to this book, including Matt Krause, whose work as a student researcher was central to the development of the section on the Chronology of the Border. This project would not have got off the ground without the work of Zalfa Feghali, to whom we owe more than just gratitude. Finally, Jeff's work would not have been possible without the constant love and support of his wife Suzanne, and the joyful company of their children, Saoirse and Cormac. David, in turn, owes eternal thanks to the love and patience of Jo, Florence and Ottilie.

Series Editors' Preface

Marking twenty-five years since Edinburgh University Press published the first titles in the BAAS Paperbacks series, we are extremely pleased to relaunch the series as Critical Insights in American Studies, in conjunction with the British Association for American Studies.

Over the last quarter-century, American Studies, as an interdisciplinary field of research and teaching, has undergone multiple transformations. Not only have we witnessed the study of the history, literature, politics and culture of the United States being expanded through transatlantic, transpacific and transnational perspectives, but scholars have probed deeper into critical interpretations of micro-histories, regional literatures, grassroots politics and cultural industries. As we approach the second quarter of the twenty-first century, we see American Studies being again reinvigorated by crucial debates on race and diversity, war and memorialisation, the environment and the economy, and digital and social media, among many other directions in the arts, humanities and social sciences.

Predicated on the belief that an interdisciplinary approach offers surprising, challenging and thought-provoking insights, this series introduces readers to leading-edge enquiries into all aspects of the Americas, reaching back to the colonial period and stretching forward to tackle present-day concerns in and beyond the United States. Each book in the series is designed to offer both a rigorous examination of its topic that will satisfy the most demanding reader within an accessible and readable narrative, ideal for undergraduates and postgraduates seeking imaginative American Studies approaches to important and intersecting topics.

We are very privileged to launch this new chapter in collaborations between Edinburgh University Press and the British Association for American Studies. It is also our privilege to work with the talented authors who will propel the Critical Insights in

American Studies series into the next quarter-century of debate and analysis.

Martin Halliwell and Joe Street
University of Leicester and Northumbria University

Introduction: Borderline Considerations, Conditions, Constructions and Contradictions

Jeffrey Orr and David Stirrup

By now, the assertion that border studies is most closely associated with the Mexico–US borderlands is not just a given but a tired cliché. That a volume of essays on the Canada–US border might justifiably open with a reminder of that, however, serves to emphasise the fact that, while other border sites have come under greater scrutiny in the most recent iterations of border studies' development, they remain undertheorised and largely absent in site-specific terms from the arc of border theory itself. As Gillian Roberts notes in her introduction to *Reading Between the Borderlines*, in 'cultural theory and cultural production, the Mexico–US borderland has been theorized as a site conducive to cultural hybridity and transgressive cultural performance and practice'.[1] Ila Nicole Sheren, meanwhile, notes that 'border thinking' is 'a mostly US phenomenon'.[2] Where border theory wrestles free of its bindings, it becomes, in the words of Sheren and the artists and thinkers she draws on, 'portable', a means of understanding a 'state of mind as well as the boundary between nations', namely 'the mental state of the permanent outsider'.[3]

This border thinking, as Sheren puts it, is expanded in a border mentality, which 'sees the entire world as consisting as layers of borders', making it 'impossible to determine who (or what) is outside versus inside'.[4] Here, we are all 'border subjects, constantly engaged in the act of obeying, crossing, or transgressing established lines'.[5] The abstract – 'border/lands theory' or 'border discourse' – derives from the concrete: the site-specific art of the Mexico–US borderlands. It is rendered 'available', in turn, when applied to other sites and spaces. The result, richly textured though it is, frequently draws from conditions and traditions that are not necessarily stable across all categories and all borders; more to the point, in the abstractions of the latter, we often lose the specificities of the former. In the transposition, in particular, of border thinking from the Mexico–US border to the Canada–US border, for instance, we lose many nuances of class, linguistic, ethnic, economic, historical and environmental difference. What place, then, does the Canada–US border site have in the sphere of border theory?

This repositioning is not entirely without precedent. The conceptual mutability of the border is perhaps best illustrated in one moment. Towards the end of the first decade of the twenty-first century, following much theoretical reflection on the post-9/11 era, the Canada–US border was presented as a potential model for future negotiations or formulations of borderlands by Canadian studies scholars while being all but symbolically erased by US-American scholars spearheading the short-lived 'hemispheric' turn in American Studies.[6] In other hemispheric moves, more resistant to the evasion of nation state logics, the borderlands have offered comparative possibility between border-spanning cultures in the Americas and between cultural production at the US's northern and southern boundaries.[7] For Indigenous scholars, the border has remained a zone of tension, both a site of strategic enunciation of sovereignty and an artificial fragment that divides and displaces.[8] More recently, meanwhile, the northern borderlands have been traversed alongside inveterate border-crossers to reframe both American Studies and Canadian cultural identity respectively.[9] In total, we have a selectively broad picture of recent book-length work beyond the social and political sciences in which the Canada–US border site figures as an object or tool for analysis.

Notwithstanding this level of critical production, much of the theoretical conversation that the Canada–US border has contributed to tends more broadly to reflect the conditions of the nation state and of citizenship within the nation state than the border more specifically or explicitly: the border as more metaphor than site. In that sense, at its most reductive, our understanding of Canada is as a kind of 'anti-US', defined as much by what it isn't – its neighbour to the south – as by what it is. The Canada–US borderlands in that context become a residual absence: a non-space for the American travelling north; a nebulous but symbolic, nation-defining space 'before the US' or 'still Canada' to the southbound Canadian. Beyond such broad brushstrokes, study of the Canada–US border has long been dominated by the political, environmental and social sciences, focused on questions of trafficking, border security and policing, and cross-border jurisdictional issues. Where the Mexico–US border is associated not only with its jurisdictional duty (most clearly embodied by talk – and construction – of walls, crossings and other infrastructure), but also with the art, literature and other philosophical-cultural material that lived experience on, around and over it produces, the Canada–US border is most commonly associated with its (misleading) status, certainly prior to 9/11, as the world's longest undefended border. Sections of the border, such as that length which separates Alaska from north-western Canada, barely figure in the wider imagination at all.

For Jack London, writing between the 1890s and 1910s, the Yukon existed as a new frontier of American expansion during a time of global US imperialism through which the receding and tamed frontier of the Wild West is relocated to the north. London figured the Alaska and Klondike borderlands as 'a single, unified territory whose undetermined borders and geopolitical location allow US adventurers unrestricted expansion'.[10] The Canadian Arctic held a romantic appeal to American expansionists, as a region they considered both geographically and cartographically blank. In this regard, the dynamics of the Northern gold rush repeated those of more southerly expansions, such as the Fraser River and the Cariboo in what is now British Columbia, where gold rushes led to conflicts between Indigenous land claims, Canadian nation state authority claims, and the mining claims of Canadian and American prospectors. For a region and a narrative body so concerned with the material specificities of borders in the matter of 'claim jumping' miners, the disregard for national and cultural territorial claims can seem especially jarring.[11] Erasing or disregarding the border in this manner is not an oversight or an accident, but rather, as Kollin notes, a narrative justification for US expansion, and a crucial staging ground for territorial struggles between Indigenous peoples, Russians, Canadians and (US) Americans.[12] The effectiveness of this approach can be partly gauged by Canadian historian Pierre Berton's reference to Dawson City, Yukon, as 'an American city on Canadian Soil' in the documentary film *City of Gold* a half-century later.[13] Obscured by this bi-national dispute are the voices of the

Indigenous people of the region. In the imagination and the instantiation, the Canada–US border often figures as a line in the forest, a weathered post in a field, or a ditch in the trees.

Where the border does figure in the wider public sphere, all too often it is for its quirkiness, although that quirkiness itself demands theorisation. A quick glance at contemporary media, for instance, will regularly return stories about the oddity of life in the pene-exclaves of the Northwest Angle, Minnesota, or the town of Point Roberts, Washington, where residents live in the US, but need to travel through Canada if they want to leave town for any other part of the States.[14] Alternatively, pick any number of stories about the Stewart, BC/Hyder, Alaska border and you can feast on articles that take a trite, small-town perspective on both international affairs and domestic politics. In Dan Levin's 2016 *New York Times* piece, 'An Alaskan Village where Grizzlies Roam and Canada Rules (if anyone does)', for example, the lead-in declares: 'If libertarians had an earthly paradise, it would probably be here in Hyder, Alaska', a small town 'wedged between two Canadian borders'.[15] This is not so much a tale of a border as it is a portrayal of carnival in the wilderness – where 'Interdependence Day' means a four-day party from Canada Day in Stewart on 1 July to Independence Day in Hyder on 4 July, and where one key distinction is that 'we're a little freer over here' on the Hyder side of the boundary, while the Canadian border station remains well staffed and vigilant for guns and contraband. It makes for a fascinating case study, undoubtedly, but it no more meaningfully represents the Canada–US borderlands, or the border-crossing experience, than any other tiny stretch.

Paradigms and Border Lines

The Canada–US border, nevertheless, provides a truly interesting paradigm. Separating two developed nation states, both settler-colonial in foundation but with very different apparatus of law and governance, the Canada–US border is also home to several other key distinctions. Not only do multiple Indigenous nations, 'domestic' and 'dependent' (descriptions imposed without consultation by US federal law), live within its borderlands, making them subject to the whims and boundary-drawing of the opposing colonial and settler-colonial powers that struck that line, but some among them also quite literally live astride the 'Medicine Line'.[16] The way the border figures in Indigenous legal and political struggles on and across this border, then, is highly uneven, its effects felt differently by different parts of the same communities. Where the borderlands to the south are home to what Gloria Anzaldúa describes as '*Los atravesados* ... the squint-eyed, the perverse, the queer, the troublesome, the mongrel, the mulatto, the half-breed, the half dead ... those who cross over, pass over, or go through the confines of the "normal"', meanwhile, it is worth remembering that close to 90 per cent of Canadians live within 100 miles of the US border.[17] In other words, here the 'borderlands' are nearly coterminous (in a population sense) with the nation state. Whilst Anzaldúa's sense of the borderlands – a 'vague and undetermined place created by the emotional residue of an unnatural boundary' – *may well* have resonance along long stretches of the US side of the 49th parallel, in Canada it has less purchase.[18] We italicise the phrase 'may well', too, because although the Canada–US borderlands frequently feature in the US imagination as just that kind of space, it is essential to remember those communities for whom the 'margins' are in fact 'centres'. The seemingly appropriately named Boundary Waters in northern Minnesota, for instance, forms a key part of the historical homelands of the Anishinaabeg. The twin cities of Sault Ste Marie, Ontario, and Sault Ste Marie, Michigan, although divided by the international border in the St Marys River, are Anishinaabe homelands in the heart of the wider fur trade territories; they remain so even as jurisdictional boundaries attempt to pull them apart. This tension between centres and margins among differentiated communities in Canada and the US becomes even more acute at Akwesasne, where Mohawk territories sit squarely on the borders separating Ontario, Quebec and New York. Echoing the labour movement's call further south, these communities do not cross the border: the border crosses them.[19] There is no refuge for *los atravesados* here, but home: *Nation*, for generations, sitting both inside and outside, both fugitive and transcendent to, the settler-state container. Kevin Bruyneel's notion of the third space of sovereignty is practically embodied in the transaction staged by every Indigenous border crossing, and amplified when said crossing occurs within the cadastral boundaries *or* the traditional range of that Indigenous nation's territories. Bruyneel notes, for instance, that the vision of Tuscarora Chief Clinton Rickard – the founder of the Indian Defense League – was of 'indigenous political space ... that overlapped the political spaces of the United States and Canada in a nonbinaristic way, as a postcolonial, inassimilable supplement to the colonial impositions of these settler-states'.[20] For Rickard, this edge was another centre – a defining marker at the core of Indigenous political struggle.

Its southern analogy is not the borderlands that Anzaldúa describes but the position in which the Tohono O'odham have found themselves, politically at least, since the settlement of the current Mexico–US border in the Treaty of Guadalupe-Hidalgo (1884). The discourse surrounding the impact of ex-US President Trump's border wall on the Tohono O'odham, whose territory straddles a 75-mile stretch of the border in the Sonoran desert – its de facto boundary in the absence of Mexican recognition – is redolent of Rickard's assertions. Such reminders are important precisely because for those Indigenous nations whose rights to cross are framed by late colonial and early Republic-era treaties such as the 1794 treaty commonly referred to as 'The Jay Treaty', the border is paradoxically most illusory *and* most obstructive. Its obstruction, in fact, inheres in its artifice for those peoples guaranteed the right to cross unimpeded – those 'Indians dwelling on either side of said boundary line'.[21] When those peoples are prevented from crossing freely, it is not only their rights as Canadian or US citizens (if, indeed, they have taken said citizenship) that are being both tested and performed but those of nations recognised as such under international law.[22] These are nations whose ancestral territories and attendant rights precede and transcend the much newer impositions of the settler states, which then render them transgressors within what is – theoretically at least, and literally at Akwesasne – their own jurisdiction. Where, as Thomas Nail emphasises, '[t]he border is "a process of social division"' in any scenario, in Indigenous contexts it enacts divisions that have profound legal, political and familial implications on top of those social/national ones, while detaching and ultimately alienating people from their land.[23]

Border theory as it has emanated from the Mexico–US border has tended to receive cool welcome further north, and particularly in Indigenous literary studies, where binarised debates around questions of hybridity and authenticity have been persistent – and, since the 'nationalist' turn of the late 1990s, fairly consistently rejected. Where figures like Anzaldúa's mestizo/a, for all their implicit power, dissolve cultural and political identities into new forms, these have tended to be seen as at odds both with the nationalist permutations of Indigenous literary studies and the wider sovereignties of Indigenous nationhood. While border theory's cultural realities often map on to contemporary Indigenous experience, in other words, its political, racialised, implications tend to blur rather than clarify what is at stake. The Canada–US border offers fertile ground for theorising this tension, as outlined above. Indeed, it is somewhat surprising that the presence of the Tohono O'odham 'on' the Mexico–US border has not prompted more thinkers to trouble some of border theory's assumptions. At the Canada–US border, however, both legal precedent and the larger volume of nations on or close to the border make experiences of Indigenous peoples within (and across) settler nations far harder to ignore. Bruyneel's third space of sovereignty proposes a model of overlapping sovereignties – a border theory that envisions and enables what can almost be described as a temporo-spatial collage of enmeshed borders.[24] Stuart Christie, meanwhile, proposes a framework of plural sovereignties in which individual agents deploy different sovereign attitudes depending on political, social or cultural context.[25] While Bruyneel approaches the subject from political science and Christie from literary studies, both centre their subjects jurisdictionally, foregrounding multiple frames of reference that remain more or less discrete even as they are interrupted and challenged by other frames – a distinctly different sense of the border than the cultural-political blend produced by older border theories.

From a geopolitical standpoint, that one further distinction is worth noting in this context, encapsulated by the notion of the Medicine Line, so designated during the Plains Wars, when fleeing warriors discovered that pursuing US soldiers would stop, suddenly, and retreat. An invisible, entirely artificial line in the sand (or rather, grass), the Medicine Line thus invokes a more complex sense of jurisdictional difference for Indigenous peoples that has gathered its own apocrypha. Although it was unsuccessful, Sitting Bull led his band of Húŋkpapȟa into Canada in 1877 – seeking refuge in the 'Grandmother's country' – in hope if not always in practice; they were eventually forced to return to the States. Nevertheless, the Canada–US border has represented precisely that demarcation between immediate danger and safety at numerous times since Canada and the US violently separated – from its role in the Underground Railroad to its appeal to Vietnam draft resisters. It carried that symbolic spirit every bit as much as its jurisdictional import at the beginning of 2020 when border blockades sprang up in support of Wet'suwet'en protests against pipelines on their lands – the latest in a long history of fighting for (and at) the line. In equivalent figurations of the Mexico–US and Canada–US borders and borderlands, it is striking the ways in which at the former both peoplehood and identity become malleable, shifting, while at the latter it is the border site itself that takes on multiple forms depending on political, legal and cultural contexts of crossing.

Terms and Conditions, Applied

The matter of theorising the Canada–US border requires a consideration of terms. Mark Salter's reconsideration of the '/' as a suture by which the border connects rather than divides is a useful counter to the seductive binary thinking into which border conceptions have often been drawn.[26] Patrick Lalonde's 2017 intervention regarding metaphors of the border and simulacra continues this work of reassessing the binaries, and draws attention to the numerous problems inherent in imagining the border as (and through) metaphor.[27] The questions of economics/identity, globalism/nationalism, localism/xenophobia, geographical/social, physical/emotional or ideational, historical/contemporary recurrently dominate discussions of the line that designates locations as either Canada or the United States.

Border metaphors and the power relationships they describe create absences or presences in the national discourse, either to fill them with the voices of power, or to silence the voices of those already there. The framing of nations by their borders elicits the question of who is left out of the frame, who the frame crosses or cuts, and what absences may be included, overlooked or buried beneath its structure. The material in this collection not only concerns itself with how the border is produced, developed, operated or lived through, but also with living the border as a door and a wall, a connection and a barrier – as 'a noisy hyphen', to adapt Chinese-Canadian poet Fred Wah's description of the borders traversed by his own identity.[28] Beyond Salter's reconsideration of the border as a suture or slash, Wah speaks of riding the hyphen whose ends connect the two parts of his identity – a border line more like a lifeline that binds them together. Beyond the hyphens of identities or the borderlines in rivers, lakes and trees, we must tread a careful linguistic line as well: the use of theory as a verb here (*theorising*) acknowledges the ongoing process and activity of creating, writing, imagining and engaging the border, but also the relationship between the border and the theory. Bordering the theory would perhaps be an apt (if unlovely) way of thinking through this process – the dangers of a book on theorising anything must certainly include the acts of abstraction and empty generalisation that risk erasure of key differences and specificities. Critical and unique experiences, geographies, infrastructures and identities have been frequently homogenised or appropriated to grand schemes and taxonomies in the name of academic theorisation. This volume tries to avoid these issues through an approach to the border that is specific, grounded and organic – the theory grows from, and is linked to, the specific realities of the Canada–US border.

The growth of infrastructure of control and exploitation around the border is an accretive process – gates make way for customs houses and border guards for airport scanners – but the growth of border theory here is, we hope, more vegetable than mineral in its metaphorical development. The historical development of the border, too, may be considered through these metaphors of process. The border is imagined, constructed and lived; in the doing it becomes both more and less real. Borders often start out as at least partially natural – elements such as rivers serve as easy means of demarcating boundaries in human territorial consciousness. Much of the border in central and eastern Canada is in fact water, a result of historical circumstances and the natural boundary-producing function of rivers, lakes and inlets (that side's yours and this side's mine). By contrast, the border in western Canada was, historically, conceptual, before it became geographical. The 49th parallel was the designated border before planners knew where it actually was on the ground, as demonstrated by the exclave of Point Roberts, or the 'Canadian' ghost town settlement of Molson in northeastern Washington State, while the Northwest Angle of northern Minnesota was the result of geographical ignorance enshrined in the Treaty of Paris (1783).[29] The Canada–US border, like many other international demarcations, is evidence on the ground of a series of political impositions, obscure negotiations between competing interests, and various calculations of money, power and identity.

The architecture of borders builds material, conceptual and geographical blind spots even as it facilitates corporate and governmental vision, surveillance and clarity. Once a border is imposed, we see through it, as the chain link fences and bollards of border infrastructure allow one to see the other side. We see imperfectly, however, in its existence at what Foucault called 'the fatal intersection of time and space'.[30] The promise of clarity from crossing over, to know and be known, is in this sense always deferred, as the border separates times and memories as well as places and people; one cannot cross the line back into the time before the border existed. The matter of lost or past borders is a recurrent theme in this collection. Chris LaLonde's work examines Gerald Vizenor's evocations of the fluid borderscapes of watery northern Minnesota; Roberts' work considers how borders of identity and geography are cast into the future through Wayde Compton's poetic reimagining of coastlines, territories and identities.

The making is not a binary term for opposition or definition – 'made' (or even 'made up') is not the opposite of 'real' nor of 'natural', nor even of 'imaginary' – for who would argue that ideas are not real? Rather, it gestures to the slow movement of power and habituation as the border is conceived and constructed; imposed and opposed; envisioned, institutionalised and interrogated. The poetic, academic and governmental metaphors that describe the border inevitably privilege some aspects or perspectives over others. These choices have consequences in government policy, in social relationships of fear or engagement, in economic integration, and in the development of community ties, individual identities and collective memory.

Another way to view the border is as a performance. The nation state asserts itself by contrast to its neighbour; here the theatre of interrogation, belonging, acceptance and rejection is enacted on the tiny stage of the border crossing, the airport, or the harbour. As the Canada–US border has begun to shift from the geographical to the electronic and from differentiation to integration, however, the infrastructural stages on which the border is performed, as well as the geographical anomalies that have defined and been defined by it, become less central to its work as a process. More recent consideration of the border has compared it to a filter or a firewall – either mechanical or digital technology of differentiation that enables the smooth exchange of goods and people acceptable to the state, while stopping those deemed undesirable.[31]

Binaries often either fall into, or indeed arise from, what Walters describes as 'a set of geographical assumptions that have combined to obscure the historicity and mutability of political space and territory'.[32] These assumptions overlap and often overlay the project of the nation state, masking the other perspectives on the border as an economic force, a security apparatus, or even as a risk management tool. The metaphors of a wall, a filter or a performance of national distinctiveness and strength can help us focus on specific aspects of border use.[33] During the Canada–US 'border closure' of the COVID-19 pandemic, for example, trade items were free to move, and flights were less strictly regulated than land crossings. Travel between Seattle and Vancouver meant, in effect, that the border closure was a strictly enforced reality for drivers, but a nominal one for flyers, who were able to travel during the land border closures in 2020 and 2021, according to the website of the US Embassy and Consulates in Canada. The border thus operated as a bio-economic filter, allowing and enabling the movement of trade goods and people with the economic power to fly, while restricting the movement of people whose economic circumstances required land travel – and more decisively curtailing localised networks of exchange and relationality.

The problem with the above metaphors for cultural theory examinations of the border is that they do not fully capture the dynamic and social aspects of the interactions at the border. Borders are not merely things; they are creative and constructive: they exist as structure and infrastructure, but their administrative implications, and the social relationships they shape, permit or forbid, define how the border is experienced. Their effects on experience (real or imagined) create, constrain and even condemn ways of discussing nation, social control and individual or collective identity. The truth values of these constructs are constrained by ways of knowing and ways of being, through 'types of discourse which [a society] accepts and makes function as true; the mechanisms and instances which enable one to distinguish true and false statements, the means by which each is sanctioned; the techniques and procedures accorded value in the acquisition of truth; the status of those who are charged with saying what counts as true'.[34] Borders normalise ways of speaking, acting and representing the self – encouraging some and penalising others – creating social control with the infrastructure of spatial control. Given recent leaps in surveillance culture, the Foucauldian panopticon has regained some of its currency as an analogy, with the borders of the nation state standing as the walls of the prison, but other metaphors of power, historicity, contingency and ideology in the construction of different kinds of border knowledge are also needed to examine the ideological substrate on which the border is discursively built. What does the US citizen of Hyder, Alaska, quoted earlier, mean by his assertion of greater freedom in comparison to the Canadians by whom he is effectively cut off from his own country? If truth 'is produced only by virtue of multiple forms of constraint . . . and it induces regular effects of power', as Foucault noted, then the theory of the border must account for such multiplicities – less linear and more a collection of facets that change with the angle of perspective.[35]

The production, creation and imposition of difference are noticeable results of the *fiat* that builds borders; structures developed and, when useful, removed, by elites whose interests they serve. There is no better symbol of this fact than the privately owned Ambassador Bridge between Detroit and Windsor, as Vincent Manzerolle's chapter here makes plain. The company's website includes the assertion that the bridge's six lanes carry 25 per cent of all merchandise between Canada and the United States, a trade worth US$612.1 billion per year, according to the office of the US trade representative.[36] As Newman points out, borders 'cannot be understood without recourse to the question of power relations and an analysis of whose interest the opening or closing of borders serve'.[37] For instance, the economic description of Canadians as 'hewers of wood and drawers of water' (a Biblical reference often attributed to Harold Innis in his 1930 *The Fur Trade in Canada*) describes a resource-extraction based economy relative to the manufacturing focus of the United States of the time, but ignores the long and continuing settler-colonial process of attempting to empty the land of Indigenous inhabitants in order to facilitate access to those very resources. The long use of this particular description of Canadian economic activity simultaneously implies a trap for the settler-colonial population, as eternal resource suppliers for the more dynamic economic behemoth to their south, inadvertently displacing accountability for settler colonialism's insatiable extractivism onto the US while at the same time helping to preserve Canada's (increasingly fragile) benevolent self-image.[38] How, then, do the discursive frames that create the border bend around or break against other discourses of identity, whether cultural, political or ideological? How do such frames focus or divert the gaze of those who would examine them?

The economic structure and infrastructure of the border shapes and reflects the experience of citizens, refugees and international travellers. Such issues are tied to larger social and ideological projects through the manifestation and projection of power, operating as capitalist machinery, as historic icon and as marker of social difference. The subtle assertion of implied superiority found in the language of 'going down to the States' in Canadian parlance, for instance, papers over insecurities about economic, military and cultural power with a glib sense of cartography as morality. The border reflects the industrial and post-industrial social contexts that it helped to define and that have made it relevant to the lives of people on both sides of the line, as well as to people who refuse to acknowledge the line at all.

In the field of international relations, concerns around ontological security – security as continuity of being and self-definition, rather than security as survival – have had a notable impact on discussions of boundaries and borders, being used to explain both interstate and intrastate relationships around policy, lawmaking and identity.[39] The state's relationship to itself, the people over whom it claims power, and to other states, are areas of concern in border studies and in ontological security. Modernity, globalisation and the recent turn towards a new, more insular nationalism in some late capitalist countries, have all contributed to the reconsideration of identities, and the boundaries around and between individuals, communities, cultures and states. These are issues of power, staged, performed and imposed on the border generally, and on the US–Canada border in very specific ways. Borders perform security and stability by delimiting the edges and limits of the nation state – its territory, its citizens and its power. Such performances impact individuals' senses of identity and security, communities' senses of collective memory and ways in which communities define themselves. As Konrad notes, changes in the border can lead to 'recognizable social breakdown in the cross-border community'.[40] The geographical impact of the border on communities' and individuals' ability to travel and interact is well documented.[41] The ontological turn has much to contribute to considerations of the border of individual identity and subjectivity formation, for which ontological security may be defined as 'a sense of continuity and order in events' that depends 'on our ability to have faith in those social narratives and routines in which we are embedded, and through which our self-identity is constituted'.[42] From the perspective of biosecurity, or the border's shift from a physical location to a matter of identity, informational dividuals and risk management, the ontological approach can risk weakening the coherence of the individual, as coherent subjectivity is dispersed through information and datapoints.[43]

Even when successful in what Foucault called 'a "regime" of truth' – the 'circular relation with systems of power that produce and sustain it' the 'truth' of the discourse of national identity is deeply problematic in its engagement of ontological security for the individual.[44] It requires conforming to a prescriptive narrative notion of selfhood, often inscribed through the working of institutionalised social power and coercive state apparatuses. Ontological security in the context of the nation state is, in effect, a disciplining of self-identity for security purposes, a discipline not infrequently imposed upon the individual and diminishing the value of or relationship to the Other.[45] The nation state's creation of the border creates criminality in the form of smuggling and entry laws, marking those undertaking such actions as illegal (or even as 'illegals'), as non-citizens, as alien and dangerous to the body politic. Looking south the Canada–US border can also signify an increased value on the Other, through the possibility of fulfilment: illicit desires (from Las Vegas casinos to gun shows), big city adventures, or career advancement, or ideological affinities. Even the lure of cultural consistency can be enticing – as if the US could be a place where TV matches reality, rather than requiring the endless acts of cultural translation that Canadians perform – from 'greenbacks' to Trader Joe's. For some Americans, meanwhile, the northern border can offer a blank canvas on which to paint fantasies of wilderness and conquest, as Jack London did, or escape – to an American frontier past, to a more liberal, communitarian future, or in narrative imaginings of the nineteenth century, a terminus marked 'freedom' on the Underground Railroad. The border did represent a geographical location of an aspiration to freedom in some nineteenth-century African American and slave discourses, as roughly 15,000 to 20,000 enslaved people are estimated to have crossed the border into British North America between 1850 and 1860.[46] Their legal status was relatively clear as a result of the Act for the Abolition of Slavery throughout the British Colonies (1833); their status as part of the social order continued to be far more actively contested.[47]

More recent spikes in American citizen threats to move to Canada during US federal elections demonstrate the border's continuing complex role in US self-perception – part hand grenade, part parachute – an escape from American life but not entirely alien, and always potentially available to American access or concern. Such threats, interestingly, come from both ends of the American political spectrum. Canada served as an escape from the Vietnam War draft in the late twentieth century, and as an escape from the effects of climate change in the early twenty-first century. Ideals of escape across the Canada–US border often attempt to resolve inconsistencies and tensions at the borders of personal identity by displacing them onto the borders of the nation state, a place where their policing, as Cash and Kinnvall note, 'has resulted in attempts to govern not only physical borders, but also ideational, emotional, and embodied borders and boundaries'.[48]

The border does not manifest itself, in spite of the naturalising rhetoric of the state. It is always contingent and, like the ontological security of the individual, the community or the state, it is at once rigid and fragile.[49] Beyond the brute impositions of national power and national infrastructure the nuances of space, time, representation and identity open a wide variety of interpretive possibilities around, about and often far from the geographical lines of the border – as demonstrated by the existence of the 100-mile US border protection zone established by the Supreme Court of the United States in 1976 – a liminal space in which rights to personal property and integrity are mitigated and in which nearly two-thirds of the US population resides. If identity or legality mark the edges of the nation state's reach as much as a line on a map, then one may carry the border within a pocket, a purse or a persona. Identities that can be carried, however, can also be dropped.

The search for ontological stability exists within, beyond and between nation state boundaries, structured by place, but also time, to the extent that nation states require a coherent narrative (often about the progress of modernity) justifying their own existence. The Canada–US border divides geographical space and historical narratives, imagined pasts and possible futures, from each other, and from the concrete realities of the present. As we have noted, the Jay Treaty guarantees the right of Indigenous peoples to cross the border, but the mute fact of the border's existence, coupled with increasingly militarised defences of border security, continually call such rights into question. Intricately connected to the project of exploration, development and nation building, the agreement defining the Canada–US border west of Lake of the Woods was a casting of political aspiration far into the future – a border imposed before the geography or temporality of the nation states imposing it were fixed. The *fiat* of nation-making that drew a line around territory also drew a line beneath the history of a relationship to land, dividing Indigenous communities and settlers, but also making suddenly unreal a pre-colonial mythological past, discursively broken from a linear and technologically driven present and future.[50] It not only defined a nebulous differentiation between British subjects and American citizens, it created communities in which 'a linear and progressive understanding of time (and borders) facilitates the representation of some collectives as modern – actors that advance history – while others are stuck in the past'.[51] Such differentiations develop further in the NEXUS programme,[52] a fast-track option for border crossing that uses background checks and surveillance technology to enable technologically engaged and financially secure citizens to bypass border-crossing lines by self-selecting for special relationships to surveillance, identity through the use of biometrics, data and virtual border crossing. In effect, the programme differentiates citizens of a future techno-state from citizens stuck in the quotidian present, acting as one of the 'critical sites where a specific notion of "safe citizens" is worked out'.[53] Such impositions of informational identity reimagine people as data sets – the border crosses their lives and experiences, imposing meaning beyond the physical place it occupies.

That space, however, remains critical to an effort at theorising the border. As Johan Schimanski notes, 'One must also be open to the possibility that the border itself is also the product of the border crossing or brought into being by border-crossers. Taken at face value – or rather, taken *only* at face value – the sentence *the border-crosser crosses the border* reveals a Descartian view of space which may be superseded by concepts of space as a social construct.'[54] Sociologically speaking, this approach may be unremarkable; objects are defined by their contextual use. The border too, and even the spaces it divides or connects, can be read in these terms, but in focusing on the lives and acts that define the border, we must also be cautious not to re-elide those lives and acts already elided by the political powers that impose and enforce the border.

If, as noted above, the Canada–US border operated as the Medicine Line which offered protection from US military action, then in more recent years it has also marked the range and territory of policies of elision and abuse, and has been more or less invisible in mainstream historiography, with the obvious exception of the Underground Railroad (see, e.g. Vernon[55] who outlines four major periods of migration into the prairies from the 1780s onwards, noting the frequent absence of Black presence from fur trade narratives, for instance).[56] Such issues are central to the matter of border studies because the border operates as a frame for the nation state: geographically, conceptually in terms of identity, culturally in terms of identity, politically in terms of policy imposition, and even aesthetically in terms of representations of nationhood, citizenship and the collective arbitration of taste.

The issues discussed here – of time and memory, of individual, community, and national identity, among others – are the building blocks of this collection. Through the lens of three broad organising themes – nation, negotiation and resistance – the chapters of this book explore the Canada–US border as both a site and figure. In doing so, they offer an alternate paradigm for developing the cultural and socio-political dimensions of transnational border studies, while shifting critical attention away from the heavily analysed perspective of the United States, and expanding North American studies at a historical moment when the control, use and re-inscription of North American borders is becoming a matter of urgent concern. They engage with legislation, artistic creation and media representation as means of considering how we make the border and how the border makes us.

The first section of the book looks at the production and enforcement of national identity through the infrastructure, geography and creative representation of the border. Opening the section, in 'Getting Played: Confession, Identity and *Border Security*' Jeffrey Orr considers the role of television in building national identity through an analysis of the television show *Border Security: Canada's Front Line* (National Geographic, 2012–14), arguing that it creates a troublingly self-congratulatory structure of citizenship as gatekeeping. Valorising the Canadian Border Services Agency with which it cooperated, the show positioned viewers as armchair border security agents themselves, offering racially, economically and culturally loaded choices as to who would be 'worthy' of entering Canada.

Extending the use of media and communications theory, in Chapter 2 Vincent Manzerolle's 'Border Media: Contributions to a Non-Linear History of the Detroit River' examines the infrastructure of the border using historical elements. His media studies approach to crossings between Detroit, Michigan, and Windsor, Ontario, includes ferries, bridges, tunnels, airports and telecommunication networks, and crafts a theoretical understanding of 'logistical media' using the work of Harold Innis and John Durham Peters. It approaches the long history of one particular border crossing: from a networking of colonial empires, through contemporary transnational movements of capital.

Finally in this section, Pierre-Alexandre Beylier's chapter 'Comparing Twin Towns along the US Southern and Northern Borders: A Historical Review' examines the economic and demographic characteristics of twin towns/cities, seeking to understand their 'duplicate' – but not always symmetrical – aspect. Comparing the logics of formation of border towns on the Mexico–US and Canada–US borders, Beylier examines their commonalities, especially in the generation of integrated systems and structures, while drawing attention to certain 'mutations' in twin town relationships as a result of the changing security landscape post-9/11.

If these first three chapters all address, in different ways, the construction of nation and regional and national identities, the book's second section considers the ways in which Indigenous communities have negotiated the border imposed upon their lands, territories, geographies and lives. Lived relationships to the border and the nation states that imposed it are a complex dance of treaty rights, historical contexts, social practices, as well cultural interactions and reimaginings through immigration and displacement. These continue to be shaped by violence at the individual, community and state levels, as well as by cultural expectations from all sides of the negotiations.

Opening up the border as a site of possibility in ways implied but not examined in the chapter that follows by David Stirrup, Chris LaLonde engages with the work of Indigenous writer and activist Gerald Vizenor in his chapter 'Continental Liberty, Natural Reason, *Survivance*: Gerald Vizenor's Sojourning in the Borderlands'. Vizenor, Lalonde argues, upsets expectations and discursive platitudes around what it means to be Indigenous (and what settler societies *think* it means) using the watery borderlands of northern

Minnesota to articulate and undermine national identities and challenge his readers to think differently about Indigenous identities.

David Stirrup's chapter 'The Logics of Border Theory: Negotiating Sovereignties at the Impasse' offers a reflection on Indigenous literary and cultural concerns, engages with the related issues of equivocation about and around border theory in the field of Indigenous studies, and considers the 'competing' claims of cultural and political sovereignty with respect to hard and soft borders as a troubled location for transgression, de-centring of national narratives, as well as for struggle and enunciation.

Building on the senses of refusal and resistance the preceding two chapters invoke, the closing section re-examines the border from other angles. All resistance necessarily engages with power, whether to claim it back, deny its effectiveness or mitigate its effects. Imagining the erasure of the border, making it tricky or illusory, or building communities that exist on the threshold of national territory: these are acts in literature, in art and in daily practice that trouble and interrogate the careful presentation of the border as natural.

That interrogation begins in Gillian Roberts' careful reading of Wayde Compton's poetic work, in her chapter 'Border Hypotheses: Speculations on Territory and Sovereignty in Wayde Compton's *The Outer Harbour*' (Chapter 7), which places the poet's community-based art projects beside the poetic fantasy of new geographies to argue that he turns the past into the future – turning historical and political questions already circulating in contemporary British Columbia towards the realm of speculative fiction. Roberts argues that by imagining a possible future for the city of Vancouver, Compton's work views the nature of borders through a lens of spectrality and recurring settler-state violence against Indigenous peoples.

Approaching border poetry from a different angle again, Tanis MacDonald's consideration in her chapter 'Grit and Grief: Wayde Compton's *49th Parallel Psalm* as borderblur elegy' (Chapter 6) takes the poet's sensitivity to place, historical memory and archive as a way to think about blurring borders of time, memory and genre. Her work reads the writing as an elegy to a dead politics through voice and silence, invoking a silenced and troubling Black North American history at the periphery of Canada's cultural narrative.

Finally, in his afterword, Border Studies geographer Victor Konrad confronts the ways in which recent world events and political shifts have reinforced borders, filtering into surveillance processes, and observing that all the while 'the border is transcended by seducing ideas and unseen pathogens, as well as those who "Can-pass"'. Taking an overview of the chapters in this book, and pondering the logics and ethics of intersection, connection, division, separation, differentiation, variation and change that the figure of the border effects in different times and spaces, Konrad concludes that 'cultures of and at the border are being renewed at time-honoured crossings and twin cities to form and enlarge these interstitial spaces'.

The exigencies and impacts of the border on the individual, the community and the state; on the environment and the economy; on history, the present and the future, are difficult to grasp beyond the statistics and structures that trace its imprint and impact. Those imprints are nonetheless a lasting element of how stories are told, how relationships are built or torn apart, and how selfhood and nationhood are understood, represented and bound together.

This volume is not an attempt at a definitive theory of borders, or of this border in particular. Indeed, the length and variation in the Canada–US border make it difficult to comprehend through a single approach. Rather, the essays collected here concern themselves with examining specific aspects of specific parts of the border in the hope that by looking closely at one part we might increase our understanding of the others. The wide range of approaches and ideas contained here offer changes in outlook, in optimism, in views to the past, present and future. Like the cartographic project they consider, they are efforts to map ideas arising from what people on both sides of the border, and those who refuse to recognise it at all, continue to refer to simply as 'The Line'.

Notes

1. Gillian Roberts, ed. *Reading between the Borderlines: Cultural Production and Consumption across the 49th Parallel* (Montreal and Kingston: McGill-Queen's University Press, 2018), 19.
2. Ila Nicole Sheren, *Portable Borders: Performance Art and Politics on the U.S. Frontera Since 1984* (Austin: University of Texas, 2015), 17.
3. Ibid., 62.
4. Ibid.

5. Ibid.
6. Victor Konrad and Heather Nicol, *Beyond Walls: Re-Inventing the Canada-United States Borderlands* (Aldershot: Ashgate Publishing, 2008); Winfried Siemerling and Sarah Phillips Casteel, ed. *Canada and its Americas: Transnational Navigations* (Montreal and Kingston: McGill-Queen's University Press, 2010); Caroline Levander and Robert F. Levine, *Hemispheric American Studies* (New Brunswick, NJ: Rutgers University Press, 2008).
7. Rachel Adams, *Continental Divides: Remapping the Cultures of North America* (Chicago: University of Chicago Press, 2009); Claudia Sadowski-Smith, *Border Fictions: Globalization, Empire, and Writing at the Boundaries of the United States* (Charlottesville: University of Virginia Press, 2008); Gillian Roberts and David Stirrup, ed. *Parallel Encounters: Culture at the Canada–US Border* (Waterloo, ON: Wilfrid Laurier University Press, 2013); Kyle Conway and Timothy Pasch, *Beyond the Border: Tensions across the Forty-Ninth Parallel in the Great Plains and Prairies* (Montreal and Kingston: McGill-Queen's University Press, 2013); Gillian Roberts, *Reading Between the Borderlines: Cultural Production and Consumption across the 49th Parallel* (Montreal and Kingston: McGill-Queen's University Press, 2018).
8. Shari M. Huhndorf, *Mapping the Americas* (Ithaca, NY: Cornell University Press, 2009); Karl S. Hele, *Lines Drawn Upon the Water: First Nations and the Great Lakes Borders and Borderlands* (Waterloo, ON: Wilfrid Laurier Press, 2008).
9. Zalfa Feghali, *Crossing Borders and Queering Citizenship: Civic Reading Practice in Contemporary American and Canadian Writing*, (Manchester: Manchester University Press, 2019); Gillian Roberts, *Discrepant Parallels: Cultural Implications of the Canada–US Border* (Montreal and Kingston: McGill-Queen's University Press, 2015).
10. Susan Kollin, 'North to the West: Jack London and the Literature of U.S. Expansion in Canada', *Canadian Review of American Studies* 26.2 (Spring 1996): 65.
11. See, for instance, Jack London's *The King of Mazy May*, 1899.
12. Ibid.
13. *City of Gold*, directed by Wolf Konig, performance by Pierre Berton. National Film Board of Canada, 1957.
14. Grant Stoddard, 'The Lost Canadians', *The Walrus*, January/February 2011. https://thewalrus.ca/the-lost-canadians/
15. Dan Levin, 'An Alaskan Village where Grizzlies Roam and Canada Rules (If Anyone Does)', *The New York Times*, 3 July 2016. https://www.nytimes.com/2016/07/03/us/canada-alaska-hyder-stewart-british-columbia.html

16. 1871 Indian Appropriations Act, US Congress.
17. Gloria Anzaldúa, *Borderlands/La Frontera: The New Mestiza* (San Francisco, CA: Aunt Lute Books, 2012, 4th edn), 3.
18. Ibid., 3.
19. For an excellent discussion of this phrase and its recent rejuvenation in protest art, see Edward J. McCaughan, '"We Didn't Cross the Border, the Border Crossed Us": Artists' Images of the US–Mexico Border and Immigration', *Latin American and Latinx Visual Culture* 2.1 (2020): 6–31.
20. Kevin Bruyneel, *The Third Space of Sovereignty: The Postcolonial Politics of U.S.-Indigenous Relations* (Minneapolis: University of Minnesota Press, 2007), 117.
21. See Article III, Jay Treaty in *United States, The Treaties between the United States and Great Britain: Viz, The Definitive Treaty, Signed at Paris, 1783: Treaty of Amity, Commerce and Navigation, Signed in London, 1794, by Mr. Jay: Monroe and Pinkney's Treaty, 1806, Rejected by Mr. Jefferson: Also the Treaty of Peace, Signed at Ghent, Dec. 24, 1814*. Boston [Mass.]: E.G. House, 1815.
22. The history of both US and Canadian citizenship for Indigenous peoples is complex and contested. It includes periods of coerced citizenship (triggered, for instance, by the act of leaving the reserve), blanket but not necessarily always welcome citizenship such as that conferred in the US by the 1924 Citizenship Act, and continued refusal of citizenship by various nations, most notably among the Haudenosaunee.
23. Thomas Nail, *Theory of the Border* (New York: Oxford University Press, 2016), 2.
24. Kevin Bruyneel, *The Third Space of Sovereignty: The Postcolonial Politics of U.S.-Indigenous Relations* (Minneapolis: University of Minnesota Press, 2007).
25. Stuart Christie, *Plural Sovereignties and Contemporary Indigenous Literature* (New York and London: Palgrave, 2009).
26. Mark B. Salter, 'Theory of the /: The Suture and Critical Border Studies', *Geopolitics* 17.4 (January 2012): 734–55. doi:10.1080/1465 0045.2012.660580. 734.
27. Patrick Lalonde, 'Cyborg Work: Borders as Simulation', *British Journal of Criminology* 58.6 (November 2018): 1361–80. doi:10.10 93/bjc/azx070.
28. Fred Wah, *Diamond Grill* (Edmonton, AB: NeWest Press, 1996), 176.
29. See 'Treaty of Paris' in *United States*.
30. Michel Foucault and Colin Gordon, 'Of Other Spaces: Utopias and Heterotopias', in *Rethinking Architecture: A Reader in Cultural Theory*, ed. Neil Leach (New York: Routledge, 1997), 330.
31. Patrick Lalonde, 'Cyborg Work: Borders as Simulation', *British*

Journal of Criminology 58.6 (November 2018): 1361–80. doi:10.10 93/bjc/azx070. 1363.
32. William Walters, 'Border/Control', *European Journal of Social Theory* 9.2 (2003): 187–203. doi:10.1177/1368431006063332. 141.
33. Patrick Lalonde, 'Cyborg Work: Borders as Simulation', *British Journal of Criminology* 58.6 (November 2018): 1361–80. doi:10.10 93/bjc/azx070. 1363.
34. Michel Foucault and Colin Gordon, 'Truth and Power', in *Power/Knowledge: Selected Interviews and Other Writings, 1972–1977* (New York: Pantheon Books, 1980), 109–33, 131.
35. Ibid., 131.
36. See https://www.ambassadorbridge.com
37. David Newman, 'Towards an Interdisciplinary Dialogue', *European Journal of Social Theory* 9.2 (May 2006): 171–86. doi:10.1177/1368 431006063331. 176.
38. The Biblical reference (Joshua 9:27 – interestingly, a condemnation to servitude by a colonial military occupier) still holds water in contemporary Canadian journalism. See, for instance, Dimitry Anastakis, 'Hew that Wood, Draw that Water', in *The Literary Review of Canada*, January 2015, or Kevin Carmichael's 'How the Hewers of Wood and Drawers of Water are Saving Canada Some Pain', *The Financial Post*, 7 April 2021.
39. Catarina Kinnevall and Jennifer Mitzen, 'An Introduction to the Special Issue: Ontological Securities in World Politics', *Cooperation and Conflict* 5.1 (2017): 4; Maria Malksoo, '"Memory Must Be Defended": Beyond the Politics of Mnemonical Security', *Security Dialogue* 46.3 (June 2015). doi:10.1177/0967010614552549. 222.
40. Victor Konrad, 'Conflating Imagination, Identity, and Affinity in the Social Construction of Borderlands Culture Between Canada and the United States', *American Review of Canadian Studies* 42.4 (December 2012): 543.
41. Ibid.
42. Anthony Giddens, *Modernity and Self-Identity: Self and Society in the Late Modern Age* (Cambridge: Polity Press, 1991), 243; Chris Rossdale, 'Enclosing Critique: The Limits of Ontological Security', *International Political Sociology* 9.4 (December 2015). doi:10.1111/ips.12103. 372.
43. Patrick Lalonde, 'Cyborg Work: Borders as Simulation', *British Journal of Criminology* 58.6 (November 2018): 1361–80. doi:10.10 93/bjc/azx070. 1368.
44. Michel Foucault and Colin Gordon, 'Truth and Power', in *Power/Knowledge: Selected Interviews and Other Writings, 1972–1977* (New York: Pantheon Books, 1980), 109–33, 132.

45. Chris Rossdale, 'Enclosing Critique: The Limits of Ontological Security', *International Political Sociology* 9.4 (December 2015): 369–89. doi:10.1111/ips.12103. 370; Carmina Yu Untalan, 'Decentering the Self, Seeing Like the Other: Toward a Postcolonial Approach to Ontological Security', *International Political Sociology* 14.1 (March 2020): 40–56. doi:10.1093/ips/olz018. 48.
46. Natasha Henry, 'Underground Railroad', *The Canadian Encyclopedia*. 2006. https://www.thecanadianencyclopedia.ca/en/article/underground-railroad
47. Slavery Abolition Act, 1833. https://www.pdavis.nl/Legis_07.htm
48. John Cash and Catarina Kinnvall, 'Postcolonial Bordering and Ontological Insecurities', *Postcolonial Studies* 20.3 (2017). doi:10.1080/13688790.2017.1391670. 270.
49. Chris Rossdale, 'Enclosing Critique: The Limits of Ontological Security', *International Political Sociology* 9.4 (December 2015). doi:10.1111/ips.12103. 370.
50. Popular 1960s Canadian folk singer Gordon Lightfoot's "Railroad Trilogy" (commissioned by the CBC for Canada's 1967 centenary) opens with an evocation of a time before the Canadian National Railway 'long before the white man and long before the wheel / when the green dark forest was too silent to be real'.
51. John Cash and Catarina Kinnvall, 'Postcolonial Bordering and Ontological Insecurities', *Postcolonial Studies* 20.3 (2017). doi:10.1080/13688790.2017.1391670. 268.
52. NEXUS (2002) is part of the Trusted Traveller Program for citizens and permanent residents of Canada and the United States, jointly administered by both governments. Members are pre-screened in a security interview by Canadian and US border officials, and they pay a fee to use dedicated processing lanes at the Canada–US border, or dedicated security check-in kiosks at airports. The NEXUS card replaces a passport for travel between Canada and the USA, at designated border-crossing locations.
53. Benjamin J. Muller, 'Unsafe at Any Speed? Borders, Mobility and "Safe Citizenship"', *Citizenship Studies* 14.1 (2010): doi:10.1080/13621020903466381. 76.
54. Johan Schimanski, 'Crossing and Reading: Notes Towards a Theory and a Method', *Nordlit* 10.1 (2010). doi:10.7557/13.1835. 45.
55. Karina Vernon, *The Black Prairie Archives: An Anthology* (Waterloo, ON: Wilfrid Laurier University Press, 2020).
56. For contextualisation of these terms and the long history of Canadian governmental violence against Indigenous people, see the Final Report of the Truth and Reconciliation Commission (2008), as well as more recent findings of previously unacknowledged abuses and deaths at Canadian residential schools.

Bibliography

Adams, Rachel. *Continental Divides: Remapping the Cultures of North America*. Chicago: University of Chicago Press, 2009.

Anzaldúa, Gloria. *Borderlands/La Frontera: The New Mestiza*. San Francisco, CA: Aunt Lute Books, 2012 (4th edn).

Avalon Project, The. [1794]. Treaty of Amity, Commerce, and Navigation. In *The Avalon Project: Documents in Law, History, and Diplomacy* [online] [accessed 1 February 2015]. Available at: http://avalon.law.yale.edu/18th_century/jay.asp

Avalon Project, The. [1848]. Treaty of Guadalupe-Hidalgo. In *The Avalon Project: Documents in Law, History, and Diplomacy* [online] [accessed 1 February 2015]. Available at: http://avalon.law.yale.edu/19th_century/guadhida.asp

Bruyneel Kevin. *The Third Space of Sovereignty: The Postcolonial Politics of U.S.-Indigenous Relations*. Minneapolis: University of Minnesota Press, 2007.

Canada. Transport Canada. *Road Transportation*. https://tc.canada.ca/en/corporate-services/policies/road-transportation. Accessed 15 October 2021.

Cash, John and Catarina Kinnvall. 'Postcolonial Bordering and Ontological Insecurities'. *Postcolonial Studies* 20.3 (2017): 267–74. doi:10.1080/13688790.2017.1391670.

Christie, Stuart. *Plural Sovereignties and Contemporary Indigenous Literature*. New York and London: Palgrave, 2009.

City of Gold. Directed by Wolf Konig, performance by Pierre Berton. National Film Board of Canada, 1957.

Conway, Kyle and Timothy Pasch. *Beyond the Border: Tensions across the Forty-Ninth Parallel in the Great Plains and Prairies*. Montreal and Kingston: McGill-Queen's University Press, 2013.

Feghali, Zalfa. *Crossing Borders and Queering Citizenship: Civic Reading Practice in Contemporary American and Canadian Writing*. Manchester: Manchester University Press, 2019.

Foucault, Michel. 'Of Other Spaces: Utopias and Heterotopias' in *Rethinking Architecture: A Reader in Cultural Theory*. Ed. Neil Leach. New York: Routledge, 1997. 330–6.

Foucault, Michel. 'Truth and Power' in *Power/Knowledge: Selected Interviews and Other Writings, 1972–1977*. New York: Pantheon Books, 1980. 109–33.

Foucault, Michel and Colin Gordon. *Power/Knowledge: Selected Interviews and Other Writings, 1972–1977*. New York: Pantheon Books, 1980.

Fox, Claire. *The Fence and the River: Culture and Politics at the US–Mexico Border*. Minneapolis: University of Minnesota Press, 1999.

Giddens Anthony. *Modernity and Self-Identity: Self and Society in the Late Modern Age*. Cambridge: Polity Press, 1991.

Hele, Karl S. *Lines Drawn Upon the Water: First Nations and the Great Lakes Borders and Borderlands*. Waterloo, ON: Wilfrid Laurier Press, 2008.

Henry, Natasha. 'Underground Railroad'. *The Canadian Encyclopedia*. 2006. https://www.thecanadianencyclopedia.ca/en/article/underground-railroad

Huhndorf, Shari M. *Mapping the Americas*. Ithaca, NY: Cornell University Press, 2009.

Innis, Harold A. and Arthur J. Ray. *The Fur Trade in Canada*. [Electronic Resource]: An Introduction to Canadian Economic History. Toronto: University of Toronto Press, 1999.

The King James Bible. King James Bible Online, 2021. https://www.kingjamesbibleonline.org

Kinnevall, Catarina and Jennifer Mitzen. 'An Introduction to the Special Issue: Ontological Securities in World Politics'. *Cooperation and Conflict* 5.1 (2017): 3–11.

Kollin, Susan. 'North to the West: Jack London and the Literature of U.S. Expansion in Canada'. *Canadian Review of American Studies* 26.2 (Spring 1996): 63–81.

Konrad, Victor. 'Conflating Imagination, Identity, and Affinity in the Social Construction of Borderlands Culture Between Canada and the United States'. *American Review of Canadian Studies* 42.4 (December 2012): 530–48.

Konrad, Victor and Heather Nicol. *Beyond Walls: Re-Inventing the Canada-United States Borderlands*. Aldershot: Ashgate Publishing, 2008.

LaDow, Beth. *The Medicine Line: Life and Death on a North American Borderland*. New York: Routledge, 2001.

Lalonde, Patrick. 'Cyborg Work: Borders as Simulation'. *British Journal of Criminology* 58.6 (November 2018): 1361–80. doi:10.1093/bjc/azx070.

Levander, Caroline and Robert F. Levine. *Hemispheric American Studies*. New Brunswick, NJ: Rutgers University Press, 2008.

Levin, Dan. 'An Alaskan Village where Grizzlies Roam and Canada Rules (If Anyone Does)'. *The New York Times*, 3 July 2016. https://www.nytimes.com/2016/07/03/us/canada-alaska-hyder-stewart-british-columbia.html

Lightfoot Gordon. 'Canadian Railroad Trilogy'. *The Way I Feel*. United Artists, 1967.

London, Jack. *The King of Mazy May*. Amazon Kindle Books, 2014.

McKinsey, Lauren and Victor Konrad. *Borderlands Reflections: The United States and Canada*. Orono: University of Maine Press, 1989.

Malksoo, Maria. '"Memory Must Be Defended": Beyond the Politics of Mnemonical Security'. *Security Dialogue* 46.3 (June 2015): 221–37. doi:10.1177/0967010614552549.
Muller, Benjamin J. 'Unsafe at Any Speed? Borders, Mobility and "Safe Citizenship"'. *Citizenship Studies* 14.1 (2010): 75–88. doi:10.1080/13 621020903466381.
Nail, Thomas. *Theory of the Border*. New York: Oxford University Press, 2016.
Newman, David. 'Towards an Interdisciplinary Dialogue'. *European Journal of Social Theory* 9.2 (May 2006): 171–86. doi:10.1177/1368 431006063331.
Roberts, Gillian. *Discrepant Parallels: Cultural Implications of the Canada–US Border*. Montreal and Kingston: McGill-Queen's University Press, 2015.
Roberts, Gillian, ed. *Reading between the Borderlines: Cultural Production and Consumption across the 49th Parallel*. Montreal and Kingston: McGill-Queen's University Press, 2018.
Roberts, Gillian and David Stirrup, ed. *Parallel Encounters: Culture at the Canada–US Border*. Waterloo, ON: Wilfred Laurier University Press, 2013.
Rossdale, Chris. 'Enclosing Critique: The Limits of Ontological Security'. *International Political Sociology* 9.4 (December 2015): 369–89. doi:10 .1111/ips.12103.
Sadowski-Smith, Claudia. *Border Fictions: Globalization, Empire, and Writing at the Boundaries of the United States*. Charlottesville: University of Virginia Press, 2008.
Sadowski-Smith, Claudia, ed. *Globalization on the Line: Culture, Capital, and Citizenship at U.S. Borders*. New York: Palgrave. 2002.
Salter, Mark B. 'Theory of the /: The Suture and Critical Border Studies'. *Geopolitics* 17.4 (January 2012): 734–55. doi:10.1080/14650045.2012 .660580.
Schimanski, Johan. 'Crossing and Reading: Notes Towards a Theory and a Method'. *Nordlit* 10.1 (2010): 41–63. doi:10.7557/13.1835.
Sheren, Ila Nicole. *Portable Borders: Performance Art and Politics on the U.S. Frontera Since 1984*. Austin: University of Texas, 2015.
Siemerling, Winfried and Sarah Phillips Casteel, ed. *Canada and its Americas: Transnational Navigations*. Montreal and Kingston: McGill-Queen's University Press, 2010.
Slavery Abolition Act, 1833. https://www.pdavis.nl/Legis_07.htm. Accessed 26 September 2021.
Stoddard, Grant. 'The Lost Canadians'. *The Walrus*, January/February 2011. https://thewalrus.ca/the-lost-canadians/
Truth and Reconciliation Commission of Canada. *Final Report of the Truth*

and Reconciliation Commission. Ottawa: Government of Canada, 2015.

United States. *The Treaties between the United States and Great Britain: Viz, The Definitive Treaty, Signed at Paris, 1783: Treaty of Amity, Commerce and Navigation, Signed in London, 1794, by Mr. Jay: Monroe and Pinkney's Treaty, 1806, Rejected by Mr. Jefferson: Also the Treaty of Peace, Signed at Ghent, Dec. 24, 1814. Boston [Mass.]:* E.G. House, 1815.

Untalan, Carmina Yu. 'Decentering the Self, Seeing Like the Other: Toward a Postcolonial Approach to Ontological Security'. *International Political Sociology* 14.1 (March 2020): 40–56. doi:10.1093/ips/olz018.

Vernon, Karina. *The Black Prairie Archives: An Anthology*. Waterloo, ON: Wilfrid Laurier University Press, 2020.

Wah, Fred. *Diamond Grill*. Edmonton, AB: NeWest Press, 1996.

Walters, William. 'Border/Control'. *European Journal of Social Theory* 9.2 (2003): 187–203. doi:10.1177/1368431006063332.

CHAPTER 1

Getting Played: Confession, Identity and *Border Security*

Jeffrey Orr

The television series *Border Security: Canada's Front Line*, is a product of Vancouver and Toronto production company Force Four Entertainment Inc. (acquired in 2014 by Entertainment One). Begun in 2012, and cancelled after its third season, *Border Security: Canada's Front Line* has been relatively successful, expanding to other regional locations in Canada and providing a surprisingly stable investment for its producers. The show follows the work of the officers of the Canadian Border Security Agency (CBSA hereafter), primarily at Vancouver International Airport and land border crossings in the Greater Vancouver, British Columbia area, presenting highly edited footage of border crossings and border-crossers.

The show provides a complex representation of the Canada–US border through reality-based 'infotainment' narratives about the CBSA, whose 'highly-trained officers must trust their instincts to investigate, educate and allow or deny access to travellers and goods of every origin'.[1] *Border Security* occupies a number of conflicting positions in relation to its own generic identity, stated intent and social positioning. The show's structure casts light on wider issues of national identity, self-identity and organisational identity, as defined and enforced at the edge of the Canadian nation state. Examining the structural relationships of social power and narrative deployed in the show casts light on its role as a tool of state and social power. Accordingly, this chapter considers some of the genre forms and structures used in the show to examine how the work of crafting stories about the border influences and imposes collective and individual identity through narrative. Generic conventions are a way of organising viewer expectations through narratives, therefore the limits of genres deployed by the show are effectively limits on how the viewers are able to imagine the border – what happens there, how it operates, what social functions it serves, and what forms of power it protects, imposes or inscribes. This chapter takes a three-step approach. First, it considers how genre structures deployed in the show shape possible understandings of border relationships (especially the relationships between CBSA agents and travellers) through narratives of power, suspicion, connection and rejection. Second, it considers the implied role for the audience as armchair CBSA agents. By affiliating the perspective of the audience with the CBSA, and then building a narrative of organisational coherence for that agency, the show effectively builds a secondary narrative of national cohesion at the same time. Third, the structure of the show, with its emphasis on audience engagement, narrative resolution and confession, offers a prize of validation and self-worth to both the CBSA agents and the audience that 'plays along' as CBSA agents, identifying with them and solving the puzzles the show presents. The tension between formal and vernacular forms of nationalism in this cohesive narrative reflects a similar tension in broader Canadian national identity development, in which the formal nationalism of Canadian multicultural policy and official practice sometimes conflict with an affective approach more based in feelings, intuitions and 'instincts' connected to ethnicities and cultural identities.[2]

The framing of the show within wider Canadian public discourse has aspired towards documentary veracity and journalistic integrity, often for the purposes of legal immunity and financial expediency. This was the line the President of Force Four Entertainment, Rob Bromley, used to defend it against accusations of racism and rights violation. A 2013 CBSA raid on a Vancouver construction site resulted in the arrest of several workers who were ultimately deemed to be in violation of immigration laws and deported; the events were filmed by a crew for *Border Security*, and a media storm broke over the film crew recording the arrest of vulnerable workers.[3] In an interview with *The Globe and Mail*, Bromley defended the show's work with the assertion that 'As good journalists, and that's what we are – this is a documentary series – . . . we documented [the arrests].'[4] Although the show survived a petition to have it cancelled, the footage of the raid was never aired. Official

CBSA support for the show, which allowed it to film in restricted government locations, was withdrawn in 2016.

Bromley's assertion of the show's objectivity invokes a journalistic tradition of impartiality and civic responsibility in potential conflict with the production company's desire to create a profitable product. This claim to documentary gravitas notwithstanding, the long history of reality TV shows like *Cops* (20th Century Fox Television, 1989–2021) or *Dog the Bounty Hunter* (A+E Networks, 2003–12) might offer more apt comparisons, given the driving introductory music, the fast-cut editing, and the show's 'law vs. crime' posture. The potential conflict between public good and private profit is hardly confined to television, but as a journalistic ideal, narrative structure is meant to ensure the clear transmission of information – this is part of what differentiates journalism from entertainment. Force Four's exclusive contract with the Federal Government of Canada (through the CBSA) which allowed the show access to locations and interactions normally off limits to public inspection, gave the producers a specific incentive to portray the CBSA's work in a positive light, in order to protect their access rights. Even more explicitly, the political review process undertaken at the yearly renewal of the series was specifically concerned with whether 'the benefits of the series warrant continued participation' by the CBSA.[5] The show was thus placed in the impossible position of claiming to provide an impartial documentary viewpoint while under contractual obligation to serve the needs of a specific state apparatus, as 'all rough footage and final episodes are reviewed and approved by the CBSA' as are 'all promotional materials'. The CBSA held '*de facto* executive production authorities' and 'would identify scenarios, sites, and storylines [. . .] and control of, all film shoots'.[6]

The questionable artistic freedom of the show undermines any claims to an objective depiction of the functioning of border infrastructure, and the episodic story structures are primarily a result of the show's editing. The production crew includes teams of both story editors and senior story editors (a total of five in the first season, reduced to three in subsequent seasons) whose job is to cut the footage into a narrative shape determined by basic archetypal story outlines.[7] This story editing work is crucial to the nature of the show because it shapes the narrative presentation of a heroic CBSA, and shapes the audience into a coherent group across demographic lines, developing a shared sense of the possible ways to understand nationalism in relation to the functioning of border infrastructure. Interviews with travellers themselves are filmed and broadcast on the show (with the signed consent of those involved) but that footage is always edited for story and narrative flow, rather than presented in raw form. This means that the show's editorial genre choices create assumptions for the audience of suspicion, innocence and guilt. Interviews are frequently contextualised by a framing statement from a CBSA officer explaining the situation, and the 'correct' way to consider it. The voiceover narrative performs a similar function by guiding the interpretive work of the audience, reminding them of previous turns in the development of the plot (created by the editing decisions), and building suspense towards the final outcome.

The public availability of the show has had a demonstrable effect on how Canadians understand themselves and the working of their own government's state apparatus, and makes a structural appeal to its audience as Canadians. The implied citizenship of the audience as Canadians is developed through the narrative and visual cues discussed above – in addition to the CBSA uniforms, flags, national insignia and establishing landscape shots feature prominently in the promotional material, B-roll and the credits. Other versions of the show in countries such as Australia or the United States have used those nations' semiotic markers to specify their implied audience.

Not only is the show widely available in re-runs on Canadian television, but a recent EKOS report indicates that

> respondents were asked if they had ever personally done any of several things to get information about crossing the border or about a CBSA program or service. Most often, they say they watched the television program *'Border Security: Canada's Front Line'* (43%). Others mentioned visiting the CBSA website (25%) or contacting CBSA by telephone (10%), in-person (10%) or email (3%).[8]

The show remains the primary source of information for Canadians about the CBSA, by an enormous margin.

The show's title hyperbolically refigures the Canada–US border – famously, the world's longest undefended border – as a war zone, implying a nation at war, and requiring loyalty and support from

Canadian citizens against an undefined threat. The rhetoric of the shared enemy or the nation under siege is a commonly used tactic in producing national affective cohesion, and, while a relatively more militaristic culture makes it a more common trope in the United States than in Canada, the importation of this rhetoric to the Canadian context of *Border Security* seems to have been effective and profitable for the production company, until its collision with legal rights led to the show's cancellation. Any shared sense of Canadian identity (always elusive to begin with) is simultaneously simplified through the vernacular nationalism of inside/outside, us/them binaries of the show's settings and characterisations. These binaries are underpinned by appeals to ethnicity and cultural inheritance, even as they are complicated by the elision the Canada's own past as a settler-invader colony, built, to a huge extent, on immigration. Margaret Atwood's invocation of garrison mentality as a Canadian trait is activated here not against the landscape, but against travellers from other lands.[9]

In addition to its outsized influence as a source of public information about the CBSA, the show's choices of genre structures influence the organisational identity of the CBSA itself. The genre of the Western, for instance, offers the CBSA a paradigm through which to define an organisation still developing its own identity independent from Canada Customs, Citizenship and Immigration Canada, or the Canadian Food Inspection Agency (the agencies from which the CBSA was formed in 2005). In the show, the recently armed CBSA agents are often portrayed as benevolent lawmen and -women, and the border-crossers as threatening outsiders. The show builds an organisational origin myth for the CBSA, smuggling the United States' national mythology of the American West into Canadian discourse: from its mixed and various background agencies, the CBSA becomes a single, new and nearly infallible armed force (*from many, one*) as its agents bring law and order to a frontier characterised as dangerous and violent (the *Front Line* of the show's title). The story itself is thus a means of satisfying a very American desire – namely, a 'nostalgia for pure origins' in the newest agency of the Canadian federal government, by connecting its present to an imagined and mythologised past.[10] This generic position implies a cultural Americanisation of a Canadian governmental agency. An approach inflected by the Canadian policy of multiculturalism – a piece of formal, rather than vernacular nationalism – might be expected to acknowledge mutually differing understandings of the world, and bring a more nuanced appreciation of the multicultural mosaic metaphor which, in Canadian identity discourse, replaces the assimilationist US melting pot. Instead, the CBSA of *Border Security* becomes uniform: as its members perform and adopt the still developing organisational identity, the show fetishises the details of CBSA uniforms (boots, badges, weapons), metonymically replacing people with the uniforms they wear.

The show thus builds an organisational identity for the CBSA itself. The show's editing produces narrative from raw footage, with frequent editing cuts in location and storyline, while recaps build suspense and allow the viewer to join the story midstream. The effect is to create a sort of action movie, in which the CBSA heroes are cast as virtuous, knowledgeable defenders of a vulnerable and innocent country; they are the knights that guard both the castle walls, and the honour of the nation. This accords precisely with Pratt and Thompson's findings that the self-perception of CBSA officers 'emboldened by the crime-security nexus, is itself shaped by a protectionist logic that represents the nation as a "damsel in distress", border officers as her guardians and the border as the thin blue line in need of constant vigilance'.[11]

A feedback loop of *esprit de corps*, reaffirmed through narrative and the self-perception of the officers, defines what it means to be a good CBSA officer. It has several other important results as well. Pratt and Thompson note the level of individual officer's discretion in border interactions, regarding who to question, and how or when to initiate security protocols. Such interactions often involve the vernacular nationalism of snap judgements based on race, identity or perception,[12] or even feeling, although they are seldom enunciated in those terms. This has a narrative generic element to it as well, for as Pratt and Thompson note, 'protectionist and quasi-chivalrous narratives [...] represent frontline border officers as benign guardians of public safety, whose preemptive and morally charged work protects the endangered nation, local communities, and innocents from harm'.[13]

The generic and cultural logic demands an innocent to protect, and indeed, 'chivalry and protectionism at the border require not only the existence of "bad men", [...] but also of dependent, innocent victims. Child pornography and paedophilia, despite the relative infrequency of such encounters, are often at the top of the list of the threats that galvanize border officers.'[14] The chivalrous benevolence assumed in this characterisation can be most readily seen 'if we assume that outside the warm familial walls are aggressors who wish to attack'.[15]

In the second season of *Border Security*, this dynamic is brought directly before the viewers, as the CBSA's Inland Enforcement Team arrests a German tourist wanted on child pornography charges. The segment takes place on the streets of downtown Vancouver, following the generic conventions of police procedural shows, in which surveillance and a chase precede the arrest. The segment reinforces the infallibility of the CBSA using the genre structures of detective stories, in which bad men are found and brought to justice. However, while most of *Border Security* takes place at the border (either the actual land crossing, or the airport) this segment takes place in the centre of a major city, suggesting that the border is not only more fluid but also more porous than it usually portrayed. No mention is made of how the German tourist was able to enter the country in the first place; the segment opens with a briefing which implies that the charges may have been newly brought (thus sidestepping the possibility of CBSA having let a sex offender into the country in the first place). Instead, the episode focuses on reinforcing the valorising and unifying narratives of CBSA identity, playing primarily to a narrow audience of CBSA officers themselves, with a secondary audience of Canadian viewers whom the voiceovers and camera angles work to affiliate with a CBSA identity by proxy.

If narrative structure here provides a path to self-understanding and representation, then affect binds together the members of the CBSA who identify in this way. Affect operates through the body, creating mutuality and fellow feeling in its identification of what constitutes the good.[16] Pratt and Thompson found that 'regardless of whether individual border officers were men or women, this protectionist discourse is gendered. It renders the job of border officers as primarily one of protection: of nation, community, family and friends – of all those innocents who exist in a permanent state of potential victimization'.[17] The threat to the bodies of loved ones or innocents (especially, perhaps, in terms of the sexual exploitation of innocence, as above) is mitigated by the willingness of officers to put their bodies on the line, and that sense of physicality is reinforced through uniform, through the emphasis (in public discourse, and in the war motif of the show) on the militarised elements of the job (weapons, body armour, boots, etc.).

Ranged against this united team of officers is a similarly connected group of 'bad people, evil people [. . .] you know, terrorists and drug smugglers' (interviewee 100703).[18] As the subtle potential for stereotyping in the description above suggests, 'the conflation of criminality and security concerns contributes to the slippage between and resultant ambiguity surrounding race and nationality at the border'.[19] The slippage means that, in Pratt and Thompson's findings, 'when asked about racial profiling, officers commonly responded by talking about nationality', but implies a feeling that criminality or specific types of criminal propensity can be read through the body, or, as officers in *Border Security* sometimes assert, 'he seemed kind of nervous', 'when he came up to the counter he seemed very nervous' and sometimes through ethnicity or gender.[20] In Pratt and Thompson's interviews with CBSA officers 'Jamaica was commonly mentioned as a high risk nationality and country of origin, as were specific countries in Africa. Vietnamese and East Indian people were frequently mentioned in relation to currency violations (often referred to as "Asians" or "Orientals").'[21] Similarly, Helleiner notes that her interview subject, a 'working class female [felt that . . .] "if you are a female going over [the border] you're pretty safe, if you're male you'd expect to be questioned"'.[22]

The narrative framing of the show, with its over-the-shoulder camera angles and implied first person perspectives, conflates the viewer's perspective with that of the CBSA officer rather than the travellers upon whose interrogation the show ultimately relies to produce the narrative conflict. Like the 2013 videogame *Papers, Please* which 'makes the player complicit in the projection of state power', the structure of the show encourages an empathetic connection to the officers on screen.[23] Positioned in an over-the-shoulder perspective as the camera follows multiple officers, the viewers are offered the chance to affiliate their point of view not only with a single CBSA officer, but with that of the organisational identity of the CBSA as a whole, which the show broadcasts as a wider Canadian identity.

Episode two, season one of the show follows a Dutch woman's attempt to enter the country, structured through her interrogation, with asides from the CBSA officer acting as narratorial guidance. In a direct-to-camera address the CBSA officer on the case confides that she has 'many concerns at this point', and that the traveller's 'story is definitely falling apart'.[24] An over-the-shoulder shot of the officer insisting to the traveller that 'you are going to have to tell me the true story' positions the viewer as a surrogate interrogator, searching for the truth along with the interviewing CBSA officer-as-detective.[25]

The most common generic approach to the show – the detective story – is developed through stories of contraband smugglers, lying interviewees and inherent tension between the personal and the systemic. Travellers deal with their expectations to be treated as individuals and/or citizens, which conflicts with their positioning as data points, as security threats or as potential criminals. Agents deal with the conflict between their roles as authority figures representing the power of the state, and as individuals who represent and wield that power. This internal conflict of the detective as individual vs. detective as agent of state power occurs frequently in the detective genre as detectives' personal lives intrude upon their professional lives for the sake of plot and character development. On a larger social scale, too, the show operates as a form of detective story in which both officers and viewers search for a narrative of stable Canadian identity. 'Every passenger has a "story" . . . it's our job to dig deeper for the truth', asserts CBSA officer Lori Miller on the National Geographic advertising website for the show.[26] There is an inherent contradiction in the show's portrayal of how the border works. *Border Security: Canada's Front Line*, like the CBSA and like Canada itself, includes officers and border-crossers of various ethnic and cultural backgrounds, complicating simple 'us vs. them' binaries and reflecting the multicultural complexities of Canadian society. However, the narrative framing produced by the breathless questions of innocence or guilt that precede and follow the advertising breaks in the show offer the opposite possibility: rather than complicating and building nuance around identity and cultural difference, they reassure the audience that these difficult and troubling questions of ambivalence can and will be resolved.

The travellers featured in the show reveal something about 'the truth' of their identity through their stories, and provide a corresponding revelation to the audience. The narrative of the Dutch woman starts as a love story; the Dutch traveller claims to be in a long-term relationship with a Canadian man, who, under questioning, later denies this connection. She is proven to be entering the country for work, 'and without a work permit, that's illegal', as the voiceover takes pains to inform the audience.[27] The CBSA officer, portrayed as suspicious but professional, is validated in her suspicions and rewarded with the satisfaction of saving the nation from exploitation. Since much of the episode is shot over her shoulder, her success is also ours. By extension, when her suspicion and scepticism are retroactively shown to have been justified, they become ours as well. Our reward for watching the show and vicariously joining in the interrogation is a justification and reinforcement of our own suspicion of non-Canadians, and a satisfying sense that our suspicions too will help protect the nation.

The generic conventions of detective fiction discussed above ascribe identities to interviewees and suspects through the uncovering of elements such as nervous physical actions, facial expressions and the literal policing of tone, as well as generaliations about nation, race and ethnicity, and harder evidence in the form of written documents, messages and material objects. The central dynamic of the show is the interaction between officer and traveller; a series of question-and-answer self-disclosures that begins with the question 'Anything to declare?' This dynamic can be usefully explored through a different set of televisual generic conventions – specifically, confessional talk shows. *Border Security* bills itself as documentary reality TV, but operates as a theatre of confessional judgement in which the viewer is invited to participate – from the opening theme song's question, seemingly addressed directly to the viewer (Annie Lennox's 1985 hit 'Would I Lie to You?'), to the slightly cathartic moments of shame, damnation and redemption that constitute the climaxes or 'turns' of the intercut border-crossing episodes.

The first episode of *Border Security* features a traveller whose entry is complicated by his having one extra, and undeclared, bottle of alcohol above the allowable limit. His interview with the CBSA officer is an example of confessional coercion of the kind Foucault describes in the *History of Sexuality*: 'we have become a singularly confessing society. The confession has spread its effects far and wide. It plays a part in justice, medicine, education, family [. . .] one confesses one's crimes, one's sins, one's thoughts and desires, one's illnesses and troubles', in a grand cultural effort to convert experience and identity into discourse.[28] The young man is asked a series of standard questions about his relationship (he has come to Canada to visit his girlfriend), his previous convictions and his past recreational drug use. The questions are straightforward, but the situation and the tone of the questioning is an exercise in building trust, as the agent's approach encourages confession, and the traveller begins his most incriminating statement with 'I won't lie to you . . .', then proceeds into a cringe-inducing litany of self-incrimination.[29] The moment of confession makes compelling television because it allows the audience two kinds of voyeuristic power: first the glimpse into another's secrets, and, second, a power to judge without accountability, granted through our perspectival affiliation with the CBSA agent, who serves as a proxy for the viewer. This second power provides the audience nationalist self-validation: it presumes their right to judge through their narrative affiliation with the CBSA agents, and it provides an un-self-critical sense of self-worth: *they* want to enter Canada; *we* are already here. Cast as armchair CBSA agents through the generic structures developed in the editing suite, *we* assume the gatekeepers' right to judgement, with none of their responsibilities. The travellers being interviewed are here because they want to join a club of which we are already members; our membership in the nation implies our superiority.

This process of judging, assessing, solving and finding (or failing to find) the truth is the structural foundation on which the show is built. Beneath its storytelling and shifting generic choices lies a relationship to the audience developed around these audience activities, specific to mass broadcast media: the gameshow. *Border Security* offers a simplified world in which two classes of people –good or bad – obtain one of two possible outcomes, ending up either successful or unsuccessful in their bid to win the prize of entering Canada. In place of evidence, the narrative editing builds suspense and conflict by deploying generic expectations that imply guilt or innocence, in order to keep the audience guessing, and the overlap between the detective genre and the gameshow genre operates to great effect – both invite the audience to play along at solving a puzzle, and both reward the audience with a sense of intellectual superiority for a 'correct' answer. Both genres operate with rules that the audience is expected to know before participating, or to pick up as they play along. This generic overlap enables the basic audience engagement with the show, as similar sets of possibilities are played out in each narrative segment: 'Good' people try to enter the country, and are accepted or rejected; 'bad' people try to enter the country, and are accepted or rejected (see Table 1.1).

Table 1.1 Possible outcomes of border encounters on *Border Security: Canada's Front Line*

Good people try to enter Canada	Bad people try to enter Canada
REJECTED System works, Canadians are enviable, and better than those seeking entry	REJECTED System works, Canadians are enviable, and better than those seeking entry
ACCEPTED System works, Canadians are generous and hospitable	ACCEPTED Not depicted

All practical outcomes of the game flatter the viewing audience and the CBSA, moulding them into a smugly satisfied but also vaguely fearful and suspicious cohesive national identity. If 'good' people get in, then we, the intended Canadian audience, are powerful and welcoming hosts, and shrewd judges of character in our proxy relationship to the CBSA officers on the show. If 'good' people get rejected, then 'we' the audience are lucky and privileged; the bar for being accepted into Canada is so high that we, as Canadians, must be exceptionally good people ourselves, since so many good people would like to come here, but sadly they cannot meet the requirements that we, as Canadians, already have both set and met ourselves – either through successful border crossing, or an accident of birth.

If bad people get rejected, then the system works; we, as Canadians of good standing (and armchair CBSA agents), are still excellent judges of character, and our vigilance is rewarded with continued safety. The only theoretical outcome not shown is bad people successfully entering the country – an outcome that would damage the credibility of the CBSA, and so endanger the show's continued access to restricted security areas. Narrative voiceover provides the show with continuity across advertising breaks and directs audience responses by reminding them how to view the border-crossers (contestants) – as good or bad respectively – and occasionally changing the initial categorisation for the purpose of dramatic narrative reversal though the use of genre expectations.

The act of being subjected to personal interrogation and confessional pressure, once considered as widespread as its Catholic predecessor, is now increasingly reserved for those who cannot afford to buy their way out of it, either through the purchase (in time, money and cultural capital) of a NEXUS card that fast-tracks Canada–US border crossings, or through the access to the social capital, legal counsel and specialised knowledge that enable an individual to assert herself in the face of state authority.[30] *Border Security* separates border-crossers into three categories (see Table 1.1 above) as a result of the need for narrative engagement and production profitability. We, the audience of *Border Security*, sit aloof in judgement of the travellers, simultaneously engaged in a form of affective rehearsal for an imagined moment in which we become the protectors of the state, emotionally affiliating ourselves with the power and perspective of the CBSA officers. We do as we are instructed, not by the officers of the law, but by the persuasive power of the medium and its narrative rhetoric which, in the show's tagline, insists that we 'follow the work of the men and women who protect Canada's borders.'[31] We follow them visually, as the camera moves with them through the performance of their duties; educationally, as we are trained in our expectations of our own border-crossing interrogations; and morally, as we fall into agreement with the officers' decisions, when the narrative editing of the show proves their virtually infallible good judgement.

For the sake of the show's clarity and closure, then, it is better if travellers being questioned are caught in a lie, confess, break down or offer some easy emotional resolution. For the CBSA agents, eliciting a confession makes their job simpler. For the show, too, eliciting confessions makes its work easier, and provides a moment of satisfying catharsis. Getting caught and made to confess produces shame, and shame produces ratings. The border-crossers shown become the subject of a double act of confessing their sins as they answer the voice of authority demanding, 'Where have you been?' 'Why did you travel?' 'How long have you been gone?' while the (Canadian) audience sits behind their screen, offering or refusing benediction from afar.

Confession in this context gives voice to the culpability of the accused while validating the suspicions and moral superiority of the interrogator, reaffirming his right to sit in judgement. It gives narrative voice to collective ideas about national superiority and tells Canadians about themselves – giving them the opportunity to participate in the work of deciding who or what is or is not acceptable in Canada. Talk shows such as *The Jerry Springer Show* or *The Jeremy Kyle Show* rely heavily on theatrical presentations of emotional distress, revealed secrets and the confession of personal indiscretions. They also invite the audience to make guesses about the interviewees' stories while passing judgement on their characters. Similarly, *Border Security*'s generic interest in confession requires the emotional involvement of the audience. Affiliating the audience's viewpoint with the CBSA officers through camera perspective and voiceovers pushes the audience into a more active role as imagined CBSA officers themselves, and they participate in the interrogation process by passing judgement on the travellers in the mode of audience involvement found in a gameshow. *Border Security* invites its Canadian audience to treat the cases it presents as participatory opportunities to judge border-crossers through the eyes of CBSA officials by correctly solving the puzzle of their guilt or innocence. Doing so requires that the audience, like the officers in the show, must 'use their instincts', but those instincts may conflict with the official duties of the CBSA and the legally stated nature of Canadian multicultural society.[32]

Moorti argues that the gameshow 'genre permits the formation of a cosmopolitan identity even as it facilitates the re-inscription of vernacular nationalisms', and that the genre creates 'a site where questions of consumption, cultural citizenship, and national identity are worked out'.[33] Though Moorti's work is specifically in regard to Tamil national identity in South Asia, the point is relevant here too; for the participants in many gameshows, the focal point is a commodity object to be won (a car, a vacation or a cash prize). *Border Security* offers a multi-perspective gameshow. For the 'contestants', who sign away their rights to anonymity under the potentially coercive gaze of a federal officer, the prize is access to Canada. For the officers of the CBSA, who compete against the travellers in the game of cat and mouse set up by the show's editing and genre choices, the prize is the individual and organisational sense of self-worth that comes from identifying 'bad people' and protecting the nation from harm. For the viewers playing along at home with this *de facto* gameshow, the prize is a renewed sense of a value and 'faith in those social narratives and routines in which we are embedded, and through which our self-identity is constituted'.[34] Where these narratives and routines differ from the official version of Canadian national identity, they constitute what Moorti calls a form of vernacular nationalism.[35] *Border Security*'s implied vernacular nationalism differs from official nationalism in several crucial ways, and builds a sense of shared national *feeling* through affect, using bodily representations and bodily reactions as a means of social connection and validation.

Much of the show's work, both in the actions of the CBSA, and in production of social cohesion, is done with bodies. The show engages the bodily affect of the viewers, defining Canadian national identity through the body politic's acceptance or rejection of travellers, and through the binary relationship between the nation and its only neighbour. Canada, unusually, only has a land border with one country, the United States, pushing border sensibilities towards clearer binary divisions of national identity. As Sara Ahmed points out, 'the social bond is always rather sensational. Groups cohere around a shared orientation toward some things being good, treating some things and not others as the cause of delight', or equally, as a cause of concern, of fear or of disgust.[36] In *Border Security*, CBSA officers 'use their instincts' or get a feeling about particular travellers whose bodies, biographies and freedoms are used to define the limits of the nation as they are interrogated, held and searched. With an implied judgement of character, the camera invites the viewer to note the travellers' nervously drumming fingers or tapping feet, and the audience learns to emulate the CBSA officers in reading physical manifestations of emotional states – to use the affective clues the show provides.

The affective power of the show is perhaps most obvious in its deployment of fear as a narrative structure. The eighth episode of season one includes a segment filmed at the Vancouver International Postal Centre, which opens with a CBSA officer's assertion that 'we see a lot of heroin particularly coming through this port; a lot of pornography that shouldn't be coming through, and we see a lot of prohibited weapons components'.[37] The officer's list not only describes her job, it also reiterates the main elements that Pratt and Thompson found to be common motivating elements in their interviews with CBSA officers.[38] Officers exhibit a clear sense of themselves as defending the country against hostile, dangerous or depraved exterior threats. The vernacular nationalism here is binary, and leads to a binary outcome – acceptance or rejection. In contrast to the official policy of multiculturalism, it often works through a cultural-, ethnic- or identity-focused lens.

The job of the CBSA, says *Border Security*'s narrator, is to intercept dangerous material, 'especially when it comes from high-risk countries'.[39] While the issue of what constitutes a 'high-risk country' is not made explicit, the packages in this particular investigation are quickly revealed to have come from Thailand and China, and are declared as children's toys – increasing the perceived threat to Canadian values that the package represents through the juxtaposition of drugs and children – and cell phones, although the first contains illegal steroids and the second illegal stun guns. In many of the show's segments, fear of violence and contamination (through drugs, pornography, etc.) are affective elements, endangering the individual viewer as they endanger the nation. If affect can be used to bind together a disparate group of citizens into a nation, then it can also be used to differentiate that identity from others – especially those that could be perceived as threats to safety or purity of the national identity. Thus the terminology of 'high-risk countries' creates discursive borders for the nation, excluding the dangerous from acceptance into the country.

As Pratt and Thompson note, the definition of racial profiling is heavily disputed, in fact and action, if not in legal precedent.[40] Their interviews with CBSA officers revealed de facto racialised assessment practices, carried out in conjunction with other assessment elements such as travel routes, modes of transportation, behavioural elements and countries of origin.[41] Without the elements of passports and ticket information available in airports, 'at land ports of entry, modes of profiling remain largely informal, symbolic, and interactive', while more recently 'conflation of criminality and security concerns contributes to the slippage between and resultant ambiguity surrounding race and nationality'.[42] The question of who gets searched, interrogated or suspected at land crossings depends, to a greater extent than in airports, on the personal judgement of the officers on duty. That judgement is coloured by masculinist (regardless of the gender of the officer), moralising and nationalist sets of assumptions that nonetheless vary between officers. Pratt and Thompson point out that 'while denying the practice of statistically based "actual" racial profiling, [a] senior manager nonetheless confirmed that if enforcement trends indicate that a certain nationality is a "known" risk for certain kinds of criminality, the they would "pay attention to that", but that this was about risk and nationality, not race – at least not exactly'.[43]

The vernacular nationalism of such activity lies in the unexamined conflation of race and nation, and in the assumptions about the nation protected by the CBSA officers. As Pratt and Thompson note, that nation is characterised through a romanticised chivalric narrative paradigm that draws heavily on imagined European values.[44] It underlay the construction of nineteenth-century Romantic nationalist discourse from 'white knights' to 'fair maidens', and is extremely resilient. These unspoken assumptions are juxtaposed to the more formal language of the Canadian Multiculturalism Act of 1988.

In episode eight of the show's first season, an unclaimed suitcase at the Vancouver airport raises suspicions amongst CBSA officers because 'the contents don't match what should be coming out of that part of the world'.[45] Whether this assertion relates to cultural preconceptions or standardised lists of searchable objects is not clear. Moorji notes that in much of the gameshow structure, 'difference is articulated from within the interstices of global cultural traffic'; in the episode under discussion here, feeling Canadian becomes tied to identifying difference and similarity within a global traffic flow.[46]

That global traffic flow is arrested within the narrative segment at what a CBSA officer calls 'the moment of truth'; first with an advertisement break, then intercut with another storyline.[47] This keeps the audience viewing, builds the narrative suspense required by the detective genre conventions, and restarts the gameshow for the viewers playing along at home. Finally, the voiceover archly explains that one of the contents of the 'unclaimed bag from the Middle East is getting special treatment from Officer Richard', because, according to the officer, some of the 'pieces appear to be more natural' than others, and the difference raises suspicions. A chemical test confirms that the suspicious pieces of charcoal are actually 'over half a kilogram of pure opium'.[48]

The vernacular and official versions of nationalism are equally at play in this episode, and the game requires the audience to resolve the tension between them – in crude terms, avoid ethnic or regional generalisations, but follow their feelings about 'what should be coming out of that part of the world'. The CBSA officers are shown to be highly professional and appear to be following standard protocol – their actions are above professional reproach. The voiceover takes an affectively engaging knowing tone, so the audience is asked to share and validate feelings of suspicion and distrust for the unclaimed baggage from the Middle East – a piece of stark metonymy given cultural weight by violence and movement of refugees from the region. The structure of the voiceover narrative raises a series of semiotic flags including blackness, opium and natural vs. unnatural appearances. The story is not just about material objects; it transposes the discourse of race onto the 'suspicious' objects described, so that the audience feels a sense of relief and reassurance as the suitcase is wheeled away behind a text-over asserting that 'CBSA and a partner agency investigated. Charges are pending against the traveller.'[49] The anonymous traveller is represented metonymically by the suitcase abandoned to its lonely, and apparently well-deserved, incarceration. As Satzewich notes, 'a broadly defined crime-security nexus, defined ideologically by the state, informs how border control officials construct and define individuals who apply for [...] status within Canada. These definitions overlap with various ethnic and racial stereotypes that are also produced discursively at the level of the state and which reinforce existing stereotypes.'[50]

In deploying and relying on the vernacular nationalism of ethnicity and race, the show (sanctioned, supported and vetted by the federal government) raises these affective individual prejudices to the level of state action. A vernacular nationalism built on ethnicity and colonial juxtapositions of 'risky' countries to those of European colonial origins continues beneath the official assertions of the Multiculturalism Act. By enjoining the audience to participate with both the formal discourse of official policy and the affective bodily focus of vernacular nationalism as they 'play along at home' as armchair CBSA officers, the gameshow structure of *Border Security* is 'able to hail the viewer simultaneously as a cosmopolitan and a vernacular subject'.[51]

Border Security develops a thematic relationship to national and individual identity through the deployment of specific genre markers from fiction. Using generic expectations to define the range of possible stories around border interactions, the show focuses and narrows audience understandings of how those interactions work. The show builds cohesion in the organisational identity of the CBSA, and the national identity of Canadian citizens, through a sense of collective pride and self-worth at the expense of those outside the designated group. For the national audience of the show, this means a sometimes-contradictory development of formal vs.

vernacular nationalism. For the development of organisational identity within the CBSA itself, it means a narrative reach for origin myths in detective stories, Westerns and war stories, as well as a re-inscription of the fears, concerns and identity points that motivate CBSA officers. The overlapping elements of gameshow and confessional generic structures make the audience complicit with officers in the interrogations, and develop a national identity based on affiliation with a state security apparatus, while encouraging an attitude of judgemental detachment towards the travellers depicted. The show was actively vetted and sanctioned by the CBSA during its run, and was given special access to restricted areas and activities. Given the potential for conflict between the disparate narrative and nationalist structures of meaning that the show deployed, it is less surprising that the show was cancelled, and more surprising that it lasted as long as it did.

Notes

1. 'Border Security', Force Four Entertainment, 4 May 2014. https://www.forcefour.com/ bordersecurity
2. Sujata Moorji, 'Fashioning a Cosmopolitan Tamil Identity: Game Shows, Commodities and Cultural Identity', *Media, Culture & Society* 26.4 (2004): 550.
3. CBC News/Radio Canada, 'Border Security TV Show Canned after Federal Watchdog Finds Privacy Violation', 13 June 2016. https://www.cbc.ca/news/canada/british-columbia/border-security-cancelled-1.3632468
4. Marsha Lederman, 'Despite Controversy, Filming of New Season of Border Security Underway', *The Globe and Mail* (Toronto, Canada), 9 May 2014. www.theglobeandmail.com
5. Denise Ryan, 'Public Safety Minister Personally Approved Border Security Reality Show', *The Vancouver Sun* (Vancouver, Canada), 18 March 2013. www.vancouversun.com/news/Public+Safety+minister+personally+approved+Border+Security+reality+show+with+video/8112338/story.html
6. Ibid.
7. 'Border Security', IMDb.com, 10 November 2017. www.imdb.com/title/tt2518480/?ref_=nv_sr_1
8. Will Daley, *Canadian Views on CBSA and Border Management* (Ottawa: EKOS Research Associates Inc., 2018).
9. Margaret Atwood, *Survival: A Thematic Guide to Canadian Literature* (Toronto: McClelland and Stewart, 1972).

10. Lynette Hunter, *Outsider Notes: Feminist Approaches to Nation State Ideology, Writers/Readers and Publishing* (Vancouver: Talonbooks, 1996), 113.
11. Anne Pratt and Sara Thompson, 'Chivalry, "Race", and Discretion at the Canadian Border', *The British Journal of Criminology* 48.5 (2008): 620.
12. Ibid.: 622.
13. Ibid.: 625.
14. Ibid.: 626.
15. Ibid.: 625.
16. Sara Ahmed, 'Happy Objects', in *The Affect Theory Reader*, ed. Melissa Gregg and Gregory J. Seigworth (Durham, NC: Duke University Press, 2010), 29–51.
17. Anne Pratt and Sara Thompson, 'Chivalry, "Race", and Discretion at the Canadian Border', *The British Journal of Criminology* 48.5 (2008): 625.
18. Ibid.: 627.
19. Ibid.
20. Ibid.: 629; *Border Security: Canada's Front Line*, season one episode one, directed by Dale Drewery et al. Force Four Entertainment, 2012.
21. Anne Pratt and Sara Thompson, 'Chivalry, "Race", and Discretion at the Canadian Border', *The British Journal of Criminology* 48.5 (2008): 629.
22. Jane Helliener, 'Whiteness and Narratives of a Racialized Canada–US Border at Niagara', *Canadian Journal of Sociology* 37.2 (2012): 118.
23. Jason Concepcion, '"Papers, Please" Is a Disturbingly Relevant Video Game About Immigration', *The Ringer*, 9 February 2017. https://www.theringer.com/2017/2/9/16045604/papers-please-is-a-disturbingly-relevant-video-game-about-immigration-96cda43156af
24. *Border Security: Canada's Front Line*, season one episode one, directed by Dale Drewery et al. Force Four Entertainment, 2012.
25. Ibid.
26. 'Border Security', *National Geographic TV*, 10 November 2017. www.natgeotv.com/ca/border-security
27. *Border Security: Canada's Front Line*, season one episode two, directed by Dale Drewery et al. Force Four Entertainment, 2012.
28. Michel Foucault, *The History of Sexuality Volume I: An Introduction*, trans. Robert Hurley (New York: Pantheon Books, 1978), 59.
29. *Border Security: Canada's Front Line*, season one episode one, directed by Dale Drewery et al. Force Four Entertainment, 2012.
30. 'Nexus', United States Customs and Border Protection, 10 November 2017. www.cbp.gov/travel/trusted-traveler-programs/nexus

31. 'Border Security', IMDb.com, 10 November 2017. www.imdb.com/title/tt2518480/?ref_=nv_sr_1
32. 'Border Security', Force Four Entertainment, 4 May 2014. www.forcefour.com/bordersecurity
33. Sujata Moorji, 'Fashioning a Cosmopolitan Tamil Identity: Game Shows, Commodities and Cultural Identity', *Media, Culture & Society* 26.4 (2004): 549.
34. Chris Rossdale, 'Enclosing Critique: The Limits of Ontological Security', *International Political Sociology* 9.4 (2015): 372.
35. Sujata Moorji, 'Fashioning a Cosmopolitan Tamil Identity: Game Shows, Commodities and Cultural Identity', *Media, Culture & Society* 26.4 (2004): 549.
36. Sara Ahmed, 'Happy Objects', in *The Affect Theory Reader*, ed. Melissa Gregg and Gregory J. Seigworth (Durham, NC: Duke University Press, 2010), 29–51.
37. *Border Security: Canada's Front Line*, season one episode eight, directed by Dale Drewery et al. Force Four Entertainment, 2012.
38. Anne Pratt and Sara Thompson, 'Chivalry, "Race", and Discretion at the Canadian Border', *The British Journal of Criminology* 48.5 (2008): 627.
39. *Border Security: Canada's Front Line*, season one episode eight, directed by Dale Drewery et al. Force Four Entertainment, 2012.
40. Anne Pratt and Sara Thompson, 'Chivalry, "Race", and Discretion at the Canadian Border', *The British Journal of Criminology* 48.5 (2008): 620.
41. Ibid.: 621.
42. Ibid.: 624, 627.
43. Ibid.: 628.
44. Ibid.
45. *Border Security: Canada's Front Line*, season one episode eight, directed by Dale Drewery et al. Force Four Entertainment, 2012.
46. Sujata Moorji, 'Fashioning a Cosmopolitan Tamil Identity: Game Shows, Commodities and Cultural Identity', *Media, Culture & Society* 26.4 (2004): 549–67.
47. *Border Security: Canada's Front Line*, season one episode eight, directed by Dale Drewery et al. Force Four Entertainment, 2012.
48. Ibid.
49. Ibid.
50. Vic Satzewich, 'Visa Officers as Gatekeepers of a State's Borders: The Social Determinants of Discretion in Spousal Sponsorship Cases in Canada', *Journal of Ethnic and Migration Studies*, 40.9 (2013): 1456.
51. Sujata Moorji, 'Fashioning a Cosmopolitan Tamil Identity: Game

Shows, Commodities and Cultural Identity', *Media, Culture & Society* 26.4 (2004): 550.

Bibliography

Ahmed, Sara. 'Happy Objects' in *The Affect Theory Reader*. Ed. Melissa Gregg and Gregory J. Seigworth. Durham, NC: Duke University Press, 2010. 29–51.
Amoore, Louise. 'Interventions on Rethinking 'The Border' in Border Studies'. *Political Geography* 30: 2 (2011): 61–9.
Atwood, Margaret. *Survival: A Thematic Guide to Canadian Literature*. Toronto: McClelland and Stewart, 1972.
'Border Security'. Force Four Productions, 4 May 2014. www.forcefour .com/ bordersecurity
'Border Security'. Global TV, 4 May 2014. www.globaltv.com/bordersecur ity
'Border Security'. Global TV, 21 April 2015. www.globaltv.com/borderse curity
'Border Security'. IMDb.com, 10 November 2017. www.imdb.com/title/tt 2518480/?ref_=nv_sr_1
'Border Security'. National Geographic TV, 10 November 2017. www.nat geotv.com/ca/border-security
CBC News. 'Border Security TV Show Canned after Federal Watchdog Finds Privacy Violation'. CBC/Radio Canada, 13 June 2016. https:// www.cbc.ca/news/canada/british-columbia/border-security-cancelled -1.3632468
Concepcion, Jason. '"Papers, Please" Is a Disturbingly Relevant Video Game About Immigration'. *The Ringer*, 9 February 2017. https://www .theringer.com/2017/2/9/16045604/papers-please-is-a-disturbingly- relevant-video-game-about-immigration-96cda43156af
Daley, Will. *Canadian Views on CBSA and Border Management*. Ottawa: EKOS Research Associates Inc., 2018.
Drewery, Dale et al., dir. *Border Security: Canada's Front Line*, season one episode one. Force Four Entertainment, 2012.
Drewery, Dale et al., dir. *Border Security: Canada's Front Line*, season one episode two. Force Four Entertainment, 2012.
Drewery, Dale et al., dir. *Border Security: Canada's Front Line*, season one episode eight. Force Four Entertainment, 2012.
Drewery, Dale et al., dir. *Border Security: Canada's Front Line*, season one episode nine. Force Four Entertainment, 2012.
Foucault, Michel. *The History of Sexuality Volume I: An Introduction*. Trans. Robert Hurley. New York: Pantheon Books, 1978.
Helliener, Jane. 'Whiteness and Narratives of a Racialized Canada–US

Border at Niagara'. *Canadian Journal of Sociology* 37.2 (2012): 109–36.

Hunter, Lynette. *Outsider Notes: Feminist Approaches to Nation State Ideology, Writers/Readers and Publishing*. Vancouver: Talonbooks, 1996.

Lederman, Marsha. 'Despite Controversy, Filming of New Season of Border Security Underway'. *The Globe and Mail* (Toronto), 9 May 2014. www.theglobeandmail.com

Moorji, Sujata. 'Fashioning a Cosmopolitan Tamil Identity: Game Shows, Commodities and Cultural Identity'. *Media, Culture & Society* 26.4 (2004): 549–67.

'Nexus'. United States Customs and Border Protection, 10 November 2017. www.cbp.gov/travel/trusted-traveler-programs/nexus

Peters, Michael A. 'Foucault, Biopolitics, and the Birth of Neoliberalism'. *Critical Studies in Education* 48.2 (2007): 165–78.

Pratt, Anne and Sara Thompson. 'Chivalry, "Race", and Discretion at the Canadian Border'. *The British Journal of Criminology* 48.5 (2008): 620–40.

Rossdale, Chris. 'Enclosing Critique: The Limits of Ontological Security'. *International Political Sociology* 9.4 (2015): 369–89. doi:10.1111/ips.12103.

Ryan, Denise. 'Public Safety Minister Personally Approved Border Security Reality Show'. *The Vancouver Sun* (Vancouver). 18 March 2013. www.vancouversun.com/news/Public+Safety+minister+personally+approved+Border+Security+reality+show+with+video/8112338/story.html

Satzewich, Vic. 'Visa Officers as Gatekeepers of a State's Borders: The Social Determinants of Discretion in Spousal Sponsorship Cases in Canada'. *Journal of Ethnic and Migration Studies* 40.9 (2013): 1450–69.

CHAPTER 2

Border Media: Contributions to a Non-Linear History of the Detroit River

Vincent Manzerolle

In 2019, a Canadian taxi driver was sentenced to sixteen months in a US prison for 'steering desperate immigrants to a railroad tunnel under the Detroit River', allowing them to enter the United States illegally.[1] This particular route was notable, not only for its illegality, but also because of the inherent danger involved given the tunnel's continued use as an essential conduit for cross-border rail cargo. During the trial it became clear that the tunnel, as dangerous as it is, was likely used an indeterminate amount of times, by the convict in this case, and perhaps others, serving as a reminder that people and cargo move across borders according to different circulatory regimes.

The Windsor-Detroit Rail Tunnel is less than a kilometre from Sandwich First Baptist Church, built in 1851, one of the oldest Black churches in Canada. Promoted by the first Black-owned newspaper in Canada, the *Voice of the Fugitive* (also founded in 1851), the church was a critical stop for the not-so-literal Underground Railroad – a formal/informal network of people, information and built infrastructure that directed enslaved people towards a promised freedom in the dominion of Canada and away from slave-holding states in the American South. A proper Canadian rail terminus in Windsor took another three years to complete. Borders are gatekeeping sites, but also horizons of escape or liberation.

Some cross-border flows have been even more difficult to control. The 'Windsor Hum' – a mysterious sub-30hz low frequency known as an 'infrasound' operating at the bottom of human hearing – has haunted these very same border communities, causing windows and walls to rumble while inducing a general state of unease in people.[2] It has been estimated that the cause of these vibrations is blast furnaces operated by US Steel on the secretive Zug Island, indirectly confirmed by the fact that the hum disappeared once the blast furnaces were idled. Zug Island – artificially created by the Henry Ford company in order to better access his once sprawling River Rouge Factory Complex – sits in the Detroit River between the construction site for the new Gordie Howe International Bridge, and the privately owned and currently operating Ambassador Bridge, built upon the historical site of the interface between European settlers and First Nations communities. It is a testament to the inseparability of economic, political and cultural forces converged and materialised in one space. Indeed, this convergence often makes this border crossing a historically significant site for understanding how these forces shape particular regimes of circulation.

In February 2022, the Ambassador Bridge – the busiest land crossing between the United States and Canada – was blockaded for a week by the so-called 'Freedom Convoy', an event which epitomised not only the reactionary political climate of the COVID-19 pandemic and its specific politics of circulation but, more materially, how integral the flow of goods across this singular land crossing is to the regional economy, and national politicians.[3] The economic disruption was so significant (between US$350–400 million worth in trade crosses per day)[4] that it led to Canadian Prime Minister Justin Trudeau invoking the never-before-used 'Emergencies Act' in order to force an end to the blockade.

Taken together, these brief scenes from the Detroit River borderlands reveal the multilayered nature of cross-border flows, inviting us to consider how these media of circulation shape and reshape the communities in which they are embedded. Furthermore, these scenes reveal how border crossings are nodal points within larger networks of circulation, they distil the contradictions of the existing spatio-temporal regimes that characterise transnational capitalism. Borders are sites that invite us to theorise the materiality of circulation, and to contextualise this materiality within broader historical and political economic formations.

The goal of this chapter is to broaden the theoretical engagement with borders as cultural, political, geographic and economic phenomena. It does this by focusing on the mediating function of borders, and, as such, develops a media theoretical perspective to understand the overlapping forms of circulation – people, goods, information, culture – that emerge out of infrastructural configurations. More generally, I argue that border regions offer an opportunity to investigate the logistical dimensions of media, shaping the circulation of products, people, information and capital; conceptualised as media, borders act as the interfaces of empire.

The chapter also does this by developing a media theoretical perspective, one that returns to the essential inseparability of communication and transportation, shaped and reshaped by infrastructure both natural and technical. In this chapter, media is here understood as circulatory infrastructure that provides the material grooves in which cross-border flows act and re-act upon each other. Borders are 'multi-media' phenomena, comprising the messy integration of mediating infrastructure that shapes the flows of people, goods, information, culture in complex ways. They are distilled circulatory thresholds. They act, whether politically or geographically (even geologically) as contradictory points of both connection and separation, places where the constitutive function of space-time binding via mediating infrastructure is materialised – often acting as circulatory nodes that can function as bottlenecks or accelerants.

The chapter argues that, from this perspective, borders not only provide nodal points for understanding the mediating effect of infrastructure – or 'border media' – but they also provide a concentrated site in which to investigate and unpack how this infrastructure reflects the shifting political economic forces that materially determine borderlands more generally. In order to develop and ground this theoretical framework, the chapter uses the example of the Detroit River as a specific site of enquiry, where the impact of the border and related infrastructure offers a synecdochic view into the circulatory pathways and barriers of the 'empire of capital'.[5] Put simply, this chapter uses a localised point on the Canada–US border, with all of its historical and material contingencies, to theorise the mediating function of borders more generally.

Borders offer concentrated sites in which political, economic, technological and cultural forces become materially instantiated. On the general significance of borders to understanding the modern world, Achille Mbembe writes, 'Borders. Everything begins with them, and all paths lead back to them. They are no longer merely a line of demarcation separating sovereign entities. Increasingly, they are the name used to describe the organized violence that underpins both contemporary capitalism and our world in general.'[6] Our contemporary global order, such as it is, is increasingly defined by the contradictions and tensions implicated in a mediating process that Mbembe calls 'borderization', whose volatility stems from pressures to simultaneously accelerate and control circulation.[7] In this case the borderisation is symptomatic of contemporary capitalism's acceleratory logic shaping the circulation of goods, people and capital across and through the Detroit River: borders are specifically bound up with circulatory functions and thresholds, they act as the receiver/transmitters across and through the Detroit River.[8]

From the perspective of theorising the mediating function of borders, Essex County is a worthwhile regional case study for a number of reasons. As the most southern county in Canada it is uniquely surrounded by both a geographic and a political border (see Figure 2.1), creating a peninsula surrounded on three sides by the United States. This particular Canadian region is acutely impacted by the Canada–US border, and its history – cultural, economic, political, infrastructural – reflects theorisations of borders both explicitly and

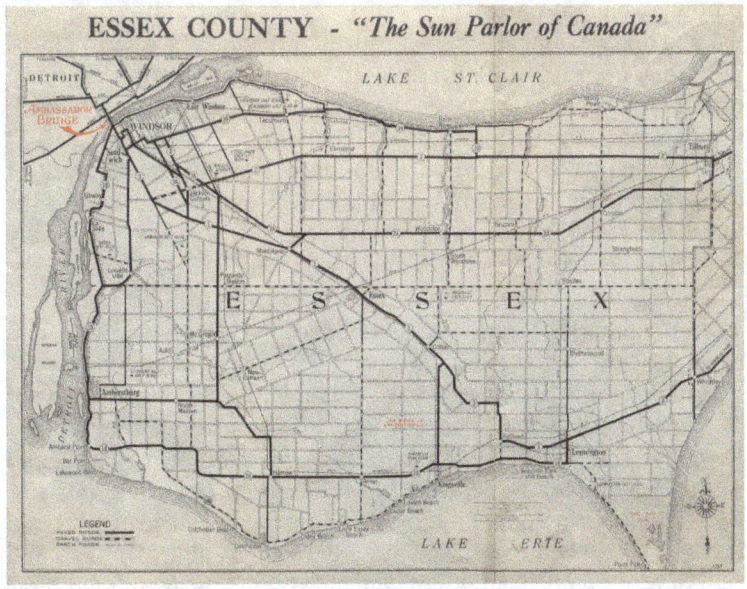

Figure 2.1 Map of Essex County c. 1930

implicitly, stretching back even before the establishment of trading posts by Europeans at the beginning of the eighteenth century. It is a region that has been profoundly shaped by the forces of borderisation sedimented within the various border infrastructure that makes up Essex County.

What follows offers conceptual and analytic signposts towards engaging with border media through their infrastructural and logistical dimensions, using the Detroit River as the ur-medium upon which this border crossing depends. Two representations of the logistical, mediated existence of this boundary point encapsulate the contradictions at the heart of its infrastructural history: the Ambassador Bridge and Michigan Central Station (MCS). While one, the Ambassador Bridge, pulses with the circulatory rhythms of cross-border supply chains and international trade, the other is a widely circulated example of contemporary urban ruins, an icon of the decay and decline of the 'Paris of the Midwest', e.g. Detroit.[9] Recently the MCS has been granted a second life as it has been purchased by the Ford Motor Company to act as the hub for future advanced automotive research and development and its years' long restoration process speaks to the multiple ways that the sedimentation of built infrastructure can be reimagined and repurposed. Among other examples of border media, we might include rail lines, ports, ferries, radio broadcasting and First Nation trails, to name only a few. These converge on the form of the Detroit River to facilitate or control particular types of circulation.

The chapter is structured as follows. First, I treat the task of theorising the Canada–US border through the specific case of the Detroit River border crossing, making the case that it is historically important and analytically useful. I will then broaden my analysis to consider the role of border media, particularly infrastructure, within a theory of empire that builds on the work of Innis and others. Next, I will discuss the crucial importance of temporality by looking at the work of Manuel De Landa, employing his method of crafting 'non-linear' histories; here I'll think through the Detroit River in terms of geological and thermodynamic dimensions. I build on this framework by returning to the concept of border media as one reflecting the 'mineralisation' of broader social structures and how these constitute the grooves within which culture, politics and economy are embedded. I will conclude by briefly examining three specific infrastructural media – river, rail and road – important to understanding the non-linear history of the Detroit River. I conclude with a few considerations regarding sustainability within the region in the face of unprecedented new localised infrastructure spending.

'Frontier Metropolis'

The strategic importance of the Detroit River has long been the source of its development as both a natural political and geographic asset, and because of this it has been acutely shaped by the imposition and reimposition of borders by a sequence of empires. Even for the pre-European settlers, the Detroit River was a natural border between territories, evidenced by massive ancient burial mounds strewn along its shores.[10] Later, in the seventeenth century, the Detroit River acted as an informal boundary between the Haudenosaunee (aligned with the British and Dutch) and the retreating Wyandot (Huron) and other western tribes (aligned with France).[11] The founding of the settlement of Fort Pontchartrain on the Detroit River by Antoine de la Mothe Cadillac in 1701 was meant to act as a border outpost (see Figure 2.2), a 'frontier metropolis' considerably deeper within the North American interior than any previous European settlement, providing an advantage both commercial and military for the Empire of France.[12] It was strategically chosen to create a buffer between the tribes allied with France, and those of the Iroquois and the British, for which a peace had just been negotiated in the year 1700.

Despite the peace treaty, the colonisation of the south shore (current Windsor) was delayed until 1749 when a Jesuit mission was founded as both a means to evangelise to Indigenous peoples, but also to serve as a trading post that added some distance from the established fort of the French (Lajeunesse). This early fort, meant to capitalise on water access to the interior via the Great Lakes and its tributaries, as well as to exploit the proximity to tribes who had access to untouched hunting grounds for furs, was also envisioned by Cadillac as a settlement comprising both European and First Nation settlers and included enslaved people throughout its early history.[13] It was conceptualised from the outset as a settlement at the boundary of two civilisations. However, the European settlements of the Detroit River, first on the north shore (Detroit) in 1701 and then on the south shore (Windsor) in 1749, were not defined by any formal border, and the communities along the river were collectively referred to as 'Detroit' for roughly ninety years, even after being ceded to the British from 1763–96.[14] It was only with the Jay Treaty of 1794 (implemented in 1796) that a formal political boundary divided the Detroit River communities. As Teasdale explains, 'In 1795, the Detroit River region was one community. There was no border to cross, no duties to pay.'[15] Yet despite this formality, flows of people, goods and money moved across the river relatively smoothly well into the early twentieth century.[16]

The rise of manufacturing in the Detroit River region on both sides of the border, associated with Fordism (Harvey) and the mass production of automobiles, stimulated rapid growth, wealth accumulation and economic integration.[17] This integration expanded considerably in the wake of the Reciprocity Treaty of 1854, and later through the Auto-Pact Treaty of 1965, then NAFTA in 1993 and its recent replacement, the USMCA, which took effect on 1 July 2020. As such, the border is an archive of various political and economic configurations, acting as a testing ground for industrial and neoliberal capitalism. A resurgent protectionism from the Trump administration (2017–21), and its USMCA free trade agreement (effective in 2020), persisting into Biden administration, with its

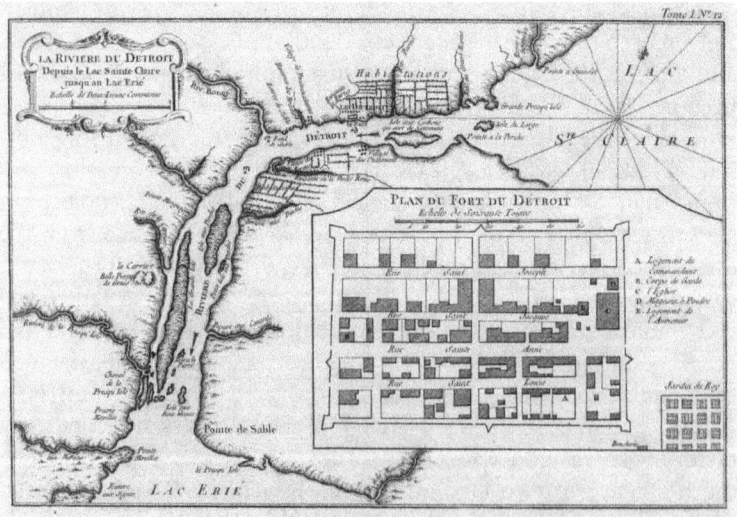

Figure 2.2 Map and plan of Fort Pontchartrain in 1764

strengthening of national interests and thickening borders, may upend the neoliberal logistical and infrastructural order that defined the end of the twentieth and beginning of the twenty-first centuries.

Given this history the Windsor-Detroit border is one of the most important points for cross-border trade between the two nations. Roughly 30 per cent of Canada–US trade flows across this border point, with 2.5 million transport trucks hauling CDN$100 billion in trade in 2016.[18] The build-up of border infrastructure, particularly recent investments in the Herb Gray Parkway in Windsor, and the forthcoming Gordie Howe International Bridge have brought an estimated CDN$7.1 billion in new infrastructure spending to the region.[19]

The Logistics of Empire

The conceptual focus on border media is rooted squarely in the historical and theoretical work of Harold Innis, a foundational figure in the discipline of media studies and part of the Toronto School of Communication Theory.[20] Canadian economic historian and media theorist Harold Innis was an internationally celebrated political economist, often described as the intellectual forebear of Marshall McLuhan.[21] Innis' legacy, however, is distinctly bifurcated, separated by his early work on Canadian Economic history usually linked to his Staple Thesis. His later work, although initially dismissed as being opaque and byzantine in nature, was popularised by McLuhan, and is currently undergoing a renaissance with several new books published in recent years.[22]

For Innis, media are infrastructural in nature (although he did not explicitly use the word).[23] Communication, as one necessary function of media, allowed Innis to identify one of the core structural features of modern Western history: a growing shift away from concerns over temporal organisation and towards those over spatial organisation. The modern West had become a 'space-binding culture . . . whose predominant interest was in space – land as real estate, voyage, discovery, movement, expansion, empire, control'. Innis' assertion about a spatial – indeed, circulatory – bias in modern Western political economies was also couched in an emphasis on the associated forms of 'leverage' that funnel 'power to elites'.[24] We can extend these core aspects of Innis' work to the theorisation of borders, both in the specific case of the Canada–US border, but also to a broader analysis of borders within a global economy marked by the contradictory flows of goods, people, information and capital.

It is in this broader horizon of applicability that Innis' intellectual legacy offers up a model for using specific historical case studies to detect larger historical patterns. As evidence of this pivot from the particular to the general, we need only compare the titles of Innis' earliest and latest published works: *A History of the Canadian Pacific Railway* and *Empire and Communications*. Innis' early work on the development of the Canadian nation state as a function of changing and contested imperial borders constituted the foundation for a more general theory of how media are infrastructural components of larger, power-laden social structures (e.g. empire). The title of his final published work – *Changing Concepts of Time* – completed just before his untimely death, captures what he believed to be the major vulnerability of modern thought: a disregard for temporality and hence a failure to understand the sustainability of this, or any, society. In order to redress this deficiency, Innis developed historically grounded conceptual tools to understand and interrogate how spatial biases became sedimented, and largely invisible, in everyday life.

Innis' concept of space-time bias (1964) is conventionally understood as pertaining to the cultural and economic implications of communication media and their impact on the sustainability/stability (or not) of a given community. For example, inscriptions in stone are time biased (emphasising durability through time), while those using papyrus are space-biased (emphasising portability across space). Bias can thus be used to understand how differences in the media supported vectors of circulation shape culture and economy. Thus, for Innis the concept of communication involves both the movement (or circulation) of physical goods and information. The question of bias, it must be noted, is not an absolute characteristic, but a relative one, and one embedded within a wider media ecology that allows historians, theorists and policymakers to consider the potentially destabilising effects of new media (and, hence, new vectors or modalities of circulation).

While the concept of bias was explicitly developed in Innis' later work dealing with communication media, especially *The Bias of Communication* and *Empire and Communications*, many recent academics returning to Innis have begun to see this early work on transportation and his later work on media as being part of one long project.[25] This was a project not limited to explaining the rise and fall of past empires, but one meant to guide current and future research and policymaking. For Innis the concept of bias is a heuristic tool meant to help us understand the 'laboratory of history' in the hopes that the resulting reflexive knowledge would enhance our collective ability to shape our shared future.[26]

Innis' perspective, developed through rigorous historical research, used concepts to better understand the materialities and particularities of prevailing media and related infrastructure. Reflexive knowledge, for Innis, emerged at the intersection of abstraction and contingency. In this regard, there are many important and unique characteristics of the Detroit River border crossing which might lend themselves to a more general set of transferrable insights (which likely reflects the truism that all border crossings have their distinguishing features). But in this case those unique characteristics not only speak to the construction of this border crossing, but they are also symptoms of the spatial and temporal biases of past and existing political economic regimes, or 'empires'. For Innis, empire is a category used to understand certain forms of political economic cultural expansion, or control. Over the course of several books and articles, Innis explained how empires emerged from (and were at the mercy of) a specific equilibrium between various monopolies of force, wealth and knowledge.[27] The specific relationship and prospective equilibrium reached among these factors would enable/constrain how a given empire could extend through space and/or time because of this *relative* stability.

Considered in this framework, the Windsor-Detroit border is an especially rich site for exploring theoretical lines of analysis about the Canada–US border as a symptom of the logistics of empire(s). It is one of the most historically important border crossing between the US and Canada, with a chaotic history of changing hands between empires political, religious or economic. It is in this last sense that the theorisation about this specific border crossing reflects the logistical 'interfaces' of empire. It also entails the expansion and incorporation of areas outside itself, to creates various means of interfacing with the outside or margins of a specific political-economic system. The boundaries and borders of empire entail the creation of media able to incorporate and subsume aspects of its productive capacities or natural resources. The logistics of empire revolve around an expanding circulatory network that incorporates new human cultures in order to extend and reproduce a particular protocol for the accumulation of wealth, power and/or knowledge.

In this sense, borders are liminal sites relying on a variety of media as key logistical infrastructure – circulation is dependent upon material forms of support, or 'mediation'. Logistics are a specific subset of infrastructure that here can be understood in terms of the arrangement and consequent circulation of people, goods, information and capital. The point here is one about both the logistical and infrastructural realities of media, as materialities that enable (or disable) certain organisational forms, thus contributing to their reproduction (or not) over space and time. Media theorist John Durham Peters has usefully elaborated on the logistical function of media:

> The job of logistical media is to organize and orient, to arrange people and property, to arrange people and property, often into grids. They both coordinate and subordinate, arranging relationships among people and things. Logistical media establish the zero points where the x and y axes converge. McLuhan's slogan 'The medium is the message' applies particularly well to them. They prepare the ground on which we can make such distinctions as nature and culture. They span ocean, ground, air, outer space, and cyberspace ... Logistical media pretend to be neutral and abstract, but they do often encode a subtle and deep political or religious partisanship.[28]

From Peters we get a sense that media offer the 'infrastructure of Being', whether personal or social.[29] Thus from the construction of media infrastructure, and in this case, infrastructure that specifically constitute the particularities of the Windsor-Detroit border, we can get a sense of the type of 'Being' that is enabled through infrastructural and logistical dimensions of media. Indeed, border logistics have played and continue to play a key role in shaping economic development and investment along the Detroit River. On the Canadian side, the entire economy has centred on the border as a competitive advantage.[30]

In the beginning, before man-made bridges, tunnels, ports and so forth, there was the river and the land. It is often claimed that geography is destiny, but I would like to suggest that it is perhaps more accurate to say that, in fact, *geology* is destiny.[31] 'Geological history is a precursor to later history'.[32] What is perhaps most interesting about John Durham Peters' understanding of the logistical aspects of media, is that they originate in what he calls 'earth' media, or what Manuel De Landa and Jussi Parikka call the geological foundations of media. In this view media are not strictly speaking man-made; bedrock, rivers, lakes, forests, tundra, etc., offer naturally occurring media, upon which humans arrange and adapt themselves.[33]

This is a position very closely aligned to Innis' own. For Innis (*The Fur Trade*), the development of European communities in North America (especially Canada) was as much about using the media of rivers and lakes to expand the European market for goods (and equally important exploiting local knowledge and technologies to do so, as in the canoe), as it was about ship building, the processing of furs, or the planting of crops. The Detroit River must itself be understood in geological terms as a medium thousands of years in the making, with its own particularities in soil, climate, flora and fauna, that have given rise to other forms of sedimentation associated with human settlement.[34] Border media such as bridges, ports, tunnels, shipping lanes and trenches, broadcasting towers, underwater cables, and highways are literally grounded in, and inseparable from, the geological constitution of the Detroit River itself.

Towards a Non-Linear History of Circulation at the Border

To provide a comprehensive history would be far too massive, and so I have 'portaged' De Landa's concept of 'non-linear history' to understand the parallel aspects of border infrastructure development. A non-linear approach to historical research admits a variety of 'attractors' and 'bifurcations' allowing for 'multiple coexisting forms of varying complexity' creating 'strong mutual interactions (or feedback) between components'.[35] What this means for the study of human society is to admit that human communities exist within a much longer time scale in which infrastructural dimensions of everyday life create situated and parallel forms of equilibrium (or disequilibrium) that lie outside of the traditional linear descriptions of history (e.g. as narrative that subsumes all phenomena within a linear causal trajectory, e.g. the 'great men of history' model). De Landa's approach allows for geological (sedimentation and mineralisation) and thermodynamic (matter-energy flows) considerations as part of a historical and theoretical framework. This approach compliments Innis' focus on the materialities that shape the vectors and modalities of circulation in time and space.[36]

Referring to the various stages of societal development, from hunter-gatherer to bureaucratic agrarian society, De Landa suggests we consider this change not as 'progressive developmental steps, each better than the previous' but rather as phases that may coexist in the same way that 'water's solid, liquid, and gas phases may coexist'.[37] He writes, 'human history did not follow a straight line, as if everything pointed toward civilized society as humanity's ultimate goal. On the contrary, at each bifurcation alternative stable states were possible, and once actualized, they coexisted and interacted with one another.'[38] These bifurcations can be thought of as moments of disruption caused by changes in geological (e.g. infrastructure) or thermodynamic (e.g. matter-energy flows) forces. As De Landa explains, 'cities arise from the flow of matter-energy, but once a town's mineral infrastructure has emerged, it reacts to those flows, creating a new set of constraints that either intensifies or inhibits them'.[39] With respect to this non-linear approach, De Landa elaborates:

> nonlinear models show that without an energy flow of a certain intensity, no system, whether natural or cultural, can gain access to the self-organization resources constituted by endogenously generated stable states (attractors) and transitions between those states (bifurcations) ... nonlinear models [also] illustrate how the structures generated by matter-energy flows, once in place, react back on those flows either to inhibit them or further intensify them ... many different types of structures can play this catalytic role: the mineralized infrastructure of cities themselves; the organizations (centralized or decentralized) that live within the mineral walls; and various other cultural materials that move in and out of cities or accumulate in them: skills and knowledge, money and credit, informal rules and institutional norms.[40]

In sum, 'From the point of view of energetic and catalytic flows, human societies are very much like lava flows; and human-made structures (mineralized cities and institutions) are very much like mountains and rocks: accumulations of materials hardened and shaped by historical processes.'[41]

Geology speaks to the material infrastructure, as well as the various layers of mineralisation that may exist in parallel with more contemporary thermodynamic regimes; for example, the shifting reliance on wind, steam, electricity, or combustion-centred transportation. Specifically, Detroit has played a key role in commercialising various thermodynamic regimes, but is most associated with the combustion engine and the mass production of the personal automobile. The various sedimentations that litter the region, for example Albert Khan's groundbreaking factory architecture, or the design of highways, bridges and inspection centres, even the abandoned buildings, neighbourhoods and crumbling infrastructure, are in many ways symptoms of the acceleratory thermodynamics enabled by the combustion engine as it was integrated by, and ultimately transformed, the circulatory flows of twentieth-century capitalism.[42]

Manuel DeLanda outlines a periodisation that extends from the years 1000 to 1700, ending at precisely the moment when the Detroit River border region is integrated into European colonialism within the founding of Fort Pontchartrain by Cadillac (later known simply as Detroit). This mineralisation is itself infrastructural to the thermodynamics of circulation that have integrated the region into a much broader political economic system – a link between extractive colonial frontiers and distant urban centres. The use of geology as a potential media framework extends the time scale of analysis to usefully emphasise the impact of infrastructure like forts, bridges, tunnels, railways and ports. Indeed, the construction of each of these along the Windsor-Detroit border crossing is a direct response to the unique geological context provided by the Detroit River.[43]

It is precisely due to this extended geological time scale that the history of the Detroit River itself, created some 14,000 years ago with the melting of the glaciers, might be incorporated into an expanded theory of media and borders. The last 300 years of the Detroit River have been marked by an acceleration of movement between, most significantly, the European empires that have colonised and exploited this crossing with the river itself acting as a key infrastructural medium – leading up to the most recent empire that is transnational capitalism and its vital circulation of goods, people and money for which the Detroit River has been a nodal point.[44]

This border, insofar as we can consider it both geological and political, requires specific types of media to bind space-time in unique ways; a perennial tension between control and flow. We can understand one element of a non-linear history of the Detroit River in geological and thermodynamic terms, through the infrastructure that has created and overcome the border. It is as an effect of the circulatory needs of this most recent empire, an empire dominated primarily by the flows of international capital. A history of the Detroit River in geological and thermodynamic terms focuses on the infrastructure that has paradoxically created and overcome the border. Building bridges and tunnels, dredging rivers and creating regional roads/highways require a geological orientation, an understanding of soil and rock mechanics, a specialised area of praxis known as geotechnical engineering. Moreover, all of these require long-term considerations.[45] In this process of instituting a specific space-time regime at the border we see the interplay between geology and thermodynamics, as new infrastructure enable and constrain certain types of flows, leading to more 'bifurcations' shaping the developmental trajectory of the region. I would like now to briefly sketch part of this non-linear history through the political economic development of the region.

After the defeat of the French by the British in 1759–60, the region was taken over by the British who continued the development of the fur trade, largely through the Hudson Bay and Northwest companies that constituted the economic and military heart of the border communities. Until 1794, and the establishment of the Jay Treaty which established borders between the British Empire and the newly constituted United States, the Detroit River was used as a conduit to transport furs out of the interior, and to deliver supplies to the border region and outposts further in the interior to maintain the trade network now controlled by British mercantile interests.

After the takeover of Detroit by the Americans in 1796, two communities were almost immediately established on the south side of the Detroit River: Amherstburg at the lower mouth of the Detroit River, which would serve as a military buffer; and Sandwich town (now just west of the Ambassador Bridge), which would continue to serve the commercial interests of the British in the region and serve as a safe haven for British loyalists fleeing American rule. Each town was developed in relation to the Detroit River as key media for the transportation of commerce and military strength.

The American takeover of Detroit distinctly changed the economic and cultural composition of the region. The development of steam powered water vehicles built specialised skill and manufacturing capacity in the region; the opening of the Erie Canal in 1825 increased migration and demand for regular transportation routes linking east coast ports, especially New York. The capacity for building and fixing steam engines was built up significantly in the area and turned it into a key shipping hub, as well as a burgeoning cross-river ferry industry for which very little has been written or documented.

The next moment of bifurcation was the building of the Michigan Central Railroad (completed in 1846) on the north shore and the Great Western Railway on the south shore (completed in 1854). Adoption of the 'Reciprocity Treaty' coincided with completion of the Great Western Railway connection in Windsor at Detroit River; the Reciprocity Treaty essentially allowed 'farm, forest, mines, and fisheries to cross the boundary line freely for a ten-year term'.[46] In 1858, the first underwater cross-border telegraph cable was laid, connecting the communities with the speed of electric information, and allowing for better coordination of cross-border movement. Much has been written on the impact of the rail system on communities, and indeed Harold Innis himself has written a great deal on this topic as it relates to Canadian economic development, although Innis seems to have had a blind spot for this border point. The economic development of the south shore, Windsor, is largely tied to the arrival of the Great Western Railway.[47] The expansion of rail capacity on either side of the Detroit River further stimulated an industry dedicated to the ferrying of goods, and indeed rail cars, across the river.

The volume of trade enabled by the rail transport stimulated demand for some quicker way to cross the river, and speculation about building a rail bridge over the river began a few short years after the completion of the Great Western Rail line.[48] The needs of merchants to move goods across the river more quickly, since increasing trade volume created a bottleneck at the Detroit River, led to calls for the construction of a bridge or tunnel over the river almost as soon as the Reciprocity Treaty was adopted in 1854.

Figure 2.3 Postcard of CPR rail car ferry and dock, Windsor, Canada, c. 1916

Yet demands for a cross-river rail bridge met with opposition both from local residents and from the ferry industry which saw it as a direct threat. Ferry interests were not as powerful in Sarnia and Fort Erie, allowing investments in rail bridges and crossings. Ferry interests in Detroit River were significantly more powerful and profitable. Local interests of varying kinds resisted the potential for a faster means of cross-border circulation. What is most interesting is how some of the opposition to the rail bridge was mobilised. As evidence of more long-standing sentiment in the region, consider this 1898 opinion piece from the *Michigan Farmer*:

> The perennial proposition to build a bridge over the Detroit River opposite the city, in the interests of various lines of railways with eastern connections, is again before congress. It seems very singular that anyone with a regard to the future welfare of Detroit would favor such a scheme. The only ones who would profit by the building of such a bridge would be the through transportation lines between the east and the west. The business interests of this city would be affected very materially, and to their detriment. That river practically makes Detroit a railway terminus, and gives its residents the business which naturally

comes from occupying such a position. With a bridge all that business will cease. The big ferryboats will be rendered useless and their crews discharge[d] ... Detroit would become a station on the route between New York and Chicago instead of a terminal point. When a railway runs through a city or town, only stopping to take on or let off passengers, business is carried away from it. That would surely be the case in Detroit with a bridge over its river.[49]

The perspective articulated above acknowledges, albeit tacitly, the role of infrastructure in shaping the spatio-temporal flows within a region, thereby affecting the sustainability of its culture and economy. Hence, for a variety of reasons, the Ambassador Bridge was considerably delayed. It is worth noting that construction of the bridge finished on 6 November 1929, almost exactly one week after the stock market crashed on 28 October 1929.[50] Furthermore, in catering only to automotive transportation powered by the combustion engine, the bridge reflected the new thermodynamic bifurcation that had been catalysed by the Detroit region itself.

A cross-river rail line would not be completed until the opening of the CP rail tunnel in 1910 (which was itself the product of several decades of failed attempts) (Cosgrove). The rail tunnel was initially called the Michigan Central Railway Tunnel, tied directly to the forthcoming Michigan Central Station.

The tunnel, for which the construction deserves its own separate analysis, was part of the infrastructural build-up that led to the construction of the new central train terminal in Detroit that would be named Michigan Central Station (MCS), designed by the same architects responsible for Grand Central Station in New York. At the time of its completion it was the highest train station in the world – a massive monolithic building meant to convey the significance of the border region as a node in the transnational rail system, and constructed specifically to handle the increased volume of traffic/trade afforded by the new rail tunnel.[51]

The MCS was completed in 1915, and, interestingly, was designed before the mass adoption of automobile traffic. It was finished when trains were the ultimate sign of speed, and steam power was the defining thermodynamic order. As such, it was designed with no parking, could not accommodate the increased volume of automobile traffic, and was built under a particular model of urban expansion that

Figure 2.4 Postcard of Detroit River Tunnel, Detroit, *c.* 1915

Figure 2.5 Postcard of the 'New' Michigan Central Station *c.* 1936

did not take into account how cars and roads would reshape the development of Detroit. Empty now for decades, Michigan Central Station has been called the 'ruin porn crown jewel'.[52]

Combustion engines built upon the early development of steam engines and unleashed a new era of economic and cultural acceleration. This bifurcation emerges in the contrast between these two iconic structures, or mineralisations, along the Detroit River: the Ambassador Bridge and the Michigan Central Station. While the Michigan Central Station represented the epitome of the influence of the rail, and the steam engine regime of logistics, the Ambassador Bridge was a testament to the rapid spread of the combustion engine and auto technology.

The Ambassador Bridge and Michigan Central Station represent two different bifurcations related to thermodynamic changes: one alive with the pulsation of vigorous international trade; the other a hollow shell now glimmering with signs of new life after a prolonged abandonment. They are two different expressions of space-time binding. They represent two forms of infrastructural mineralisation, holdovers from specific moments in the development of this border. Their persistence reminds us of the various ways that

Figure 2.6 Ambassador Bridge looking north towards Detroit, January 2016. Photo by James Pineau, with permission

Figure 2.7 Michigan Central Station, February 2016. Photo by James Pineau, with permission

infrastructural/logistical media bind space-time within the context of wider political economic demands.[53]

A Plea for Time: Border, Infrastructure, Sustainability

The process of developing this border as a circulatory nodal point critical to the national economies of Canada and the United States continues to define the region, particularly the Canadian side. Current initiatives include the new much touted Gordie Howe International Bridge at a cost of CDN$5.7 billion, the threatened construction of a twin span bridge by the privately held Ambassador Bridge Company and upgrades to the existing train and car tunnels to increase both traffic for autos and train cargo, as well as a recently proposed pedestrian ferry that will link downtown Windsor with Detroit (resurrecting a long forgotten industry that dominated the region for years before the bridge and tunnel took over). While the region once at the centre of the automotive industry has shed much of economic capacity in the area, including a steep fall off in capital investments to build autos in the region, there has been a concurrent rise in investment related specifically to developing and accelerating the movement of international trade. Recent economic revitalisation in the auto sector[54] has exacerbated a tension between the existing infrastructure premised on international trade in manufactured goods (largely cyclical in nature), and a post-industrial vision of the region that forecasts a less volatile and more sustainable future. Detroit/Windsor expressions of the type of decline forewarned by Innis. It is not surprising that many anticipate the region being converted into an expansive 'logistical hub'.[55] The perception is that these investments are not only good for the national economies of Canada and the US (and others) but that they will provide a regional stimulus.

The Detroit/Windsor border is perhaps the canary in the coal mine when it comes to the broader effects of unchecked acceleration in service of political economic necessity (despite the forms of inequality and asymmetry). Yet the Detroit River is littered with the ruins of empire. This should foreground that the goal of sustainability is as much a theoretical question as it is an economic, cultural and indeed ethical imperative. Theorising sustainability requires theoretical frameworks that push back against this unchecked acceleration. Innis held that it was at the margins and borders of empire that rebirth and revitalisation might occur. Seen through the prism of the Detroit River's infrastructural and logistical history,

Figure 2.8 Conceptual design for the proposed Gordie Howe International Bridge and customs plaza. Image courtesy of the Windsor-Detroit Bridge Authority

Innis' insights direct our attention to the temporal considerations by which a sustainable future for the region might be possible.

Acknowledgements

Thanks are due to James Pineau for providing photographs of the Ambassador Bridge and Michigan Central Station and to the Windsor-Detroit Bridge Authority for providing the conceptual image of the Gordie Howe International Bridge. Thanks to Edward Comor for reviewing and providing valuable feedback on an earlier draft of this chapter. Thanks to James Steinhoff for drawing my attention to DeLanda's work.

Notes

1. Ed White, 'Judge Sends Canadian to US Prison for Sending Immigrants Through Windsor Rail Tunnel', *Detroit Free Press*, 15 April 2022.
2. CBC, 'Infamous "Windsor Hum" Finally Dies Down as US Steel Idles', CBC, 27 July 2020. https://www.cbc.ca/news/canada/windsor/windsor-hum-zug-island-us-steel-1.5665100
3. Miriam Berger, Amanda Colletta, Annabelle Timsit and Bryan Pietsch, 'US–Canada Border Crossing, Reopens, After Six-Day Blockade By "Freedom Convoy" Protesters', *Washington Post*, 14 February 2022. https://www.washingtonpost.com/world/2022/02/13/canada-freedom-convoy-border-blockades-truckers/
4. Craig Lord, 'Ambassador Bridge Blockades Will Have "Lasting Effect" On Supply Chain, Experts Say', *Global News*, 9 February 2022. https://globalnews.ca/news/8607316/ambassador-bridge-freedom-convoy-blockade-grocery-auto-prices/
5. Ellen Meiksins Wood, *Empire of Capital* (New York: Verso, 2003).
6. Achille Mbembe, *Necropolitics* (Durham, NC and London: Duke University Press, 2019).
7. Ibid.
8. For more on the acceleratory logic of contemporary capitalism, see Robert Hassan, *Empires of Speed: Time and the Acceleration of Politics and Society* (Leiden and Boston, MA: Brill, 2009), and Vincent R. Manzerolle and Atle Mikkola Kjøsen. 'The Communication of Capital: Digital Media and the Logic of Acceleration', *tripleC: Communication, Capitalism & Critique. Open Access Journal for a Global Sustainable Information Society* 10.2 (2012): 214–29.
9. Matthew May, 'Leaving Detroit', *The American Thinker*, 19 April 2011.

10. Clarence Monroe Burton, *The City of Detroit, Michigan, 1701–1922* (Detroit and Chicago: The SJ Clarke Publishing Company, 1922).
11. Stephan C. Demeter, Kent C. Taylor and Donald J. Weir, *Archaeological Phase I and II Investigations of the Detroit River International Crossing (DRIC) Project Detroit, Wayne County, Michigan* (Commonwealth Cultural Resources Group, Inc, 2008).
12. Brian Leigh Dunnigan, *Frontier Metropolis: Picturing Early Detroit, 1701–1838* (Detroit, MI: Wayne State University Press, 2001). Print. Great Lakes Books.
13. Stephan C. Demeter, Kent C. Taylor and Donald J. Weir, *Archaeological Phase I and II Investigations of the Detroit River International Crossing (DRIC) Project Detroit, Wayne County, Michigan* (Commonwealth Cultural Resources Group, Inc, 2008); Tiya Miles, *Dawn of Detroit: A Chronicle of Bondage and Freedom in the City of the Straight* (New York: New Press, 2017).
14. Lisa Philips Valentine and Allan K. Mcdougall, 'Imposing the Border: The Detroit River from 1786 to 1807', *Journal of Borderlands Studies* 19.1 (2004): 13–22. Primo. Web.
15. Guillaume Teasdale, *Fruits of Perseverance: The French Presence in the Detroit River Region, 1701–1815* (Montreal and Kingston: McGill-Queen's University Press, 2018).
16. Brandon Dimmel, '"South Detroit, Canada": Isolation, Identity and the US–Canada Border, 1914–1918', *Journal of Borderlands Studies* 26.2 (2011): 197–209. Primo. Web.
17. Ford of Canada was incorporated as a public company and established its first Canadian auto plant on the south shore in 1904, one year after Henry Ford incorporated his company and began production in the United States (Anastakis); Ibid.
18. Bill Anderson, Laurie Tannous, Roger Hamlin, Daniel Lynch and Bob Armstrong, *The Gordie Howe International Bridge and the Bi-National Great Lakes Economic Region: Assessing Economic Impacts and Realizing Economic Opportunities* (Cross-Border Institute, 2016). https://www.cbinstitute.ca/wp-content/uploads/2021/01/Gordie-Howe-Internation-Bridge-Full-Report.pdf (accessed 26 November 2021).
19. Jordan Press, 'Low Loonie Could Increase Cost of New Canada–US Border Crossing by $2B', CBC News, 4 January 2016. http://www.cbc.ca/news/canada/windsor/gordie-howe-bridge-cost-may-rise-2b-as-a-result-of-low-loonie-trudeau-told-1.3388954
20. R. Watson and M. Blondheim, ed. *The Toronto School of Communication Theory: Interpretations, Extensions, Applications* (Toronto: University of Toronto Press, 2008).
21. Indeed, McLuhan famously wrote in the introduction to the 1964

22. edition of the *Bias of Communication* that his work was merely a footnote to Innis' own (Innis 1964).
22. For more recent considerations of McLuhan's work and legacy, see Robert E. Babe, *Wilbur Schramm and Noam Chomsky Meet Harold Innis: Media, Power, and Democracy* (Lanham, MD: Lexington Books, 2015). John Bonnett, *Emergence and Empire: Innis, Complexity, and the Trajectory of History* (Montreal: McGill-Queen's University Press, 2013). Print. William J. Buxton, ed. *Harold Innis and the North: Appraisals and Contestations* (Montreal: McGill-Queen's University Press, 2013).
23. Infrastructure here understood through its etymological roots as referring to the foundation or basis for 'any operating system'; http://www.etymonline.com/index.php?allowed_in_frame=0&search=infrastructure. For more on McLuhan's understanding of infrastructure, see John Durham Peters, *The Marvelous Clouds: Toward a Philosophy of Elemental Media* (London: The University of Chicago Press, 2015). Print. Also Liam Cole Young, 'Innis's Infrastructure: Dirt, Beavers, and Documents in Material Media Theory', *Cultural Politics* 13.2 (2017): 227–49.
24. John Durham Peters, *The Marvelous Clouds: Toward a Philosophy of Elemental Media* (London: The University of Chicago Press, 2015). Print.
25. John Bonnett, *Emergence and Empire: Innis, Complexity, and the Trajectory of History* (Montreal: McGill-Queen's University Press, 2013). Print.
26. Edward Comor, 'Harold Innis and "The Bias of Communication"', *Information, Communication & Society* 4.2 (2001): 274–94. Primo.
27. Edward Comor, 'Harold Innis's Dialectical Triad', *Journal of Canadian Studies* 29.2 (1994): 111–27.
28. John Durham Peters, *The Marvelous Clouds: Toward a Philosophy of Elemental Media* (London: The University of Chicago Press, 2015). Print.
29. Ibid.
30. Bill Anderson, *The Border and the Ontario Economy* (Windsor, ON: Cross-Border Transportation Centre, 2012).
31. Benjamin Schwarz, 'Geography Is Destiny', *The Atlantic*, December 2008.
32. Harold Adams Innis and Mary Quayle Innis, *Essays in Canadian Economic History* (Toronto: University of Toronto Press, 1956).
33. See for instance Jussi Parikka, *A Geology of Media* (London: University of Minnesota Press, 2015). Print. And Manuel De Landa, *A Thousand Years of Nonlinear History* (New York: Swerve Editions/Zone Books, 1997).

34. As mentioned in the introduction, the infamous 'Windsor Hum' – a low-frequency vibration emanating from Zug Island on the American side of the border that can be felt by residents in certain neighborhoods within Windsor – is a result of the interaction between blast furnaces (or other manufacturing processes) with the particular low frequency propagating qualities of the bedrock under the Detroit River. It is a unique example of cross-border noise pollution, albeit at a frequency that can only be felt and not heard (CBC).
35. Manuel De Landa, *A Thousand Years of Nonlinear History* (New York: Swerve Editions/Zone Books, 1997).
36. Ibid.
37. Ibid.
38. Ibid.
39. Ibid.
40. Ibid.
41. Ibid.
42. Federico Bucci, *Albert Kahn: Architect of Ford* (New York: Princeton Architectural Press, 1993).
43. Building on this notion of the geological foundations of media, and in this case border media, Jussi Parikka (2015) explains that media are intimately tied into the long history that is represented in the geological record. Understanding the operation of an iPhone is as much about the rare earths and extractive industries that produce the material substrate of the device as it is about the software that enables its operations.
44. In a different context, David Harvey (1990) would call this space-time compression, a way of using particular relations of time and space to sustain and expand the global reach of capital's circulation and reproduction. This fact is reflected in the massive importance of the combustion engine as the motive force for the current global market and at the heart of ongoing ecological and climate degradation.
45. Geological particularities also played an important role in developing specific industries within the region; for example, the discovery of extensive salt deposits in the region, or the availability of rich topsoil suitable for commercial farming.
46. Neil F. Morrison, *Garden Gateway to Canada: One Hundred Years of Windsor and Essex County, 1854–1954* (Toronto, ON: Ryerson Press, 1954), 16. Print.
47. Ibid., 22.
48. Philip P. Mason, *The Ambassador Bridge: A Monument to Progress* (Detroit, MI: Wayne State University Press, 1987).
49. Anonymous, 'Bridging the Detroit River', *Michigan Farmer*, 17 December 1898: n.p. Print.

50. The completion of the Ambassador Bridge was soon accompanied by a tunnel for vehicle traffic. The cross-border ferry industry only survived a few decades, and had almost totally disappeared by the mid-1950s.
51. Kelli B. Kavanaugh, *Detroit's Michigan Central Station* (Charleston, SC: Arcadia, 2001).
52. Matt Tucker, 'Meet Your Local Billionaire: Matty Moroun', *Critical Moment*, 1 December 2014: n.p.
53. Interestingly, both were, until recently, owned by the entity, the Ambassador Bridge Company, a testament to the power of transnational capital, but also of its internal contradictions. The Ambassador Bridge Company has fought vigorously against the creation of a second, publicly funded competing bridge. The role of private interests, specifically the Ambassador Bridge Company, run by billionaire Matty Moroun, could be the topic of an entire paper on the political economy of the Windsor-Detroit border crossing. Moroun has been at war with public transportation officials on both sides of border, and has resisted building an updated, government operated, international crossing that could cut into his profits. He has begun acquiring property around the bridge and Old Sandwich via numbered companies, significantly delaying construction of the Gordie Howe International Bridge. Many claim that his land speculation in relation to building a second private bridge has led to the degradation of urban neighbourhoods and infrastructure. See, for example, the conflict over Indian Road in Windsor, a case adjudicated by the Supreme Court of Canada. See Battagello (2016) for a primer.
54. For example, Windsor was recently announced as the home of the first electric vehicle battery factory in Canada, reflecting a shift towards electric vehicle production and what purports to be the cornerstone of a new cross-border supply chain (see La Grassa 2022).
55. Joe Gullien, 'Michigan Might Create Logistics District in Detroit', *Detroit Free Press*, 5 September 2015.

Bibliography

Anastakis, Dimitry. 'From Independence to Integration: The Corporate Evolution of the Ford Motor Company of Canada, 1904–2004'. *The Business History Review* 78.2 (2004): 213–53.

Anderson, Bill. *The Border and the Ontario Economy*. Windsor, ON: Cross-Border Transportation Centre, 2012.

Anderson, Bill, Laurie Tannous, Roger Hamlin, Daniel Lynch and Bob Armstrong. *The Gordie Howe International Bridge and the Bi-National*

Great Lakes Economic Region: Assessing Economic Impacts and Realizing Economic Opportunities. Cross-Border Institute, 2016. https://www.cbinstitute.ca/wp-content/uploads/2021/01/Gordie-Howe-Internation-Bridge-Full-Report.pdf. Accessed 26 November 2021.

Anonymous. 'Bridging the Detroit River'. *Michigan Farmer*, 17 December 1898: n.p. Print.

Anonymous. 'What's behind Irritating Windsor Hum? Blame Michigan's Zug Island'. *CBC News*, 23 May 2014. http://www.cbc.ca/news/canada/windsor/mysterious-windsor-hum-traced-to-zug-island-mich-1.2651783

Babe, Robert E. *Wilbur Schramm and Noam Chomsky Meet Harold Innis: Media, Power, and Democracy*. Lanham, MD: Lexington Books, 2015.

Battagello, Dave et al. 'Moroun Files Lawsuit against Windsor over West-End Homes'. *Windsor Star*, 29 January 2016.

Benfield, Kaid. 'Detroit: The "Shrinking City" That Isn't Actually Shrinking'. *The Atlantic*, 10 June 2011.

Berger, Miriam, Amanda Colletta, Annabelle Timsit and Bryan Pietsch. 'US–Canada Border Crossing, Reopens, After Six-Day Blockade By "Freedom Convoy" Protesters'. *Washington Post*, 14 February 2022. https://www.washingtonpost.com/world/2022/02/13/canada-freedom-convoy-border-blockades-truckers/

Bonnett, John. *Emergence and Empire: Innis, Complexity, and the Trajectory of History*. Montreal: McGill-Queen's University Press, 2013. Print.

Bucci, Federico. *Albert Kahn: Architect of Ford*. New York: Princeton Architectural Press, 1993.

Burton, Clarence Monroe. *The City of Detroit, Michigan, 1701–1922*. Detroit, MI and Chicago: The SJ Clarke Publishing Company, 1922.

Buxton, William J., ed. *Harold Innis and the North: Appraisals and Contestations*. Montreal: McGill-Queen's University Press, 2013.

CBC. 'Infamous "Windsor Hum" Finally Dies Down as US Steel Idles'. CBC, 27 July 2020. https://www.cbc.ca/news/canada/windsor/windsor-hum-zug-island-us-steel-1.5665100

CBC News, 4 January 2016. http://www.cbc.ca/news/canada/windsor/gordie-howe-bridge-cost-may-rise-2b-as-a-result-of-low-loonie-trudeau-told-1.3388954

Comor, Edward. 'Harold Innis's Dialectical Triad'. *Journal of Canadian Studies* 29.2 (1994): 111–27.

Comor, Edward. 'Harold Innis and "The Bias of Communication"'. *Information, Communication & Society* 4.2 (2001): 274–94. Primo.

Cosgrove, Bob. 'A Tunnel Turns 100'. *Michigan History Magazine* 94.4 (2010): 44.

De Landa, Manuel. *A Thousand Years of Nonlinear History*. New York: Swerve Editions/Zone Books, 1997.

Demeter, Stephan C., Kent C. Taylor and Donald J. Weir. *Archaeological Phase I and II Investigations of the Detroit River International Crossing (DRIC) Project Detroit, Wayne County, Michigan*. Commonwealth Cultural Resources Group, Inc, 2008.

Dimmel, Brandon. '"South Detroit, Canada": Isolation, Identity and the US–Canada Border, 1914–1918'. *Journal of Borderlands Studies* 26.2 (2011): 197–209. Primo. Web.

Dunnigan, Brian Leigh. *Frontier Metropolis: Picturing Early Detroit, 1701–1838*. Detroit, MI: Wayne State University Press, 2001. Print. Great Lakes Books.

Government of Canada. 'Detroit River International Crossing'. 23 March 2011. http://actionplan.gc.ca/en/initiative/detroit-river-international-crossing

Gullien, Joe. 'Michigan Might Create Logistics District in Detroit'. *Detroit Free Press*, 5 September 2015.

Harvey, David. *The Condition of Postmodernity: An Enquiry into the Origins of Cultural Change*. Oxford and New York: Blackwell, 1990.

Hassan, Robert. *Empires of Speed: Time and the Acceleration of Politics and Society*. Leiden and Boston, MA: Brill, 2009.

Innis, Harold Adams. *A History of the Canadian Pacific Railway*. London: P. S. King, 1923.

Innis, Harold Adams. *Changing Concepts of Time*. Toronto: University of Toronto Press, 1952.

Innis, Harold Adams. *Empire and Communications*. Oxford: Clarendon Press, 1950.

Innis, Harold Adams. *The Bias of Communication*. Toronto: University of Toronto Press, 1964.

Innis, Harold Adams. *The Fur Trade in Canada; an Introduction to Canadian Economic History*. Toronto: University of Toronto Press, 1956 (rev. edn).

Innis, Harold Adams, and Mary Quayle Innis. *Essays in Canadian Economic History*. Toronto: University of Toronto Press, 1956.

Kavanaugh, Kelli B. *Detroit's Michigan Central Station*. Charleston, SC: Arcadia, 2001.

La Grassa, Jennifer. 'Electric Vehicle Battery Plant Set For Windsor, Ont., Signals Canada is a "Player" in Auto Industry's Future'. *CBC*, 24 March 2022. https://www.cbc.ca/news/canada/windsor/electric-vehicle-battery-plant-windsor-1.6394444

Lajeunesse, Ernest J. *Windsor Border Region: Canada's Southernmost Frontier, a Collection of Documents*. Toronto: The Champlain Society, 1960.

LeDuff, Charlie. *Detroit: An American Autopsy*. New York: Penguin Books, 2014 (reprint edn).
Lord, Craig. 'Ambassador Bridge Blockades Will Have "Lasting Effect" On Supply Chain, Experts Say'. *Global News*, 9 February 2022. https://globalnews.ca/news/8607316/ambassador-bridge-freedom-convoy-blockade-grocery-auto-prices/
Manzerolle, Vincent R. and Atle Mikkola Kjøsen. 'The Communication of Capital: Digital Media and the Logic of Acceleration'. *tripleC: Communication, Capitalism & Critique. Open Access Journal for a Global Sustainable Information Society* 10.2 (2012): 214–29.
Marx, Gary. 'Preface' in *Routledge Handbook of Surveillance Studies*. Ed. David Lyon, Kevin D. Haggerty and Kirstie Ball. New York: Routledge, 2012.
Mason, Philip P. *The Ambassador Bridge: A Monument to Progress*. Detroit, MI: Wayne State University Press, 1987.
May, Matthew. 'Leaving Detroit'. *The American Thinker*, 19 April 2011.
Mbembe, Achille. *Necropolitics*. Durham, NC and London: Duke University Press, 2019.
Miles, Tiya. *Dawn of Detroit: A Chronicle of Bondage and Freedom in the City of the Straight*. New York: New Press, 2017.
Morrison, Neil F. *Garden Gateway to Canada: One Hundred Years of Windsor and Essex County, 1854–1954*. Toronto, ON: Ryerson Press, 1954. Print.
Parikka, Jussi. *A Geology of Media*. London: University of Minnesota Press, 2015. Print.
Parkins, Almon Ernest. *The Historical Geography of Detroit*. Port Washington, NY: Kennikat Press, 1970.
Peters, John Durham. *The Marvelous Clouds: Toward a Philosophy of Elemental Media*. London: The University of Chicago Press, 2015. Print.
Press, Jordan. 'Low Loonie Could Increase Cost of New Canada–US Border Crossing by $2B'. CBC News, 4 January 2016. http://www.cbc.ca/news/canada/windsor/gordie-howe-bridge-cost-may-rise-2b-as-a-result-of-low-loonie-trudeau-told-1.3388954
Schwarz, Benjamin. 'Geography Is Destiny'. *The Atlantic*, December 2008.
Szewczyk, Paul. 'The Mound Builders'. *Detroit Urbanism*, 21 December 2015. http://detroiturbanism.blogspot.ca/2015/12/the-mound-builders.html
Teasdale, Guillaume. *Fruits of Perseverance: The French Presence in the Detroit River Region, 1701–1815*. Montreal and Kingston: McGill-Queen's University Press, 2018.
Tomlinson, John. *The Culture of Speed: The Coming of Immediacy*. London: Sage, 2007.

Tucker, Matt. 'Meet Your Local Billionaire: Matty Moroun'. *Critical Moment*, 1 December 2014: n.p.

Valentine, Lisa Philips and Allan K. Mcdougall. 'Imposing the Border: The Detroit River from 1786 to 1807'. *Journal of Borderlands Studies* 19.1 (2004): 13–22. Primo. Web.

Valéry, Paul. *Oeuvres*. Paris: Gallimard, 1965.

Watson, R. and M. Blondheim, ed. *The Toronto School of Communication Theory: Interpretations, Extensions, Applications*. Toronto: University of Toronto Press, 2008.

White, Ed. 'Judge Sends Canadian to US Prison for Sending Immigrants Through Windsor Rail Tunnel'. *Detroit Free Press*, 15 April 2022.

Wood, Ellen Meiksins. *Empire of Capital*. London and New York: Verso, 2003.

Young, Liam Cole. 'Innis's Infrastructure: Dirt, Beavers, and Documents in Material Media Theory'. *Cultural Politics* 13.2 (2017): 227–49.

CHAPTER 3

Comparing Twin Towns along the US Southern and Northern Borders: A Historical Review

Pierre-Alexandre Beylier

Back in the 1960s, then-president John Fitzgerald Kennedy used two similar expressions to depict the relations that the United States had developed over time with Canada, on the one hand, and with Mexico, on the other hand: 'Geography has made us neighbors, tradition has made us friends. Economics has made us partners. And necessity has made us allies [. . .] Those whom nature has so joined together, let no man put asunder.'[1]

This quote suggests that not only does the United States share a particular relationship with its two land neighbours, but that both relationships seem to bear some similarities, in the form of some kind of closeness. There is maybe no better, more concrete example of this closeness than a phenomenon that is present along both the Mexico–US border and the Canada–US border: the phenomenon of twin towns.

Twin towns are specific kinds of border towns that have garnered growing attention on the part of scholars.[2] They are characterised by the fact that they have a counterpart on the other side of the border. But they are defined by more than just their geographic proximity:

> First of all, [they are] towns located on a border and directly neighboring each other. Twinning is in this case about their historical origins and current mutual relations, but also about their potential for future cooperation. And secondly, cases are brought to the fore that employ a creative approach in cultivating an identity transcending state border.[3]

This means that they nurture interdependent ties that bring them closer together, transcending the border. Besides, these ties exist not only because of the border – like any border town – but also in spite of it.[4] In other words, they have managed to overcome the obstacle that the border constitutes by building on it.

Twin towns can have two origins. They can either be 'duplicated cities' – 'where the establishment of one border settlement sooner or later was followed by the rise of a second settlement on the other side of the border' – or 'partitioned cities', i.e. 'previously united cities [that] were divided into two different entities'.[5]

If some scholars think that the expression 'twin towns' is used improperly – because it suggests the idea of similarity, equal size and 'biculturalism', three conditions that are rarely achieved – they have put forward other terms to describe them.[6] They can be 'coupled settlements', 'double towns' or 'border-crossing cities'.[7] For the purpose of this chapter, we will stick with the term 'twin city' in its broader sense to reflect on the links that have developed across the border over time, imparting some kind of specificity to these towns.

In addition to their physical closeness, the specificity of these towns lies in the multifaceted dimension of their integration across the border that characterises them.[8] They were built on both sides of an international border or, in some cases, they are 'straddling across the border [and are thus] instantly recognizable as a single, integrated metropolis'.[9] In other words, morphologically, they are border towns that organised around an international border, and more specifically around a border crossing that traditionally became 'the core of the cities'.[10] Gradually, this international border was integrated by the ties that developed over time between the two urban entities, thus contributing to the emergence of a 'region-wide urban network'.[11] This functional integration means that they are shaped by cross-border ties that impart them some coherence, unity and dynamism.[12] Gay, for instance, emphasises the fact that they form a 'string of points of exchanges, of dynamic and prosperous locations'.[13] These interactions and exchanges give them the opportunity to develop cooperative initiatives to address some common issues. Although these initiatives can be more or less formal, they eventually further bring them together, giving birth to ties that are more political or even institutional.[14]

All these characteristics make twin towns an 'original socio-spatial system [shaped by] flows and interactions', which 'turn this double space into a unique networked space'.[15] Ultimately, this unique space is marked by its cross-border dimension, in that the multiplicity of links that connect the two 'doubles' erase or transcend the border.

In other words, twin cities are 'duplicated' urban centres that have developed on both sides of – as well as across – an international border and have given birth to a coherent urban entity. This urban entity, perceptible through some kind of continuity of the urban fabric, is animated by various flows and interactions – cross-border migrations and cross-border economic exchanges – sustained by an integrated transportation system organised around the border crossing(s) that structures and polarises those flows. Cooperative initiatives can also develop to impart an institutionalised framework to the functional links that bind twin cities together. In the end, as a result of those interactions and ties, the people living on both sides can share a particular bicultural identity or a 'feeling of belonging together'.[16]

While this phenomenon is very well-documented along the Mexico–US border, it has received less – and more recent – attention along the Canada–US border.[17] Besides, no comparative studies have been conducted on the topic. This chapter analyses the way in which twin cities have developed over time in a cross-border functional way, following a comparative approach between the Canada–US border and the Mexico–US border. The goal is to provide a historical overview of twin towns in order to explore the relations that have gradually emerged. The aim is not to be comprehensive but to identify some processes to better understand twin towns. After going back to the aforementioned 'shared history' that characterises twin cities by examining their origins and their early developments, this chapter will dwell on their growth in the twentieth and twenty-first centuries, looking more specifically at their economic and demographic evolutions.

The 'Shared History' of North American Border Twin Towns

To begin with, examining the history of border twin towns will allow us to adopt a diachronic approach in order to identify the forces that underlay their creation and that would determine their development.

The two US land borders were respectively established by two bilateral treaties: the 1783 Treaty of Paris as far as the Canada–US border is concerned, and the 1848 Treaty of Hidalgo Guadalupe as far as the Mexico–US border is concerned.[18] However, not only did the establishment of urban settlements in North America precede the creation of borders, but population patterns in what would become the borderlands started far earlier in certain places. Going back to the inception of these settlements will enable us to contextualise the birth of border towns and to analyse the impact the creation of borders had on communities that had already began to develop, inserting a divisive logic in previously united regions.

The Origins of Twin Towns

Twin towns along the Mexico–US border: the emergence of a bicultural region

When the Spanish arrived in the New World, cities played a central role in their conquest of Central America, and it was even more the case for what would become border cities since they marked the northernmost limit of New Spain. But the settlement of those towns had, from the very beginning, a religious dimension. The process amounted to what Dear calls a 'spiritual conquest'.[19] Indeed, the first towns were originally founded by Catholic missionaries in the mid-seventeenth century. It started with the establishment of a Franciscan mission, called Paso Del Norte – what is now known as Ciudad Juarez – in 1659. And several other missions would follow, such as another religious settlement in 1683 that would lead to the founding of Ojinaga.[20] This missionary process went on until the end of the seventeenth century and accompanied the creation of a great number of border towns in the eastern part of what would become the Mexico–US border.

From these initial settlements, a wave of new towns emerged, but they followed another complementary logic: a defensive one. The Spanish established cities on the south bank of the Rio Grande River as places of protection against the Indians, who were coming from the north.[21] Even if these settlements were never devoid of religious functions, they were mostly entrusted with this defensive function, serving as military outposts (*presidios*).[22] By the end of the eighteenth century, the region consisted of a 'string of border cities'.[23]

All in all, the settlement of what would become a border region started far before the establishment of the international boundary, and it occurred following a 'frontier' logic. It was characterised by some kind of 'marginality' – for lack of any mine discoveries – with only a few sparse pockets of population in a wild, deserted region mostly dominated by Indigenous people.[24] The borderland was therefore a peripheral region, the northernmost limit of New Spain's sphere of influence. For almost two centuries, it was only inhabited by Spanish conquistadors and Indigenous people. It was not until the 1820s that the American presence was significantly reinforced north of the Rio Grande River.[25] From that time on, interactions multiplied, thus imparting a bicultural dimension to this frontier area, notably through intermarriages.[26] What had been a buffer zone was gradually turning into a zone of contact between two populations that developed more and more economic and social ties.

Consequently, the border region was structured around a north/south logic. Even before the arrival of Spanish conquistadors, the Indigenous groups that inhabited the region were already organised in a north/south logic – at cross purposes with the separation line that the international border would represent in the nineteenth century.[27] Dear terms this logic 'north-south connectivity', a phenomenon that went on during the colonial period with some kind of 'north gaze' on the part of Spanish settlers. These were drawn by the economic opportunities that the northern part of the continent represented, even though they were not officially allowed to trade with foreign nations until the independence of Mexico.[28] When Mexico became independent in 1821, trade was legalised, thus reinforcing these north/south links. Economic integration was thereby provided with significant momentum.[29]

The establishment of the international border at the end of the Mexican-American War in 1848 did not entirely reverse those deeply rooted trends that had been developing for almost two centuries. Quite to the contrary, it was the founding event that gave birth to twin cities. Since it had been rumoured for a while that the Rio Grande River would be used as an international border, some people, mainly Americans, had already started investing on the north bank, founding settlements across already-existing cities.[30]

But when the border was established – since it was brought by war – it was imparted a defensive role that led to the militarisation of the international line. Again, even before the end of the war, the process had started with the construction of a number of forts designed to protect this soon-to-be border, such as Fort Polk and Fort Texas across from Matamoros, Fort Stockton in 1846 across from San Diego, or even Fort Ringgold across from Camargo in 1848, and Fort McIntosh, in Laredo, the following year. This phenomenon became systematic after the war and more forts were built for defensive purposes.[31]

The origin of most twin cities in the eastern part of the region is therefore to be found in the establishment of the border, through a duplication process.[32] When the separation line was established, it led to the duplication of those formerly frontier towns into twin towns, and they were imparted a military function that would be a defining characteristic for the rest of the century, thus at once creating links and putting a strain on their relationship.

Within two centuries, the region had moved from being a neglected 'frontier-land' to a more dynamic 'borderland' shaped by a bicultural dimension.[33] This *bicultural region border zone* with border towns being the epicenter of contacts between Mexico and the United States.[34]

The birth of twin towns along the Canada–US border:
a not-so-different story

The Canadian borderland was structured by a similar logic. Before the arrival of European settlers, the northern part of the North American continent was organised following a north/south logic as well. Indeed, for Indigenous people – and later, for European settlers – the Great Lakes were rather a meeting place than a separating line.[35] Therefore, when the border was established by the Treaty of Paris in 1783, at the end of the American War of Independence, the border inserted a new logic. However, contrary to what happened along the southern border, the Canada–US border came to intersect areas that had already been settled before its establishment. It led to the separation of communities, following a 'partition' phenomenon.[36] The most telling example is that of Detroit. After building Fort Pontchartrain on the north bank of the river in 1701, the French then went on to settle on the south bank in 1749. The two settlements that were to become Detroit and Windsor developed very close ties and soon lived as a single community 'linked by the same language, the same religion, by blood and by the same political allegiance'.[37]

That was until 1796, when Detroit became American by order of the British Crown. After enjoying a central position in the Great Lakes region, the town of Detroit therefore found itself cut off from its hinterland.[38] From that moment on, contacts with Windsor diminished tremendously and, for the first part of the nineteenth century, the development of Detroit proceeded while turning its back on Canada.[39] As a consequence, in a process that was different from what happened along the Mexican border, the twin towns of Detroit and Windsor were created by the border. The international boundary cut one town in two, and the two resulting towns evolved following two different paths, at first maintaining no links with each other.

In the eastern part of Canada, however, between Quebec and the States of New York, Vermont and New Hampshire, the establishment of the border preceded the settlement of the region. The border, which follows the 45th parallel, dates back to the Royal Proclamation of 1763 after the fall of New France, and it became an international border with the Treaty of Paris in 1783. But in some places where no one had settled yet, the border was not demarcated. Therefore, when settlers arrived in the border region, some houses or buildings were constructed on the wrong side of it. That was the case of an American fort – Fort Montgomery – which was built in Canada as a result of miscalculations.[40] In other places, the border was demarcated before settlement began, but it did not prevent people from acting as though it did not exist, as evidenced by the case of the eastern townships in southern Quebec. After keeping the region as a buffer zone for defensive purposes in the wake of the American Revolution, the British Crown allowed people to settle in the region as of 1792. The American side had already been settled by the end of the eighteenth century – the town of Derby Line was chartered on 29 October 1779; that of Stanstead was not founded until 1796 by the Taplin family, who were in search of cheaper land.[41] From that moment on, the two towns started developing and, when the two populations came into contact, they lived as if the border did not exist. Trade moved freely across the international line, members of the same families lived on both sides of the 45th parallel, and the inhabitants of the area shared a similar culture, very close traditions and cultural behaviours regardless of their citizenship.[42]

Along the Canada–US border, one can note two different situations in the emergence of border twin towns: in the case of Detroit and Windsor, the border was established after the area had been settled, and the international boundary intersected one community that used to live as one, thus giving birth to two different towns. In the eastern part – and in the west – the border was established before the area was settled, but when people founded cities and came up against the border they transcended the international line, regardless of the political tensions that dominated the relations between their own countries, in a similar way to what happened on the US–Mexican border.

In brief, both in the north and the south, twin towns originally conveyed a frontier dimension. In addition, in both cases, what prompted the establishment of twin towns was the north/south logic that had historically structured the continent and the attraction that drew settler communities towards each other. This logic provided a historical, almost natural, basis that would fuel the founding and the development of twin towns. Therefore, when they were established, borders inserted a cut in the 'natural logic' of the three countries, without however entirely reversing north/south flows.

The Early Development of Twin Cities: Building on Open Borders

Once the two borders were established they became more than just political lines. Different functions developed around them, the functions that are inherent to any international border – i.e. strategic/military, economic, migratory and cultural.[43] But these functions were not put in place all at once, as some were present from the very beginning while others were added later. The balance subsequently reached between those functions thus determined the evolution of cross-border links and, through them, that of twin cities. Indeed, a border is, by nature, an ambivalent institution, at once a meeting place and a separation line. Therefore, depending on the balance you reach, the border can become a basis for cross-border cooperation or not.

As emphasised above, the first function that accompanied the establishment of the Mexican border was the military function with the construction of forts, and it was the fortification of the border that gave birth to numerous twin cities. In other words, as pointed out by Kearney and Kopp, 'twin cities [were] born in trauma'.[44] From that moment on, relations between twin towns oscillated between friendship and rivalry. Tensions emerged and they were sometimes fuelled by domestic events that were occurring in the United States or Mexico, such as the American Civil War or the Mexican Revolution, with plots and raids taking place in some border towns that led to a further militarisation of the border at times.[45] Consequently, throughout the nineteenth century, the border retained a strong strategic function that impacted border towns negatively.

Along the northern border, the situation stabilised far more quickly, and the international line soon became known as the 'longest undefended border in the world'. Even if some authors argue that its demilitarisation dates back to the Rush Bagot Agreement of 1817, the border remained militarised for the most part of the nineteenth century.[46] A number of forts were built by England in the wake of the American Revolution in a context of latent tensions between the New Republic and the former Motherland. This proceeded until 1871.[47] The United States did not start fortifying its side of the border until 1839, but with the threat of rebellions in British North America, it paid more attention to the defence of its northern border and the trend accelerated. In 1839, Congress allocated funds to modernise existing forts such as Fort Niagara and Fort Ontario, in Oswego, NY. Then, from 1841 onwards, new forts were built to defend the border: Fort Wayne near Detroit, Fort Porter in Buffalo, and Rouses Point near Lake Champlain in 1844.[48] Some Canada–US border towns developed from this military legacy. However, even if this military policy would continue until the early 1870s – when the last fortifications were built or upgraded – bilateral relations were quite warm between the United States and British North America, with the exception of the brief military episode of the War of 1812, and they got warmer and warmer by the end of the century.[49] Consequently, the Canada–US border gradually lost its strategic function, which soon gave way to its reputation as the 'longest undefended border in the world', a reputation it retained until the terrorist attacks of 9/11.

The second function that experienced some significant change throughout the nineteenth century was economic/commercial.

Indeed, both the northern and southern borders of the United States saw some form of free trade develop – albeit at different levels. Unlike the Canada–US border which only experienced a short free-trade episode between 1854 and 1865 with the Reciprocity Treaty, which was abrogated in an attempt to annex British North America, or to drive it to seek admission to the United States, the Mexican border saw free trade develop in the second half of the nineteenth century.[50] It started in 1858, with the establishment of a local free trade zone in Matamoros, which was then extended to the Tamaupilas region and, finally, by 1885, to the entire border.[51] Free trade was dismantled in 1905 in order to protect the Mexican economy, but it had a rather positive impact on the development of twin towns.[52] Not only did free trade boost the economy and population of border towns – within a decade Matamoros grew from 12,000 people to 40,000 people – but it also fuelled cross-border ties, stimulating integration between twin towns.[53] Free trade was thus very beneficial for them. It brought them prosperity and it became a factor of growth. As far as the Canada–US border is concerned, the abrogation of the Reciprocity Treaty in 1865 re-established the border's economic function, but did not undermine economic ties altogether. Even if protectionism remained in place throughout the rest of the century – as well as for the first half of the twentieth century – economic ties took on the form of foreign direct investments that especially boomed as of 1900 to overcome the protectionist wall that had been erected between the two countries.[54] In a more surreptitious way, the economies of the two countries – and of some twin towns – began to mingle together, with American ownership of some sectors increasing tremendously. This was for instance the case of the auto industry in the Windsor region, which was taken over by American companies. In 1930, three cars out of four were built by Ford, General Motors or Chrysler, thus driving independent Canadian manufacturers into bankruptcy.[55]

The northern border experienced another factor of growth and integration: transportation networks. A corollary to the peaceful dimension of the international boundary, cross-border transportation developed earlier on the Canadian border than on its Mexican counterpart. After turning their backs on the border in the first decades of the nineteenth century, the United States and Canada started building bridges and railways as of the middle of the nineteenth century. In 1848, the first cross-border bridge was built in the Niagara region, followed by a second one between Queenston, Ontario, and Lewiston, New York, in 1851. In parallel, in the 1850s, cross-border railways developed with the Great Western that linked Buffalo to Windsor in 1855 and the Grand Trunk Railway that linked Portland to Montreal and then to Point Edward – today's Sarnia – in 1856.[56] Not only did this cross-border transportation network give the St. Lawrence River and Great Lakes region some form of coherence, but border towns benefitted from cross-border transportation becoming nodal points that polarised flows of both people and goods. This contributed to the integration of the region and, on a smaller scale, of twin towns that found themselves with an integrated transportation network as well as some kind of continuity of their urban fabric. Detroit, MI and Windsor, ON, Niagara Falls, ON and Niagara Falls, NY or Stanstead, QC and Derby Line, VT became cities – or villages – living as one with their counterparts on the other side of the border, a trend that intensified through the twentieth century.

Although the first bridge across the Rio Grande River – which was to become an international border – was built as early as 1797 in Paso Del Norte, it was not until a century later that cross-border infrastructures developed. Indeed, there was at first some resistance to the establishment of cross-border rail connections. But by the end of the nineteenth century, the arrival of the American railroad on the southern border fuelled cross-border connections. It occurred gradually, with the Southern Pacific Railroad first reaching El Paso in 1881, then Nogales in 1888, Brownsville in 1904, and Reynosa and Matamoros in 1905. In 1910, a high railroad bridge was built between the Laredos.[57] In addition, the railway also contributed to the founding of new towns – on both sides of the border. In 1883, the arrival at Yuma of the Atchison, Topeka and Santa Fe Railway not only brought prosperity to this former military outpost, but it also prompted Mexico to found a town just across the border, Los Algodones, in 1887. The two Nogales also 'sprang up from scratch' in 1880 and 1884 as a result of the arrival of the railroad. So did Mexicali and Calexico in 1901.[58]

Along with free trade, the railroad constituted a factor of growth – but also of creation. It brought incredible growth to twin cities that became, like their cousins along the northern border, nodal points.[59] Today, some of them are the busiest border crossings in North America and in the world.

The development of such numerous cross-border ties was also made possible by the absence of controls. Throughout the nineteenth century, both the northern and southern borders were devoid of any migratory function. The North American continent thus enjoyed some kind of free mobility that encouraged cross-border ties between the United States and its two neighbours, thus reinforcing the north/south logic that had been structuring the continent ever since the pre-colonial period – to some extent even during some punctual episodes of bilateral tensions when the two borders had become much more militarised. Even when the United States created the Border Patrol in 1924, its main mandate was the control of contraband in the context of Prohibition. Likewise, when the United States started restricting immigration, both Mexicans and Canadians remained exempted from the US immigration policy all through the 1960s.[60] This late semi-functionalisation of the migratory function of both borders fuelled a tradition of migrations. Both borders were virtually open and, as a result, people crossed them for economic purposes, to get better job opportunities – most of the time from Canada and Mexico to the United States.[61] The patterns were very similar along the northern and southern borders. And those migrations entailed a mingling of populations that reinforced the bicultural dimension of border cities, with frequent social relations, intermarriages and exchanges.

In all, in the first half of the twentieth century, both the Mexico–US and the Canada–US borders were 'incomplete' borders, hardly guarded – even undefended – with no immigration controls, two functions – strategic and migratory – that did not exist until later. With this openness and their specificities, both borders constituted the foundation for cross-border interactions that interweaved a specific socio-economic fabric between twin towns, while creating enormous advantages that would be exploited throughout the twentieth century and further contribute to their development.

Twin Towns in the Twentieth and Twenty-first Centuries – Between Link and Separation

In Europe, it is customary to say that border towns are 'laboratories of European integration'. More generally, not only are border towns around the world affected the most by the changes that borders experience, but they are also microcosms of the processes that are taking place at borders. When borders gradually opened up to trade in the context of the globalisation of the world economy, border towns acquired a 'new centrality', while they had traditionally been inhibited in their development by the presence of a border and by their peripheral position on the margin of a country's territory.[62]

In North America, this trend began a bit earlier insofar as, given their history, border towns have a dual specificity. In addition to being 'paired'– with a counterpart across the border – only a minority of them do not have a counterpart across the border – they traditionally also had the advantage of being located at relatively open borders, as was highlighted in the previous section. As a result, as early as the 1960s, this dual advantage, along with advantages linked to the differentials induced by the border, was exploited along both the Mexico–US border and the Canada–US border, thus further contributing to the growth of twin cities. Finding themselves on the front line of globalisation, they became central to North American prosperity.

The Economy of Twin Cities

To begin with, twin towns have based their development on certain economic systems that now represent the foundation of their growth. Indeed, the main *raison d'être* of most of those duplicated cities lies in the economic 'resource'[63] that the border represents in terms of the economic differences that it induces, which is known as 'comparative advantages'. As a result, the two borders gave birth to two different systems based, for the most part, on the exploitation of those advantages.

First, well before the implementation of the North America Free Trade Agreement (NAFTA), which was recently replaced by the United States Mexico and Canada Agreement (USMCA), the system that emerged along the southern border had become known as the *maquiladoras* system. Using the border as a north/south interface, American companies started setting up factories, *maquiladoras*, on the Mexican side of the border in 1965, more specifically in border twin towns, with the Border Industrialization Program.[64] This system was based on some kind of 'structural complementarity' between the economies of the two countries.[65] The United States provided capital and technology while Mexico offered a cheap – seven times as cheap originally, back in the 1960s – and numerous workforce.⁶⁶ The system corresponded to a process of outsourcing of the production on the other side of the border, the establishment of what Foucher calls 'off-shore production'.⁶⁷ Assembly plants were set up in Mexico, while the American twin city specialised in high-value services such as banking, research and development, marketing, etc.⁶⁸ This system was based on a local, limited free-trade agreement: in-bound products and in-bound components could cross the border duty-free – except for the Mexican value-added tax (VAT). In the end, though it was assembled in Mexico, the product remained American because it was made for the American market.⁶⁹ Originally, most *maquiladoras* concentrated in Tijuana/San Diego or Mexicali/Calexico (35 per cent), Ciudad Juarez/El Paso (28 per cent), and Matamoros/Brownsville or Laredo/Nuevo Laredo (21 per cent).⁷⁰

Not only did this system fuel the growth of border twin towns, but it also stimulated cross-border flows: American executives who live on the American side and work in Mexico, Mexican workers who cross to the United States to shop – generally Mexican workers spend 35 per cent of their salary in the US.⁷¹ Another activity that is specific to Mexican border towns is medical tourism: the cost of healthcare is so high in the United States that it prompts people to cross the border for doctors' appointments, medical procedures, medicine purchases, and so on.⁷² Some border towns, such as Los Algodones, across from Yuma, specialise in this activity and when one crosses the border, one is welcome by a street lined with dentists' and doctors' offices, opticians and clinics.⁷³ *Maquiladoras* have become one of the defining features of the Mexico–US border and one of the sources of the dynamism of this international line.

On the northern border, the system that was put in place was different, though based on similar comparative advantages. Historically, it was not just twin cities that were integrated into the American economy, but entire regions, namely southern Ontario, in the Great Lakes region that became, in the course of the twentieth century, the 'annex of the Manufacturing Belt'.⁷⁴ It started with Ford, which established its first assembly plant in Windsor, in 1904. Its goal was to overcome Canadian protectionism and to take advantage of Canada's cheap and skilled workforce. Soon, other sectors followed in the footsteps of the auto industry, such as the chemicals industry, the paper pulp industry, and other sectors.⁷⁵ But the real turning point occurred with the Auto Pact, which was signed in 1965 between Canada and the United States. This sectorial free trade agreement allowed auto parts to cross the border duty-free. As a result, certain plants specialised in the production of some auto parts to rationalise production costs and, gradually, the two countries started building cars together and integrated their supply chain across the border. Relying on just-in-time delivery, it depended on a border that was open, fluid and predictable, thus allowing companies to cut their inventories and therefore become more competitive. Currently, a car crosses the border no fewer than seven times in its production process.[76] The twin cities that benefitted the most from this agreement are Detroit and Windsor, which experienced a tremendous growth: between 1965 and 1978, the number of Canadians employed in the auto sector nearly doubled, from 70,600 to 125,000.[77] This integrated system of production became a model for other industries that soon followed the example of the auto sector, such as the food-processing sector.

Twin towns became the sites of dynamic economic relationships between the US and its two neighbours, which followed different patterns: between Canada and the United States, the two economies developed close ties through the integration of the supply chains of different sectors, thus leading the two countries to manufacture products for both markets; whereas the *maquiladoras* system made Mexico an industrial backyard for the American market. But since they were built on some kind of complementarity between the US and its two neighbours, both systems brought growth to border towns, which increased their power of attraction, especially on the southern border.

The Demography of Twin Cities

In the last 200 years, not all border cities have experienced the same growth. First of all, one can note some imbalance between the northern and the southern border. There are twenty-one 'double cities' between Mexico and the United States, whereas there are thirty-four 'double cities' between the United States and its northern neighbour. As a preliminary approach, it can be interesting to try and categorise them in a purely quantitative way.

The first element of analysis lies in the fact that, demographically speaking, there is no real symmetry between American and Mexican twin cities or between American and Canadian cities. Along the

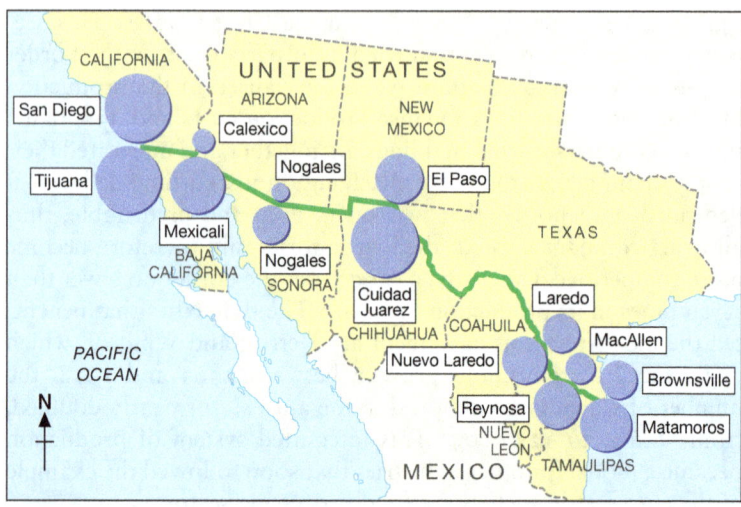

Figure 3.1 The major twin cities along the Mexico–US border

Mexico–US border, the Mexican city is always larger than its American counterpart. Sometimes, the imbalance is huge as in the case of Mexicali, the population of which almost exceeds 1 million people (1,120,872 inhabitants), and of Calexico, which only has 38,633 inhabitants (cf. Figure 3.1).[78] Even, San Diego, which had been historically larger than Tijuana, was overtaken by its twin city in terms of population, over ten years ago. What's more, Mexican border cities have experienced a huge demographic growth, especially in the last ten years, that sometimes exceeds 20 per cent (e.g. Tijuana and Reynosa). This testifies to a huge power of attraction due to, among other things, the opportunities offered by the *maquiladoras* system as well as the prospect of crossing to the United States.

On the Canadian border, we can note one instance of 'real' twin towns: Lewiston/Queenston-Niagara-on-the-Lake (15,944 and 19,088 inhabitants).[79] As explained above, the expression 'twin cities' is misleading in almost all cases, and they could thus be rebranded 'sister cities'. Besides, compared to Mexican twin cities, Canadian twin cities are only medium-size or small-size cities. There are no examples of large, i.e. over 100,000 inhabitants, demographically balanced twin cities along the northern border, like San Diego/Tijuana or Laredo/Nuevo Laredo, on the southern border,

Table 3.1 Twin cities with over 10,000 inhabitants along the Mexico–US border

American city	Population 2010	Population 2020	Variation (%)	Mexican city	Population 2010	Population 2020	Variation (%)
San Diego, California	1,307,402	1,386,932	6.08	Tijuana	1,754,403	2,140,398	22.00
Calexico, California	38,572	38,633	0.16	Mexicali	938,246	1,120,872	19.46
Nogales, Arizona	20,837	19,770	−5.12	Nogales	215,551	261,137	21.15
El Paso, Texas	649,121	678,815	4.57	Ciudad Juarez	1,333,603	1,519,214	13.92
Laredo, Texas	236,091	255,205	8.10	Nuevo Laredo	384,522	446,724	16.18
McAllen, Texas	129,877	142,210	9.50	Reynosa	728,457	899,084	23.42
Brownsville, Texas	175,023	186,738	6.69	Matamoros	489,770	562,755	14.90

Sources: World Population Review, 'World City Populations 2021', 2021, https://worldpopulationreview.com/world-cities (accessed 8 December 2021); and US Census Bureau, '2021 Census', 2021, https://www.census.gov/quickfacts/fact/table/US/PST045219 (accessed 1 December 2021).

except maybe for Detroit and Windsor (639,111 and 229,660 inhabitants), which were the cradle of the auto industry. On top of that, there is no regular pattern between American cities and their Canadian counterparts. Sometimes, the larger city is to be found on the American side, and sometimes it is to be found on the Canadian side. There is an exception, however, which concerns the largest metropolitan areas which, most of the time, are American, such as Detroit (639,111 inhabitants) and Buffalo (278,349 inhabitants) – with the exception of Surrey, BC (568,322 inhabitants) and Abbotsford, BC (153,524 inhabitants) which are larger than their American counterparts, respectively Blaine, WA (5,884 inhabitants) and Sumas, WA (1,629 inhabitants), but both are in Vancouver's suburbs. Additionally, in terms of demographic growth, we can note that the Canada–US border is far less dynamic than the southern border. On the American side, almost all border towns have experienced a loss of population – except for Sumas and Blaine, which may be benefitting from Vancouver's power of attraction, across the border, and to a lesser extent, Buffalo. On the Canadian side, the picture is more diverse but rather stable, with some border towns experiencing limited increases (e.g. Cornwall, Saint Bernard de Lacolle, Edmundstun), while others experience major population gains (e.g. Surrey, Abbotsford, Niagara-on-the-Lake). Some, finally, experience population losses (e.g. Sault St Marie, Prescott, Sarnia).[80]

Overall, border towns are far smaller on the northern border than they are on the southern border: only five cities – two American cities and three Canadian cities – have over 100,000 inhabitants: Detroit, Windsor, Buffalo, Surrey and Abbotsford. Most border cities are medium-size – fourteen cities have between 10,000 and 80,000 inhabitants (cf. Table 3.1) – the rest have fewer than 10,000 people – forty-eight cities/towns – and one can find a lot of very small towns and even villages with fewer than 1,000 inhabitants – twenty towns/villages – such as Norton, VT (153 inhabitants), Dundee, QC (372), Sweet Grass, MT (58). Most of them are located in the east and in the Great Plains, whereas all the largest urban centres are located – for historical and economic reasons – in the Great Lakes region.

Finally, interestingly enough, one can note that some border cities – along both borders – do not have a counterpart across the international line. This is the case of Tecate, Baja California: on the American side, one just has a port of entry and parking lots. Over

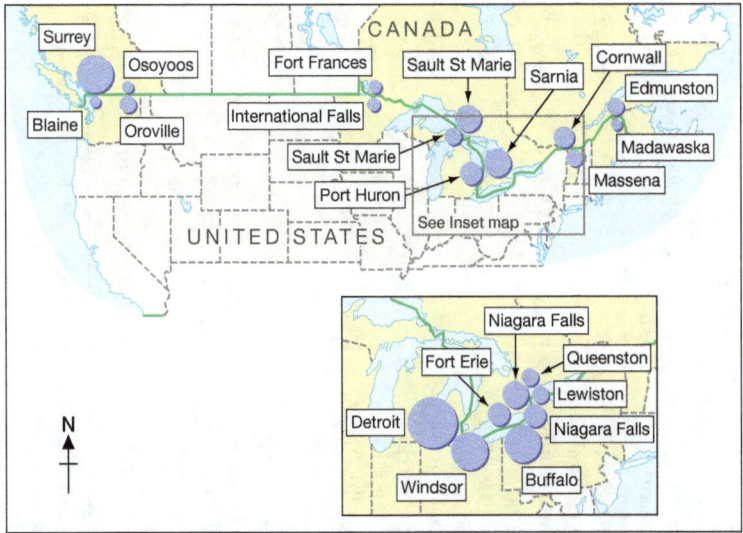

Figure 3.2 Selected twin cities along the Canada–US border

twenty towns are in such a 'twinless situation' along the southern border. Sometimes, some cities were built across from each other, but there is no connection between them: no bridge, no border crossing. Therefore, they cannot really qualify as sister cities. One could mention Falcon Heights, Texas and Nuevo Ciudad Guerrero, or Tamaulipas.

Similarly, along the Canadian border, there are fifteen 'twinless' border cities. For instance, there is a string of small border towns, south of Edmundston, New Brunswick, without any American counterparts. Grand Falls, New Brunswick, with a population of 30,000, is in a similar situation. Furthermore, as is the case along the southern border, there are border towns that face each other but do not have any connections. There is no bridge, for instance, between Niagara-on-the-Lake, ON and Youngstown, NY, or between Brockville, ON and Morristown, NY. The historical reasons for such phenomena as the existence of twinless towns or the lack of cross-border connections remain underexplored.

From a demographic perspective, different patterns have emerged on both borders, in terms of size and in terms of distribution, which mirror different levels of dynamism and attraction. Further research

Table 3.2 Population of twin cities with over 10,000 people along the Canada–US border

American city	Population 2010	Population 2020	Variation (%)	Canadian city	Population 2010	Population 2021	Variation (%)
Blaine, Washington	4,684	5,884	25.62	Surrey/Douglas, British Columbia	468,251	568,322	21.37
Sumas, Washington	1,307	1,629	24.64	Abbotsford, British Columbia	133,497	153,524	15.00
Sault Sainte Marie, Michigan	14,144	13,337	-5.71	Sault Sainte Marie, Ontario	75,141	72,051	-4.11
Port Huron, Michigan	30,184	28,983	-3.98	Sarnia, Ontario	72,366	72,047	-0.44
Detroit, Michigan	713,777	639,111	-10.46	Windsor, Ontario	210,891	229,660	8.90
Buffalo, New York	261,310	278,349	6.52	Fort Erie, Ontario	29,960	32,901	9.82
Niagara Falls, New York	50,193	48,671	-3.03	Niagara Falls, Ontario	82,997	94,415	13.76
Lewiston, New York	16,262	15,944	-1.96	Queenston/Niagara-on-the-Lake, Ontario	15,400	19,088	23.95
Ogdensburg, New York	11,128	10,064	-9.56	Prescott, Ontario	4,284	4,078	-4.81
Massena, NY	12,883	12,443	-3.42	Cornwall, Ontario	46,340	47,845	3.25
Champlain, NY Rouses Point NY	7,963	7,853	-1.38	Saint Bernard de Lacolle, Quebec	1,477	1,542	4.40
Madawaska, Maine	2,967	2,769	-6.67	Edmundston, New Brunswick	16,032	16,437	2.53

Sources: Statistique Canada, Recensement 2011, https://www12.statcan.gc.ca/census-recensement/2021/dp-pd/prof/index.cfm?Lang=E (accessed 7 March 2022); and US Census Bureau, 2021 Census, https://www.census.gov/quickfacts/fact/table/US/PST045219 (accessed 1 December 2021).

will be needed to explain the reasons for the growths or declines of some pairs or some cities/towns.

The Culture of Twin Cities

As a result of their long-standing history, twin cities or sister cities have developed countless social ties. This has led to the emergence of a shared common identity: biculturalism, or a 'feeling of belonging together'.[81] Biculturalism is a term used by Oscar Martínez in his study of 'borderlanders' at the Mexico–US border. He identifies several types, depending on their interactions with the other side, among them biculturalists, who are defined as follows:

> The typical Mexican-American who lives in the border environment is by definition a bicultural person, given that she or he has a firm grounding in Mexican culture and, through long-term residence in the United States, has become substantially Americanized. The Mexican-American biculturalist maintains this biculturalism through constant interaction with others of similar background and through frequent trips to Mexico as a shopper, tourist, or family visitor.[82]

Daily contacts, tourism, intermarriages, integrated economy: all those factors have led to the emergence of cross-border communities.[83] This sense of connectivity has 'rooted [people's lives] in both sides of the border'.[84] For instance, in Eagle Pass, Texas, the economies of the twin cities were so integrated that the majority of the population had dual citizenship in the 1970s: they were Mexican-American.[85] Those links led to the emergence of what Dear calls a 'Third Nation', i.e. Mexamerica. Border towns have their own specific culture that is different from either Mexico's or the United States'. No other cities can better illustrate this than Tijuana and San Diego, in that they are not representative of either Mexico nor the United States.[86] The emergence of *Spanglish* is another good example of this particular culture. Even if the presence of this syncretic language is not limited to the borderland, it is nonetheless symptomatic of this mingling of cultures.

This phenomenon may be more obvious on the southern border because of the cultural, linguistic and ethnic differences that exist between the United States and Mexico – whereas Canada and the

United States share a common colonial past, a common language, and, to a certain extent, a common culture. Yet, the particular situation of Quebec should not be left aside. And in southern Quebec, one can note the emergence of a similar binational border culture marked by bilingualism and dual citizenship. The most telling example is the specific situation in which Stanstead, QC, and Derby Line, VT, find themselves. The two towns share more than just a culture: they function as one. They were deliberately built on the international boundary as a sign of friendship between Canada and the United States. The two towns share some public services and they have one unified cross-border water treatment system. One street – CANUSA Street – is built on the border, with houses on the right-hand side of the road being in Canada and the houses on the left-hand side of the road being in the Unites States. Likewise, some houses and even a library, the Haskell Library, straddle the border. This particular configuration led to more opening, and more diverse ties, than anywhere else along the northern border.[87] Further research should be carried out to apply Martinez's typology to the Canada–US border and to assess this cross-border identity that manifests itself along the border.

Conclusion

In spite of their differences, northern twin cities and southern twin cities share a number of common features in their history as well as in their functioning that make them 'unique urban spatial configuration[s]'.[88] They are the sites of intense flows – of people and goods – which they polarise. They have given rise to production systems that have enabled the three countries to exploit the comparative advantages induced by the two borders. They have fuelled cross-border ties and have seen the emergence of intertwined cross-border communities that share a bicultural border identity – although more present on the Mexican border. And more importantly, the underlying force they share has been the integration of the border: functional integration, as well as the integration of their transportation systems and of their urban fabric, and a feeling of 'belonging together'.[89] To some extent, most twin cities are functioning as one city. Another aspect that could be the object of future research is how they have built on these links and launched cooperative initiatives to work together on common issues.

However, far from this ideal portrait, relations between twin cities have been experiencing some kind of mutation over the last twenty years. Ever since 9/11, Washington has led a policy of border fortification aimed at better protecting the American homeland against the terrorist threat. But border communities have become the collateral damage of this enterprise, and twin cities are at the front line of the War on Terror. As a result, cross-border flows have been impacted negatively: people have moved away from the border, while companies have found it more difficult to trade with the other country. In addition to that, a fence has been built on the southern border, thus materialising an international line that had historically been much more of a meeting place.

This shift in paradigm has given way to 'changing relations' and what had contributed to the prosperity of twin towns – the border – is now turning into an obstacle that threatens their very specificity.[90]

Notes

1. Kennedy said this on his official visit to Mexico, in June 1962. When he visited Ottawa in 1961, he used a similar sentence: 'Geography has made us neighbors. History has made us friends. Economics has made us partners. And necessity has made us allies. Those whom nature hath so joined together, let no man put asunder.' John Fitzgerald Kennedy, '192 – Address Before the Canadian Parliament in Ottawa May 17, 1961', 27 November 2015. http://www.presidency.ucsb.edu/ws/?pid=8136
2. See for example, Kearney and Knopp 1995; Vanneph 1995; Buursink 2001; Furmankiewicz 2005; Joenniemi and Jańczak 2017; Ganster and Collins 2017.
3. Pertti Joenniemi and Jarosław Jańczak, 'Theorizing Town Twinning – Towards a Global Perspective', *Journal of Borderlands Studies* 32.4 (2017): 423. https://doi.org/10.1080/08865655.2016.1267583
4. Jan Buursink, 'The Binational Reality of Border-Crossing Cities', *GeoJournal* 54 (2001): 7–19.
5. Ibid.: 8.
6. Ibid.: 10.
7. See for instance, Jan Buursink, 'The Binational Reality of Border-Crossing Cities', *GeoJournal* 54 (2001): 7–19; for more discussion of this issue, see Joenniemi and Jańczak 2017: 425; Gay 2004, 70.
8. Bernard Reitel, 'Border Temporality and Space Integration in the European Transborder Agglomeration of Basel', *Journal of*

Borderlands Studies 28.2 (2013): 245. https://doi.org/10.1080/0886 5655.2013.854657

9. Michael Dear, *Why Walls Won't Work – Repairing the US–Mexico Divide* (Oxford: Oxford University Press, 2013), 73.
10. Bernard Reitel, 'Border Temporality and Space Integration in the European Transborder Agglomeration of Basel', *Journal of Borderlands Studies* 28.2 (2013): 245. https://doi.org/10.1080/0886 5655.2013.854657; ibid.: 245.
11. Michael Dear, *Why Walls Won't Work – Repairing the US–Mexico Divide* (Oxford: Oxford University Press, 2013), 173.
12. See for instance Bernard Reitel, 'Border Temporality and Space Integration in the European Transborder Agglomeration of Basel', *Journal of Borderlands Studies* 28.2 (2013): 239–56. https://doi.org /10.1080/08865655.2013.854657; Alain Vanneph, 'Villes frontalières Mexique-Etats-Unis', in *La Frontière Mexique/Etats-Unis, mutations économiques, sociales et territoriales*, ed. P. Gondard et al. (Paris: Editions de l'IHEAL, 1995), 246–59; Jean-Christophe Gay, *Les Discontinuités spatiales* (Paris: Economica, 2004); Yehuda Gradus, 'Is Eilat-Aqaba a Bi-national City? Can Economic Opportunities Overcome the Barriers of Politics and Psychology?', *GeoJournal* 54.1 (2001): 85–99.
13. Jean-Christophe Gay, *Les Discontinuités spatiales* (Paris: Economica, 2004), 70.
14. See for example, Thomas Lundén and Dennis Zalamans, 'Local Co-operation, Ethnic Diversity and State Territoriality – The Case of Haparanda and Tornio on the Sweden–Finland border', *GeoJournal* 54.1 (2001): 33–42; Pertti Joenniemi and Jarosław Jańczak, 'Theorizing Town Twinning – Towards a Global Perspective', *Journal of Borderlands Studies* 32.4 (2017): 423–8. https://doi.org/10.10 80/08865655.2016.1267583; Paul Ganster and Kimberly Collins, 'Binational Cooperation and Twinning: A View from the US–Mexican Border, San Diego, California, and Tijuana, Baja California', *Journal of Borderlands Studies* 32.4 (2017): 497–511. https://doi.org/10.1080 /08865655.2016.1198582
15. Alain Vanneph, 'Villes frontalières Mexique-Etats-Unis', in *La Frontière Mexique/Etats-Unis, mutations économiques, sociales et territoriales*, ed. P. Gondard et al. (Paris: Editions de l'IHEAL, 1995), 246–59.
16. Marie-Carmen Macias, 'L'Espace frontalier Etats-Unis/Etats-Unis après le 11 septembre 2001 – entre processus transfrontaliers et trans-nationaux', *La frontière Etats-Unis/Etats-Unis après 15 ans d'Alena* (Cahier des Amériques Latines, 2009), 83–97; Jan Buursink, 'The Binational Reality of Border-Crossing Cities', *GeoJournal* 54 (2001): 7–19.

17. It is worth noting that this phenomenon is also well-documented in Europe, whether as twin towns or as cross-border metropolitan areas (Ehlers 2001; Lundén and Zalamans 2001; Matthiesen and Bürkner 2001; Letniowska-Swiat 2002; Furmankiewicz 2005; Reitel 2013); Emmanuel Brunet-Jailly, 'Globalization, Integration, and Cross-border Relations in the Metropolitan Area of Detroit (USA) and Windsor (Canada)', *International Journal of Economic Development* 2.3 (Ottawa, Policy Research Initiative, 2000): 379–401; Nick Baxter-Moore and Munroe Eagles, '"Living Apart Together": Challenges of Urban Governance Across the Canada–US Border in the Twin Cities of Niagara Falls' (paper prepared for presentation to the 15th Border Regions in Transition (BRIT) Conference 'Cities, States, and Borders: From the Local to the Global', Hamburg, Germany and Sonderborg, Denmark, 17 May 2016); Frédéric Lasserre, Patrick Forest and Enkeleda Arapi, 'Politique de sécurité et villages-frontière entre États-Unis et Québec', *Cybergeo* (March 2012). https://doi.org/10.4000/cybergeo.25209
18. See the section 'Chronology of the Canada–US Border' at the end of the book for more historical detail.
19. Michael Dear, *Why Walls Won't Work – Repairing the US–Mexico Divide* (Oxford: Oxford University Press, 2013).
20. Milo Kearney and Anthony Knopp, *Ciudad Cuates – A History of the US–Mexican Twin Cities* (Austin, TX: Eakin Press, 1995).
21. Ibid., 13.
22. Alain Vanneph, 'Villes frontalières Mexique-Etats-Unis', in *La Frontière Mexique/Etats-Unis, mutations économiques, sociales et territoriales*, ed. P. Gondard et al. (Paris: Editions de l'IHEAL, 1995), 246–59.
23. Milo Kearney and Anthony Knopp, *Ciudad Cuates – A History of the US–Mexican Twin Cities* (Austin, TX: Eakin Press, 1995).
24. Alain Vanneph, 'Villes frontalières Mexique-Etats-Unis', in *La Frontière Mexique/Etats-Unis, mutations économiques, sociales et territoriales*, ed. P. Gondard et al. (Paris: Editions de l'IHEAL, 1995), 246–59.
25. Milo Kearney and Anthony Knopp, *Ciudad Cuates – A History of the US–Mexican Twin Cities* (Austin, TX: Eakin Press, 1995).
26. Ibid., 41–3.
27. Brenden W. Rensink, *Native But Foreign: Indigenous Immigrants and Refugees in the North American Borderlands*, College Station (Texas: A&M University Press, 2018, 1st edn).
28. Michael Dear, *Why Walls Won't Work – Repairing the US–Mexico Divide* (Oxford: Oxford University Press, 2013).
29. Milo Kearney and Anthony Knopp, *Ciudad Cuates – A History of the US–Mexican Twin Cities* (Austin, TX: Eakin Press, 1995).

30. Ibid., 63–6.
31. Ibid.
32. Jan Buursink, 'The Binational Reality of Border-Crossing Cities', *GeoJournal* 54 (2001): 7–19.
33. Alain Vanneph, 'Villes frontalières Mexique-Etats-Unis', in *La Frontière Mexique/Etats-Unis, mutations économiques, sociales et territoriales*, ed. P. Gondard et al. (Paris: Editions de l'IHEAL, 1995), 246–59.
34. Lawrence A. Herzog, *Where North Meets South: Cities, Space, and Politics on the U.S.–Mexico Border* (Austin, TX: Center for Mexican American Studies, University of Texas at Austin, 1990, 1st edn), 35.
35. J. J. Bukowczyk, 'Trade, War, Migration and Empire, 1650–1815', in *Permeable Border: The Great Lakes Basin as Transnational Region* (Pittsburgh, PA: University of Pittsburgh Press, 2005), 10–28.
36. Jan Buursink, 'The Binational Reality of Border-Crossing Cities', *GeoJournal* 54 (2001): 7–19.
37. Olivier Milhaud, 'La Contre-urbanité: Windsor face à Detroit – ou comment se construit l'identité à la frontière', in *Tropisme des frontières – Tome 1*, ed. Hélène Velasco-Graciet and Christian Bouquet (Paris: L'Harmattan, 2005), 229–44.
38. J. J. Bukowczyk, 'Trade, War, Migration and Empire, 1650–1815', in *Permeable Border: The Great Lakes Basin as Transnational Region* (Pittsburgh, PA: University of Pittsburgh Press, 2005), 10–28.
39. Emmanuel Brunet-Jailly, 'Globalization, Integration, and Cross-border Relations in the Metropolitan Area of Detroit (USA) and Windsor (Canada)', *International Journal of Economic Development* 2.3 (Ottawa: Policy Research Initiative, 2000): 379–401.
40. Frédéric Lasserre, Patrick Forest and Enkeleda Arapi, 'Politique de sécurité et villages-frontière entre Etats-Unis et Québec', *Cybergeo*, March 2012. https://doi.org/10.4000/cybergeo.25209
41. Matthew Farfan, *Images of America, the Vermont-Quebec Border – Life on the Line* (Charleston, SC: Arcadia Publishing, 2009).
42. Frédéric Lasserre, Patrick Forest and Enkeleda Arapi, 'Politique de sécurité et villages-frontière entre Etats-Unis et Québec', *Cybergeo*, March 2012. https://doi.org/10.4000/cybergeo.25209
43. Michel Foucher, *Fronts et Frontières* (Paris: Fayard, 1991).
44. Milo Kearney and Anthony Knopp, *Ciudad Cuates – A History of the US–Mexican Twin Cities* (Austin, TX: Eakin Press, 1995), 95.
45. Ibid., 180–3.
46. In fact, the Rush-Bagot Agreement only concerned the demilitarisation of the Great Lakes.
47. C. P. Stacey, 'The Myth of the Unguarded Frontier 1815–1871', *The American Historical Review* 56.1 (October 1950): 1–18.

48. Ibid.
49. Ibid., 17.
50. John Thompson and Stephen Randall, *Canada and the United States: Ambivalent Allies* (Montreal: McGill-Queen's University Press, 2008).
51. Milo Kearney and Anthony Knopp, *Ciudad Cuates – A History of the US–Mexican Twin Cities* (Austin, TX: Eakin Press, 1995).
52. Ibid.
53. Ibid.
54. John Thompson and Stephen Randall, *Canada and the United States: Ambivalent Allies* (Montreal: McGill-Queen's University Press, 2008).
55. Ibid.
56. J. J. Bukowczyk, 'Trade, War, Migration and Empire, 1650–1815', in *Permeable Border: The Great Lakes Basin as Transnational Region* (Pittsburgh, PA: University of Pittsburgh Press, 2005), 10–28.
57. Milo Kearney and Anthony Knopp, *Ciudad Cuates – A History of the US–Mexican Twin Cities* (Austin, TX: Eakin Press, 1995).
58. Ibid.
59. Conversely, the twin towns which remained away from railroad connections, such as Mier/Roma or Ojingia/Presidio, experienced a relative decline. The railroad only reached Presidio in 1930 and, in 1950, a cross-border bridge was built (Kearney and Knopp 1995: 138).
60. Both Mexicans and Canadians were exempt from the *Emergency Immigration Act* of 1921 and from the *Immigration Act* of 1924 that established an immigration system based on quotas (cf. David R. Smith 'Structuring the Permeable Border', in *Permeable Border: The Great Lakes Basin as Transnational Region*, ed. John J. Bukowczyk et al. (Pittsburgh, PA: University of Pittsburgh Press, 2005), 120–51).
61. Milo Kearney and Anthony Knopp, *Ciudad Cuates – A History of the US–Mexican Twin Cities* (Austin, TX: Eakin Press, 1995).
62. Jean-Pierre Renard, 'Villes et frontières: antagonismes et convergences sémantiques', *Hommes et Terres du Nord* 2.1 (2001): 112–22. https://doi.org/10.3406/htn.2001.2769
63. This is a concept theorized by Christophe Sohn.
64. Christian Leblond, *L'Accord de Libre-Echange Nord-Américain*, PhD dissertation, University of Nice, 1999.
65. Michel Foucher, *Fronts et Frontières* (Paris: Fayard, 1991).
66. Jean-Christophe Gay, *Les Discontinuités spatiales* (Paris: Economica, 2004).
67. Michel Foucher, *Fronts et Frontières* (Paris: Fayard, 1991).
68. Alain Vanneph, 'Villes frontalières Mexique-Etats-Unis', in *La Frontière Mexique/Etats-Unis, mutations économiques, sociales et territoriales*, ed. P. Gondard et al. (Paris: Editions de l'IHEAL, 1995): 246–59.

69. Ibid.
70. Michel Foucher, *Fronts et Frontières* (Paris: Fayard, 1991): 418.
71. Christian Leblond, *L'Accord de Libre-Echange Nord-Américain*, PhD dissertation, University of Nice, 1999.
72. Jennifer Miller-Thayer, 'Health Migration: Crossing Borders for Affordable Health Care', *Field Actions Science Reports*, Special Issue 2 (2010).
73. Elisabeth Fauquert, 'Sometimes the Treatment You Seek is Just One Flight Away: causes et limites des nouvelles mobilités de santé étatsuniennes au xxie siècle', *IdeAs* 18 (2021). https://doi.org/10.4000/ideas.11735
74. Michel Foucher, *Fronts et Frontières* (Paris: Fayard, 1991).
75. John Thompson and Stephen Randall, *Canada and the United States: Ambivalent Allies* (Montreal: McGill-Queen's University Press, 2008).
76. Pierre-Alexandre Beylier, *Etats-Unis/Etats-Unis: Enjeux d'une frontière* (Rennes: Presses Universitaires de Rennes, 2016), 247.
77. David Crane, 'Canada-US Automotive Products Agreement', in *The Canadian Encyclopedia*, 2011. http://www.thecanadianencyclopedia.com/index.cfm?PgNm=TCE&Params=A1ARTA0001245 (accessed 8 June 2011).
78. The statistics were found on World City Populations 2021, https://worldpopulationreview.com/world-cities (accessed 8 December 2021); and US Census Bureau, 2021 Census, https://www.census.gov/quickfacts/fact/table/US/PST045219 (accessed 1 December 2021)
79. The statistics were retrieved from Statistique Canada, 2011 Census, https://www12.statcan.gc.ca/census-recensement/2021/dp-pd/prof/index.cfm?Lang=E (accessed 7 March 2022); and US Census Bureau, 2021 Census, https://www.census.gov/quickfacts/fact/table/US/PST045219 (accessed 1 December 2021).
80. Ibid.
81. Michael Dear, *Why Walls Won't Work – Repairing the US–Mexico Divide* (Oxford: Oxford University Press, 2013).
82. Oscar J Martínez, *Border People: Life and Society in the U.S.-Mexico Borderlands* (Tucson: University of Arizona Press, 1994), 110.
83. It is worth noting that not all residents of border towns are biculturalists. Martínez demonstrated that there were people – Americans and Mexicans – who were 'nationalists', believing in the superiority of their country and never interacting with the other side (Martínez 1994: 61).
84. Michael Dear, *Why Walls Won't Work – Repairing the US–Mexico Divide* (Oxford: Oxford University Press, 2013), 101.
85. Milo Kearney and Anthony Knopp, *Ciudad Cuates – A History of the US–Mexican Twin Cities* (Austin, TX: Eakin Press, 1995).

86. Michael Dear, *Why Walls Won't Work – Repairing the US–Mexico Divide* (Oxford: Oxford University Press, 2013), 101.
87. Pierre-Alexandre Beylier, "Sécurité et reterritorialisation de l'identité transfrontalière [...]", in Marie Christine Michaud and Mariannick Guennec (eds), *Sentiments d'appartenance dans les Amériques*, Paris: Edition du Cygne, 2019), 42–55.
88. Lawrence A. Herzog, *Where North Meets South: Cities, Space, and Politics on the U.S.-Mexico Border* (Austin: Center for Mexican American Studies, University of Texas at Austin, 1990, 1st edn), 1.
89. Jan Buursink, 'The Binational Reality of Border-Crossing Cities', *GeoJournal* 54 (2001): 7–19.
90. Michael Dear, *Why Walls Won't Work – Repairing the US–Mexico Divide* (Oxford: Oxford University Press, 2013), 101.

Bibliography

Baxter-Moore, Nick and Munroe Eagles. '"Living Apart Together": Challenges of Urban Governance Across the Canada–US Border in the Twin Cities of Niagara Falls'. Paper prepared for presentation to the 15th Border Regions in Transition (BRIT) Conference 'Cities, States, and Borders: From the Local to the Global', Hamburg, Germany and Sonderborg, Denmark, 17 May 2016.

Beylier, Pierre-Alexandre. *Etats-Unis/Etats-Unis: Enjeux d'une frontière*. Rennes: Presses Universitaires de Rennes, 2016.

Brunet-Jailly, Emmanuel. 'Globalization, Integration, and Cross-border Relations in the Metropolitan Area of Detroit (USA) and Windsor (Canada)'. *International Journal of Economic Development* 2.3 (2000): 379–401.

Bukowczyk, John J. 'Trade, War, Migration and Empire, 1650–1815' in *Permeable Border: The Great Lakes Basin as Transnational Region*. Ed. John J. Bukowczyk et al. Pittsburg: University of Pittsburg Press, 2005. 10–28.

Buursink, Jan. 'The Binational Reality of Border-Crossing Cities'. *GeoJournal* 54 (2001): 7–19.

Crane, David. 'Canada-US Automotive Products Agreement' in *The Canadian Encyclopedia* (2011), 1. http://www.thecanadianencycloped ia.com/index.cfm?PgNm=TCE&Params=A1ARTA0001245. Accessed 8 June 2011.

Dear, Michael. *Why Walls Won't Work – Repairing the US–Mexico Divide*. Oxford: Oxford University Press, 2013.

Ehlers, Nicole. 'The Utopia of the Binational City'. *GeoJournal* 54.1 (2001): 21–32.

Farfan, Matthew. *Images of America, the Vermont-Quebec Border – Life on the Line*. Charleston, SC: Arcadia Publishing, 2009.

Fauquert, Elisabeth. 'Sometimes the Treatment you Seek is Just One Flight Away: causes et limites des nouvelles mobilités de santé étatsuniennes au xxie siècle'. *IdeAs* 18 (2021). https://doi.org/10.4000/ideas.11735

Foucher, Michel. *Fronts et Frontières*. Paris: Fayard, 1991.

Furmankiewicz, Marek. 'Town-twinning as a Factor Generating International Flows of Goods and People – The Example of Poland'. *Belgeo* 1.2 (June 2005): 145–62. https://doi.org/10.4000/belgeo.12466

Ganster, Paul and Kimberly Collins. 'Binational Cooperation and Twinning: A View from the US–Mexican Border, San Diego, California, and Tijuana, Baja California'. *Journal of Borderlands Studies* 32.4 (2017): 497–511. https://doi.org/10.1080/08865655.2016.1198582

Gay, Jean-Christophe. *Les Discontinuités spatiales*. Paris: Economica, 2004.

Gradus, Yehuda. 'Is Eilat-Aqaba a Bi-national City? Can Economic Opportunities Overcome the Barriers of Politics and Psychology?'. *GeoJournal* 54.1 (2001): 85–99.

Hamez, Gregory. 'Les espaces frontaliers, des espaces à la marge?'. In *La France des marges, Rennes*. Ed. Martine Candelier-Cabon et Solène Gaudin. Rennes: Presses Universitaires de Rennes, 2017. 217–29.

Herzog, Lawrence A. *Where North Meets South: Cities, Space, and Politics on the U.S.-Mexico Border*. Austin, TX: Center for Mexican American Studies, University of Texas at Austin, 1990 (1st edn).

Herzog, Lawrence A. and Christophe Sohn. 'The Co-Mingling of Bordering Dynamics in the San Diego–Tijuana Cross-Border Metropolis'. *Territory, Politics, Governance* 7.2 (2019): 177–99. https://doi.org/10.1080/21622671.2017.1323003

Joenniemi, Pertti and Jarosław Jańczak. 'Theorizing Town Twinning – Towards a Global Perspective'. *Journal of Borderlands Studies* 32.4 (2017): 423–8. https://doi.org/10.1080/08865655.2016.1267583

Kearney, Milo and Anthony Knopp. *Ciudad Cuates – A History of the US–Mexican Twin Cities*. Austin, TX: Eakin Press, 1995.

Kennedy, John Fitzgerald. 'Address by the President at a Luncheon Given in His Honor by President López Mateos', 29 June 1962. http://www.jfk link.com/speech es/jfk/pubpublicpapers/1962/jfk264_62.html. Accessed 27 November 2015.

Kevaco. 'Welcome to Derby, Vermont'. http://derbyvt.org/. Accessed 13 September 2013.

Lasserre, Frédéric, Patrick Forest and Enkeleda Arapi. 'Politique de sécurité et villages-frontière entre États-Unis et Québec'. *Cybergeo* (March 2012). https://doi.org/10.4000/cybergeo.25209

Leblond, Christian. *L'Accord de Libre-Echange Nord-Américain*. PhD dissertation, University of Nice, 1999.

Letniowska-Swiat, Sylvie. 'Pratiques et perceptions d'une métropole transfrontalière: l'exemple lillois' in *Villes et Frontières*. Ed. Bernard Reitel et al. Paris: Anthropos, 2002. 99–113.

Lundén, Thomas and Dennis Zalamans. 'Local Co-operation, Ethnic Diversity and State Territoriality – The Case of Haparanda and Tornio on the Sweden–Finland Border'. *GeoJournal* 54.1 (2001): 33–42.

Macias, Marie-Carmen. 'L'Espace frontalier Mexique/Etats-Unis après le 11 septembre 2001 – entre processus transfrontaliers et transnationaux'. *La frontière Mexique/États-Unis après 15 ans d'Alena*, Cahier des Amériques Latines (2009): 83–97.

Martínez, Oscar J. *Border People: Life and Society in the U.S.-Mexico Borderlands*. Tucson: University of Arizona Press, 1994.

Matthiesen, Ulf and Hans-Joachim Bürkner. 'Antagonistic Structures in Border Areas: Local Milieux and Local Politics in the Polish-German Twin City Gubin/Gube'. *GeoJournal* 54.1 (2001): 43–50.

Milhaud, Olivier. 'La Contre-urbanité: Windsor face à Detroit – ou comment se construit l'identité à la frontière' in *Tropisme des frontières – Tome 1*. Ed. Hélène Velasco-Graciet and Christian Bouquet. Paris: L'Harmattan, 2005. 229–44.

Reitel, Bernard. 'Border Temporality and Space Integration in the European Transborder Agglomeration of Basel'. *Journal of Borderlands Studies* 28.2 (2013): 239–56. https://doi.org/10.1080/08865655.2013.854657

Renard, Jean-Pierre. 'Villes et frontières: antagonismes et convergences sémantiques'. *Hommes et Terres du Nord* 2.1 (2001): 112–22. https://doi.org/10.3406/htn.2001.2769

Rensink, Brenden W. *Native but Foreign: Indigenous Immigrants and Refugees in the North American Borderlands*. College Station, Texas: A&M University Press, 2018 (1st edn).

Smith, David R. 'Structuring the Permeable Border' in *Permeable Border: The Great Lakes Basin as Transnational Region*. Ed. John J. Bukowczyk et al. Pittsburgh, PA: University of Pittsburgh Press, 2005. 120–51.

Sohn, Christophe. 'Modelling Cross-Border Integration: The Role of Borders as a Resource'. *Geopolitics* 19.3 (2014): 587–608. https://doi.org/10.1080/14650045.2014.913029

Sohn, Christophe and Francisco Lara-Valencia. 'Borders and Cities: Perspectives from North America and Europe'. *Journal of Borderlands Studies* 28.2 (2013): 181–90. https://doi.org/10.1080/08865655.2013.854662

Stacey, C. P. 'The Myth of the Unguarded Frontier 1815–1871'. *The American Historical Review* 56.1 (October 1950): 1–18.

Thompson, John and Stephen Randall. *Canada and the United States: Ambivalent Allies*. Montréal: McGill-Queen's University Press, 2008.

Vanneph Alain. 'Villes frontalières Mexique-Etats-Unis' in *La Frontière Mexique/Etats-Unis, mutations économiques, sociales et territoriales*. Ed. Pierre Gondard et al. Paris: Editions de l'IHEAL, 1995. 246–59.

CHAPTER 4

Continental Liberty, Natural Reason, *Survivance*: Gerald Vizenor's Sojourning in the Borderlands

Chris LaLonde

The border beckons. Whether thought of in terms of the other time and space of liminality, a là Victor Turner; as contact zone, first formulated by Mary Louise Pratt; as borderlands, thanks to the work of Gloria Anzaldúa and its continuing legacy; or as linked to a way of thinking that makes delinking from Western thought conceivable, as Walter Mignolo would have us understand it; borders are sites of possibility. There, we think, we believe, alternative articulations are possible. What Mignolo terms 'border thinking' is, by nature, 'epistemically disobedient', calling into question the constructions of the West and its definition of modernity as part of an effort to see and think differently.[1] Border thinking, then, 'is by definition thinking in exteriority, in the spaces and time that the self-narrative of modernity invented as its outside [in order] to legitimize its own logic of coloniality'.[2] The plural needs to be noted, for spaces differ, obviously, and without a recognition of and attention to those differences, in space and in and across time, we run the risk of eviscerating the promise of our border work even as we begin. Mignolo seems keenly aware of this, reminding us that when we truly 'become epistemically disobedient' [we are] 'dwelling and thinking in the borders of local histories confronting global designs'.[3] Or to put it another way, place matters.

In search of alternative articulations of the border and border thinking when that which beckons is the international boundary between Canada and the United States, one could do worse than turning to the work of White Earth Anishinaabe writer and theorist

Gerald Vizenor. In a body of work that stretches from the 1960s to the present, Vizenor has continually challenged his readers to think differently about natives. Moreover, Vizenor's sojourns into the borderlands resonate with his ongoing commitment to and articulation of native sovereignty and resistance, commitment and articulation frequently phrased in such tricky Vizenor terms as continental liberty, natural reason and *survivance*.

Recognising that 'some upsetting is necessary', Vizenor turns to trickster and trickster discourse, the former embodied in the Anishinaabe figure Naanabozho and the latter theoretically informed and resonant articulations of what Vizenor long ago characterised as 'an imaginative liberation in comic narratives', in order to help his readers see that the *indian* is a sign created and perpetuated by the dominant society, on either side of the borderline.[4] 'American *indians*', Vizenor writes in *Fugitive Poses: Native American Indian Scenes of Absence and Presence* (1998), 'are never the same as natives. The *indians* are that uncertain thing of discoveries, and the absence of natives ... the *indigene*, that real sense of presence, memories, and coincidence is born in native stories. The trick is to create a new theater of native names.'[5]

Borderland Spaces

Both native and non-native scholars of Vizenor's work have long recognised his attention to and interest in borders and borderlands. For instance, Choctaw-Cherokee-Irish writer Louis Owens noted in *Mixedblood Messages* (2000) that Vizenor both deconstructs signs of the border in the novel *Bearheart: The Heirship Chronicles* (1978) as his pilgrims head south and west from northern Minnesota to the pueblos of New Mexico and through his texts offers the reader characters for whom the borderland is embodied in their mixed- or crossblood identity.[6] In 2012 White Earth Anishinaabe Kimberly Blaeser highlighted the role played by borders, literal and otherwise, in Vizenor's poetry and their link to transformation. In her words, 'whether through mixedblood or trickster embodiments or literary and linguistic innovation, Vizenor writes to disrupt the idea of difference that fortifies frontiers, to dissolve false frames of separation, and to liberate both meaning and the marginalized inhabitants of all "other" edges of these Americas'.[7]

Some years ago, I pointed out that time and again Vizenor situates scenes and characters in liminal situations and that borders figure prominently in his work, no matter the genre. For example, Stone Columbus anchors the *Santa Maria Casino*, the *Nina* restaurant, and the *Pinta* tax free market on the international border between the United States and Canada in his alternative quincentennial commemoration of Columbus' 1492 voyage, *The Heirs of Columbus* (1991). In *The Trickster of Liberty* (1998), Slyboots Browne situates his 'tribe boats' on the same border and an old trickster and tribal shaman inhabits a cabin on an island there as well.[8] More recently, in Vizenor's *Bear Island: The War at Sugar Point* (2006), a book-length poem that also has a cabin near a lakeshore as an important locale, the treeline is tellingly highlighted early on, for that both/and location of indeterminacy and possibility is a place where, if I may echo Blaeser, other articulations become possible. Fittingly, dawn is accentuated in the poem as well, for 'first light' both illuminates the battlefield and the pinned-down soldiers and newspapermen the morning following the initial skirmish on the shores of Leech Lake between soldiers of the U.S. Seventh Calvary and Anishinaabe warriors and, critically, is the light with which the reader can see for the first time the context within which that conflict unfolded and through which it is to be understood.[9]

In *Blue Ravens* (2014), Vizenor's historical novel that imagines the lives of White Earth Anishinaabeg and other natives in the years leading up to the First World War, during the war to end all wars, and after, the borderland is invoked yet again, this time to ground the White Earth Reservation and subtly to invoke the motivation behind its location: 'The Ogema Station was built near the grain elevator at the very edge of the woodland and the peneplain.'[10] The phrasing is revealing, as it makes clear that White Earth, situated in the parkland belt of the state, is where the rich flatland of the Red River basin, oak savannah, and mixed-hardwood and coniferous forests meet. Call it a contact zone. The federal government's thought in 1867 was that those Anishinaabeg already successfully assimilated and ready to adopt the country's agrarian ideal would gravitate to the western part of the new reservation where they could find ample tillable ground for row crops. Those still immersed in the seasonal round of hunting-gathering-gardening would make their homes in the woodlands where they could hunt, trap and fish;

gather berries and medicinal plants; harvest wild rice; and tap maple trees for sap to make into syrup and sugar.

The grain elevator and railway station signal both the market economy and the network of expansion and transportation that shaped the country on either side of the turn of the century. It is the railroad, moreover, that starts the Beaulieu brothers Aloysius and Basile on their journey to Europe as soldiers of the United States Expeditionary Forces. The name of the town from which they set out is telling, finally, for the Anishinaabe word for chief or leader serves to indicate early on that the young men will carry with them a critical element of traditional Anishinaabe culture and society. Historically, Anishinaabe leaders came from the avian clans and were recognised for both their ability to take the long view on matters and their facility with language. They were esteemed as orators. Small wonder then that Aloysius' paintings feature blue ravens and that Basile becomes a writer – like Vizenor, a native storier.

Tricky Phrases

It is both fitting and insightful that Blaeser calls our attention to word and phrase in Vizenor's poetry, for as she notes, Vizenor's 'literary works investigate the boundaries of language as readily as they indict political, legalistic, legislative, and other more recognized avenues used to limit freedom'.[11] Blaeser also highlights how words and phrases in *Bear Island: The War at Sugar* Point, for instance, resonate with articulations to be found in earlier Vizenor texts. For example, the phrase 'manifest manners' calls to mind Vizenor's earlier use of that phrase and his critique of Manifest Destiny, while 'pillagers of liberty' echoes his earlier trickster of liberty. Critically, the critique of the dominant society and the invocation of trickster are indicative of what language can do, of the ends to which Vizenor deploys word and phrase in the name of 'survival in story'.[12]

Vizenor's is a rich and evocative vocabulary, to be sure, both in English and in Anishinaabemowin; it strikes me that central to his efforts to disrupt, dissolve and liberate in and with words are what Vizenor terms continental liberty, natural reason and *survivance*. Indeed, the three turns of phrase are so fundamental to Vizenor's sense of identity and of sovereignty that they have pride of place in the Preamble to the Constitution of the White Earth Nation, for which he was the principal writer: 'The Anishinaabeg of the White

Earth Nation are the successors of a great tradition of continental liberty, a native constitution of families, totemic associations. The Anishinaabeg create stories of natural reason, of courage, loyalty, humor, spiritual inspiration, *survivance*, reciprocal altruism, and native cultural sovereignty.'[13] *Survivance* brings together survival and resistance, continuance, endurance and remembrance, the last playfully to be sure in as much as Vizenor deplores act or edifice that leads and amounts to static memorialisation, but it is more than the union of those words. It is an active presence. In Vizenor's words, the native stories of *survivance* are successive and natural estates; *survivance* is an active repudiation of dominance, tragedy and victimry.[14] Dominance is precisely the position the settler-colonial society creates for itself, and in doing so relegates natives to the subordinate position. In the prevailing master narrative of the state, the *indian* was all too often doomed to meet a tragic end. Whether death or assimilation, the end point inscribed offers up the static position of *indian* as victim. As Basile Beaulieu tells us early in *Blue Ravens*, he and his brother sold more copies of the reservation newspaper the *Tomahawk* to passengers when the train stopped at Ogema Station the 'greater the stories of shame, coincidence, and native victimry' the issue contained.[15] This is what readers want, both within and beyond *Blue Ravens*, in 1908, before, and since. Vizenor will have nothing of it, announcing instead, as he writes in *Native Liberty* (2009), 'Native *survivance* is an active sense of presence over absence, deracination, and oblivion in history; *survivance* is the obvious continuance of stories, not a mere reaction, or a survivable cultural name.'[16]

Continental liberty, that is to say the freedom to move about the continent, serves to at the very least call into question, if not undo, the hegemony of the Western nation states laying claim to North America and the borders they have created and seek to perpetuate and police. Vizenor sees the story of the Nez Perce, pressured from their homeland in the decade after the Civil War, pursued by the US military through the borderlands of the Rocky Mountain Pacific Northwest, and denied the right to return to Oregon's Wallowa Valley following their surrender, as a *survivance* narrative. Although 'The common authority of continental native liberty, reciprocity, and visionary sovereignty was "diminished" by discovery, occupation, removal to reservations, denial of national citizenship, and by the plenary power of the United States Congress', a painfully succinct phrasing of what the natives of North America have been subject to, Vizenor recognises that 'The Nez Perce are truly the patriots of a continental native liberty' as together with their leader Chief Joseph they engage in an act of fundamental, indeed foundational, resistance.[17] With movement through their ancestral homeland without regard for the borders created by what Vizenor terms mercenary sovereignty – be they reservation, state or territory boundaries – the Nez Perce are effectively realising, however fleetingly, their presence on the land and the continental liberty that has long been theirs.

The Nez Perce flight east and north towards Canada in 1877 embodies resistance in the name of survival, to be sure. Theirs is a fugitive pose, to invoke both the title of Vizenor's *Fugitive Poses: Native American Indian Scenes of Absence and Presence* and the 'fugitive indigeneity' that Jarrett Martineau and Eric Ritskes identify as a characteristic of contemporary Indigenous art. Deploying Vizenor's idea of the fugitive pose, Martineau and Ritskes identify an Indigenous aesthetic that refuses inclusion in the dominant paradigms and epistemologies of settler colonialism culture, choosing instead 'refusal and flight as a mode of freedom'.[18] Like the flight of the Nez Perce, fugitive indigeneity highlights movement, and thus it resonates both with what Vizenor imagines to be the active presence in native stories and the centrality of movement for the Anishinaabe both past and present as they move within their traditional homelands with the seasons. For Vizenor, motion, or what he terms transmotion, and sovereignty go hand in hand. That natives have been and are present on this continent is obvious, no matter the efforts of the dominant society to either eradicate the people or relegate them to the past, and with what Vizenor calls their 'natural right of motion, or transmotion' comes a sovereignty that is linked to something other than merely territoriality or victimry.[19] Rather, 'Native transmotion is an original natural union in the stories of emergence and migration that relates humans to an environment and to the spiritual and political significance of animals and other creations.'[20]

So it is that Aloysius early on paints blue ravens and continues to do so even after the priest at the Catholic mission on the White Earth Reservation tells the boy to use black for the bird's head, body, wings and tail. The priest cannot see what Aloysius can, that 'Ravens are blue, the lush sheen of blues in a rainbow, and the transparent blues that shimmer on a spider web in the morning rain. Blues are ironic, the tease of natural light. The night is blue not black.'[21] Character, narrator and author are aware of their environment, can see the play and tricky tease inherent in the natural world thanks to changes in both what is before us and in our position and perspective, changes themselves linked to chance. Shimmer is the critical word, subtly sounding motion while highlighting the connection between light, object, reflection and observer. Blue ravens can guide us, then, for they are 'the new totem of native motion'.[22]

The relation of humans to and indeed with an environment is marked by natural reason, that is to say, with creation rather than closure and at all times with an element of chance. Vizenor's stories 'honor chance' and in doing so 'create a sense of presence, and celebrate *survivance*'.[23] Far from 'a mere romance with nature', *survivance* is 'character by natural reason'.[24] Vizenor gives us a sample of what he means when he writes of

> a consciousness and sense of incontestable presence that arises from experiences in the natural world, the turn of season, sudden storms, migration of cranes, the ventures of tender lady's slippers, chance of moths overnight, unruly mosquitoes, and the favor of spirits in the water, rimy sumac, wild rice, thunder in the ice, bear, beaver, and faces in the stone.[25]

This is being with the world: one is attuned to the quick change of weather, the movements and rhythms of life and its unpredictability, one understands that the natural world is unruly and recognises the importance of venturing forth nevertheless, and, critically, one is willing to do so. Natural reason recognises that there is always an element of uncertainty, of indeterminacy, of chance, and with that recognition comes both possibility and, crucially, the need, always, to take care.

Writing attuned to traditional stories, to storying, Vizenor aims to 'create a distinctive literary aesthetics of natural reason and *survivance* inspired by native stories, oral, in translation, and original'.[26] His Anishinaabe ancestors, Vizenor notes, articulated 'a natural presence by sound, motion, the traces of seasons, a summer in the spring', by the relationship with animals made manifest by 'totemic associations', and by an awareness of the transformations, tease and play inherent in the world and embodied in trickster stories.[27] Early in *Blue Ravens* the narrative makes clear that natural reason stands against arbitrarily drawn borders that do not take into account the chancy nature and rhythms of the natural world. In a move that resonates with the contemporary conflict over rights that were made clear in nineteenth-century treaties, Honore Beaulieu, described as 'native by natural reason ... disregarded the federal treaty that established the White Earth Reservation. Honore refused to honor the boundaries and continued to hunt, trap, fish, gather wild rice, and maple syrup in the manner of his ancestors'.[28]

That ancestral native manner stands in telling contradistinction to that of the West, writ large in *Blue Raven*'s depiction of the Great War's horrors. Millions die, yes, millions more were wounded, yes, villages and cities were destroyed, yes; Vizenor would have us see, too, the devastation of the natural world. Birds return with caution to shattered forests on the afternoon of the Armistice, three ravens caw, 'a tease of presence, and then a haunting silence'.[29] The narrative renders the ravaged landscape as surely as it does the piles of corpses beside roads and in French fields. It reminds the reader that, contra Sandburg's grass, 'the native forests and fields would bear forever the blood, brain, and cracked bones in every season of the fruit trees and cultivated sugar beets'.[30] Both the empire demon that provoked the conflict and the war itself are the 'enemy of natural reason'.[31] What holds for Germany and the First World War, moreover, holds for past wars as well; this is made clear in the narrative's depiction of the Marne, which 'flowed in silence, an ancient course and motion through the cruel memories of many wars. The shoreline was bruised with battens and memories of the dead. The glance of rockets shivered on the dark water, and revealed the steady flow of leaves, broken trees, and human debris from the nearby war upriver near the city of Chateau-Thierry.'[32]

'Trickster Plover of Liberty'

At first glance seemingly a curious choice of words, one typically thinks not of shores but of banks when a river's borders come to mind, the shoreline rendered above is a reminder of the contact zone that Vizenor plays in and with throughout his corpus. The shoreline is also the habitat of a particular species appearing, I like to think, early and late in *Blue Ravens*, *Charadrius melodus*, the piping plover.³³ Basile Beaulieu tells us that the first stories he writes were plover stories, and those three visionary stories of guise and guile, tease and trickery, start Basile, twelve at the time, on the road to becoming a writer. His depiction of the broken wing dance of the plover, of the wobble of a plover with a wounded foot, and of the erratic and acrobatic feigning performances of the bird capture the experience of natives on the White Earth Reservation. At the novel's end, Basile returns to his first stories. With that return, he and Vizenor stress that they 'were visionary trickster stories. The most inspired and deceptive plover dances were a variety of feigns and guises as evasive entertainment, and not a predictable pattern or liturgy.'³⁴

What is true of the plover's dances holds for *Blue Ravens* as well. While announcing itself a historical novel on the dust jacket and title page, *Blue Ravens* refuses to be bound by the historical event that is the First World War. Indeed, in a text that dips back to the mid-1800s and whose chapter titles run from 1907 to 1924, less than a quarter of the work deals with the war years and the time the Beaulieu brothers and other White Earth natives spent as members of the armed forces or its support groups. As part of its effort to have the reader see the bigger picture, the text also deploys *The Odyssey* throughout, a text Aloysius reads and quotes from and which has *Blue Raven*'s final word. In moving between historical fiction and epic, ultimately lighting on the latter, Vizenor's text is mindful of the importance of culture and worldview to stories, their articulation, and one's understanding of both.

Basile tells us that Frances Densmore's work at White Earth recording native songs and stories helped him along the path to become a writer because the recordings made by the turn-of-the-century ethnographer and ethnomusicologist served as sources of inspiration, spurred him on, and made easier his efforts to write stories. The particular song to which Basile refers is a mere eight Anishinaabemowin words, rendered in English as *'little plover, it is said, has walked by'* (italicised in the original), but it need be no longer because the 'listeners understood the story'.³⁵ A traditional singer, an audience and the dynamic nature of the song itself as well as its articulation and reception are emphasised, critically, because what is absent, in this case the plover that 'has walked by', is made present thanks to the song and an engaged audience. Making what is absent present is what Vizenor has been labouring to do throughout his long career, as he works to articulate for and to his audience natives and native stories.

Vizenor fancies two species of plovers, the other being *Charadrius vociferus*, the killdeer, but I'm highlighting *Charadrius melodus* because it calls from the shores of one place in Minnesota: the borderlands sheet of water called by most the Lake of the Woods. It is there in the northernmost part of the United States through which runs the border between that nation and Canada that Vizenor sets the novel *Treaty Shirts* (2016). Set in 2034, *Treaty Shirts* tells the story of eight native exiles, seven of them from White Earth, and the text's narrators, who go to the Lake of the Woods, or rather the Lake of the Sand Hills (or better still Pub-be-kwaw-waung-gaw Sau-gi-e-gun), in the name and spirit of continental liberty after being banished from the White Earth Reservation immediately after the US Congress abrogated all treaties between the United States and native nations and did away with reservation boundaries. In *Treaty Shirts*, as is the case with others of his works – *Hiroshima Bugi* springing immediately to mind – Vizenor makes clear a concern with and concern over peace, freedom and liberty, particularly continental liberty. What's more, *Treaty Shirts* makes clear early on the awareness of the devastation the fur trade wrought on the North American beaver population, especially, and its ecosystem. Archive, whose voice opens and closes the text, is painfully clear in his phrasing, noting that the 'historical union and memorable peace treaty' that is La Grand Paix de Montreal (1701) 'was directly connected to the decimation of totemic animals in the empire fur trade'.[36] Later in the chapter he states in no uncertain terms that 'The new totems and cultural burdens of natives are hardly significant when compared with the decimation of animals, and demise of the original totemic associations in the furious continental fur trade of the past three centuries.'[37] Not simply nation states and predatory economic practices are indicted, moreover, for Archive includes the very underpinnings of the West: neither 'tiresome overcompensations of monotheism, [n]or the romantic tread of enlightenment would absolve the outright cruelty and slaughter of animals for felt hats and furry fashions'.[38]

Committed to creature justice and animal rights, Justice Molly Creche, an elected judge of the constitutional tribal court, held hearings devoted to the legal standing and natural rights of animals after the White Earth Constitution was ratified. The hearings conducted prior to the US government's termination of the treaties between it and native nations were telling – never more so than when 'the most persuasive testimony ... about the outright murder of animals in the fur trade and the murder of birds in the freaky fashion trade of decorative feathers' was voiced.[39] The 'plume hunters ... murdered' birds from a wide range of species, Creche tells us, everything from eagles and egrets to cardinals and hundreds more.[40]

Count the piping plover in that number. Although never common to the state, the migratory piping plover had at one time more than a single area that it called home when it was in the state to breed and raise its young. Migration is an example of natural motion, and the seasonal journey of the piping plover, movement that does not recognise national borders it crosses and re-crosses, is a telling instance of continental liberty. As was the case with other avian species, while the piping plover was hunted as a food source, it was targeted especially for its feathers. The 1918 Migratory Bird Act to which Creche refers when recounting the animal rights hearings for the readers afforded the piping plover and other species some protection. Still, threats remained. Indeed, in the years since the passage of the Migratory Bird Act the primary cause of the piping plover's decline in Minnesota and elsewhere throughout the Great Lakes region was and is loss of habitat. When not migrating, the piping plover spends its time between the water's edge and the line where the sandy area meets the grass or forest line. Shoreline development has transformed sandy habitats. Grooming beaches results in the loss of the vegetation and rocks that would provide the species cover from predators. Where sandy areas with sparse vegetation remain, human presence on beaches and sand spits disturbs the nesting areas. Populations decline. The piping plover and its liberty are threatened by all that fail to apprehend the natural world and humankind's place in it. The bird's tricky tease, its feigning, deceptive behaviour, is Vizenor's as well.

'*survivance* in our stories'

Aboard the *Baron of Patronia* houseboat plying the waters of the lake and crossing and re-crossing the international border, 'The eight exiles envisioned on those marvelous nights a constitution of continental liberty that was in motion, and not restrained by the metes and bounds of any treaty.[41] The exiles had recovered the spirit of the voyageurs and the natural motion of liberty.'[42] The vision and spirits of the exiles is broadcast over the airwaves by the 'Giant Wave of Panic Radio', a 'native' and 'nervy wave' of the clouds that 'became the new wave of the exiles of *survivance* and liberty.[43] The stories on the wave became the unforgettable literature of our time, the end of treaties and feigned sovereignty, and a necessary return to native stories and memories in natural motion.'[44]

Broadcasting from the watery borderlands of the north, Panic Radio serves to stress the importance of transmission, in particular oral transmission, and the role information and communication technology (ICT) plays in spreading the word, which is to say, in spreading native stories. It is the 'last original voice of native continental solidarity and liberty' because its voice, heard both sides of the arbitrary international boundary, gives the lie to the border while also celebrating and making manifest the liberty and freedom of the borderlands.[45] Although he has written for both the stage and the screen, Vizenor is a storier who uses the printed word to tell his stories of liberation, in no small measure, I think, because he knows that those tales of native *survivance* will resonate, as he writes in *Bear Island: The War at Sugar Point*, 'forever in the book'.[46] In *Treaty Shirts* what resonates forever in the book is an awareness that the betwixt-and-between space of the border, that contact zone analogous to the literary text where presencing is possible, is where *survivance* is best articulated. It is there that Chewy Browne creates the White Earth Anthem aboard 'the *Baron of Patronia* the first night' she and her fellow exiles crossed 'the international border of Lake of the Woods'.[47] With its chorus, the anthem, similar to the French anthem in melody and cadence, sounds the centrality of stories from the border to liberty:[48]

> *survivance* in our stories
> natural motion
> *survivance* in our dreams
> spirits of resistance
> forever in the favor of liberty[49]

Within the borderland that is the literary text, the exiles set forth to confound the border in the name of natural reason and continental liberty from an abandoned and weathered dock near the allotment of John Kakageesick, an Anishinaabe who lived there, Vizenor tells us in *The Everlasting Sky: Voices of the Anishinabe People* (1972, 2000), before Minnesota become a state and before the white community of Warroad was established. A healer and elder, Kakageesick was 124 years old when he died, or rather he was thought to be 124 years old, for Warroad declared that his birthday was 14 May 1844. Like his birth date, Kakageesick's identity as an *indian*, pictured on postcards wearing a turkey feather headdress and a green blanket draped over a blue suit, was the product of Warroad's imagination, 'invented', in Vizenor's words, 'by the dominant society for recreational value'.[50] Vizenor first wrote about Kakageesick in 1968, covering his funeral for the Minneapolis *Tribune*, and for more than fifty years he has been labouring to replace the invented *indian* with natives and their stories of *survivance*. Thus, it is fitting that the exiles would leave from a shore coloured by the dominant society's attempt to claim Kakageesick as its redman.

With telling word and phrase, Vizenor counters the invention that would fix the native as *indian*. Just after John Kakageesick first appears in *Treaty Shirts* the narrative links together song, dream song and trickster to indicate the critical role song, that is to say artistic utterance grounded in Anishinaabe culture and story, plays in articulating stories of *survivance*. Indeed, the piping plover is an apt choice for Basile, and for Vizenor, given that its scientific name, *Charadrius melodus*, emphasises both place and song. Years earlier, Vizenor listened as the Midewewin healer Daniel Raincloud offered chanting prayers honouring the spirit after Kakageesick passed. Now, in and with words, Vizenor would have us hear the healing song and the accompanying rattle: as the character Moby Dick says in *Treaty Shirts*, 'the presence of that sound has lasted forever in Lake of the Woods'.[51] If we join Raincloud, Kakageesick and Vizenor, if we join the Anishinaabe in being attuned to natural reason, perhaps there is hope for the endangered piping plover, perhaps there is hope for us.

Notes

1. Walter Mignolo, 'Geopolitics of Sensing and Knowing: On (De) Coloniality, Border Thinking, and Epistemic Disobedience', *Postcolonial Studies* 14.3 (2011): 277.
2. Ibid.: 282.
3. Ibid.: 277.

4. Neal Bowers and Charles Silet, 'An Interview with Gerald Vizenor', *MELUS* 8.1 (Spring 1981): 46; Gerald Vizenor, 'Introduction', in *Narrative Chance: Postmodern Discourse in Native American Indian Literatures*, ed. Gerald Vizenor (Norman: University of Oklahoma Press, 1993), 9.
5. Gerald Vizenor, *Fugitive Poses: Native American Indian Scenes of Absence and Presence* (Lincoln: University of Nebraska Press, 1998), 69.
6. Louis Owens, *Mixedblood Messages: Literature, Film, Family, Place* (Norman: University of Oklahoma Press, 1998), 85–6.
7. Kimberly Blaeser, 'The Language of Borders, the Borders of Language in Gerald Vizenor's Poetry', in *The Poetry and Poetics of Gerald Vizenor*, ed. Deborah Madsen (Albuquerque: University of New Mexico Press, 2012), 1.
8. Gerald Vizenor, *The Trickster of Liberty* (Minneapolis: University of Minnesota Press, 1988), 126, 9.
9. Gerald Vizenor, *Bear Island: The War at Sugar Point* (Minneapolis: University of Minnesota Press, 2006), 16.
10. Gerald Vizenor, *Blue Ravens* (Middletown, CT: Wesleyan University Press, 2014), 23.
11. Blaeser, 'Language of Borders', 1.
12. Ibid., 5.
13. *Constitution of the White Earth Nation*, 1.
14. Vizenor, *Fugitive Poses*, 15.
15. Vizenor, *Blue Ravens*, 23.
16. Gerald Vizenor, *Native Liberty: Natural Reason and Cultural Survivance* (Lincoln: University of Nebraska Press, 2009), 138.
17. Ibid., 108, 66.
18. Jarrett Martineau and Eric Ritskes, 'Fugitive Indigeneity: Reclaiming the Terrain of Decolonial Struggle through Indigenous Art', *Decolonization: Indigeneity, Education & Society* 3.1 (2014): IV.
19. Vizenor, *Fugitive Poses*, 181.
20. Ibid., 183.
21. Vizenor, *Blue Ravens*, 2.
22. Ibid., 14.
23. Vizenor, *Native Liberty*, 17.
24. Ibid., 88.
25. Ibid.
26. Vizenor, *Native Liberty*, 6.
27. Ibid.
28. Vizenor, *Blue Ravens*, 5. Those contemporary conflicts include the rights enshrined in treaties between the federal government and the Anishinaabe of Minnesota recognising that Anishinaabeg can hunt

and fish outside both the contemporary boundaries of the state's Chippewa reservations and the fish and game seasons defined and regulated by the state, for example. In 1999 the United States Supreme Court upheld the rights of the Mille Lacs Chippewa to hunt and fish that were articulated in the Treaty of 1837. As recently as 2015, the Eighth Circuit Court of Appeals found for both the Leech Lake band and the White Earth band on the matter of fishing rights recognised in the same treaty. Native rights to harvest wild rice also figure in current debates in Minnesota over GMOs and wild rice, its harvesting, and its protection from contamination from the genetically modified seed.

29. Ibid., 141.
30. Ibid.
31. Ibid., 109.
32. Ibid., 110–11.
33. The quotation in this section's subheading comes from Vizenor's *Blue Ravens*, 13.
34. Ibid., 275.
35. Ibid., 13.
36. Gerald Vizenor, *Treaty Shirts: October 2034 – A Familiar Treatise on the White Earth Nation* (Middletown, CT: Wesleyan University Press, 2016), 2.
37. Ibid., 18.
38. Ibid.
39. Ibid., 102.
40. Ibid.
41. The quotation in this section's subheading comes from Vizenor's *Treaty Shirts*, 123.
42. Ibid., 35.
43. Ibid., 68.
44. Ibid.
45. Ibid., 96.
46. Vizenor, *Bear Island*, 16.
47. Vizenor, *Treaty Shirts*, 122.
48. Ibid.
49. Ibid., 123.
50. Gerald Vizenor, *The Everlasting Sky: Voices of the Anishinaabe People*, (Minneapolis: University of Minnesota Press, 2000 [first published 1972]), 132.
51. Vizenor, *Treaty Shirts*, 46.

Bibliography

Anzaldua, Gloria. *Borderlands: The New Mestiza/La Frontera*. San Francisco: Aunt Lute Books, 1987.

Blaeser, Kimberly. 'The Language of Borders, the Borders of Language in Gerald Vizenor's Poetry' in *The Poetry and Poetics of Gerald Vizenor*. Ed. Deborah Madsen. Albuquerque: University of New Mexico Press, 2012. 1–22.

Bowers, Neal and Charles Silet. 'An Interview with Gerald Vizenor'. *MELUS* 8.1 (Spring 1981): 41–9.

Constitution of the White Earth Nation. Approved 19 November 2013.

Haig, Susan and Lewis Oring. 'Distribution and Dispersal in the Piping Plover'. *The Auk* 105.4 (October 1988): 630–8.

Haig, Susan and Lewis Oring. 'Distribution and Status of the Piping Plover throughout the Annual Cycle'. *Journal of Field Ornithology* 56.4 (Autumn 1985): 334–45.

LaLonde, Chris. 'The Ceded Landscape of Gerald Vizenor's Fiction'. *Studies in American Indian Literature* 9.1 (Spring 1997): 16–32.

Martineau, Jarrett and Eric Ritskes. 'Fugitive Indigeneity: Reclaiming the Terrain of Decolonial Struggle through Indigenous art'. *Decolonization: Indigeneity, Education & Society* 3.1 (2014): I–XII.

Meyer, Melissa. *The White Earth Tragedy: Ethnicity and Dispossession at a Minnesota Anishinaabe Reservation*. Lincoln: University of Nebraska Press, 1994.

Mignolo, Walter. 'Geopolitics of Sensing and Knowing: On (De)Coloniality, Border Thinking, and Epistemic Disobedience'. *Postcolonial Studies* 14.3 (2011): 273–83.

Mignolo, Walter. *Local Histories/Global Designs: Coloniality, Subaltern Knowledges, and Border Thinking*. Princeton, NJ: Princeton University Press, 2000.

Mignolo, Walter. *The Darker Side of Western Modernity: Global Futures, Decolonial Options*. Durham, NC: Duke University Press, 2011.

Owens, Louis. *Mixedblood Messages: Literature, Film, Family, Place*. Norman: University of Oklahoma Press, 1998.

Pratt, Mary Louise. *Imperial Eyes: Travel Writing and Transculturation*. London: Routledge, 1992 (2nd edn 2008).

Ryan, Mark, Brian Root and Paul Mayer. 'Status of Piping Plovers in the Great Plains of North America: A Demographic Simulation Model'. *Conservation Biology* 7.3 (September 1993): 581–5.

Turner, Victor. 'Liminality and the Performative Genres' in *Rite, Drama, Festival, Spectacle*. Ed. John MacAloon. Philadelphia: ISHI, 1984. 19–41.

Turner, Victor. 'Social Dramas and Stories About Them' in *On Narrative*.

Ed. W. J. T. Mitchell. Chicago: University of Chicago Press, 1981. 137–64.

Vizenor, Gerald. *Bearheart: The Heirship Chronicles*. Minneapolis: University of Minnesota Press, 1978.

Vizenor, Gerald. *Bear Island: The War at Sugar Point*. Minneapolis: University of Minnesota Press, 2006.

Vizenor, Gerald. *Blue Ravens*. Middletown, CT: Wesleyan University Press, 2014.

Vizenor, Gerald. *Fugitive Poses*. Lincoln: University of Nebraska Press, 1998.

Vizenor, Gerald. 'Introduction' in *Narrative Chance: Postmodern Discourse in Native American Indian Literatures*. Ed. Gerald Vizenor. Norman: University of Oklahoma Press, 1993.

Vizenor, Gerald. *Native Liberty: Natural Reason and Cultural Survivance*. Lincoln: University of Nebraska Press, 2009.

Vizenor, Gerald. *The Everlasting Sky: Voices of the Anishinaabe People*. Minneapolis: University of Minnesota Press, 2000 (first published 1972).

Vizenor, Gerald. *The Heirs of Columbus*. Middletown, CT: Wesleyan University Press, 1991.

Vizenor, Gerald. *The Trickster of Liberty*. Minneapolis: University of Minnesota Press, 1988.

Vizenor, Gerald. *Treaty Shirts: October 2034 – A Familiar Treatise on the White Earth Nation*. Middletown, CT: Wesleyan University Press, 2016.

Walker, Rachel Durkee and Jill Doerfler. 'Wild Rice: The Minnesota Legislature, a Distinctive Crop, GMOs, and Ojibwe Perspectives'. *Hamline Law Review* 499 (2009): 500–27.

CHAPTER 5

The Logics of Border Theory: Negotiating Sovereignties at the Impasse

David Stirrup

In *Mohawk Interruptus*, Kahnawake scholar Audra Simpson includes an anecdote ironically titled 'On not passing at the border', in which she describes 'the most aggressive exchange I have ever had'. In transit from Montreal to New York for research, Simpson stands before a border agent, who flips her status card over, asking, 'Are you 100 per cent Indian?' Indefatigable, Simpson's interrogator finally draws a confession: '"Look,"' Simpson says, '"I was born down there . . . I am not an immigrant; I am part of a *First Nation*, and this is the card that proves it!"' The exchange that follows – while not entirely unfamiliar – is profoundly illustrative of what she calls the 'moment of articulation between law, history, and the body that constitutes Iroquois peoples' experiences of "crossing"'.[1] The closing scene reveals the tone of the exchange and the atmosphere in which this crossing occurs: 'as I was walking toward the door, she yelled across the border house to me. / "*You are an American.*" / And I yelled back. / "*I am a Mohawk.*" / And she yelled, / "*No. / You are an American.*"'[2]

Writing later about the refusal of Mohawk lacrosse players to travel to Britain on Canadian papers in 2010, Simpson asserts that

> sovereigns must be willing to pay a price when [historical] connections [predicated on treaties, and prior equivalencies] do not achieve the desired outcome. This price is demobilization . . . However, this may not be a price at all if the gains exceed it. Here the gain is the assertion of the principle, the sign of the

other political authority, vibrant and insistent, and the suggestion of possibilities beyond the horizon of what we may think is [the 'gift'] of citizenship.[3]

In both instances, the refusals Simpson articulates relate to the right of a people to move properly through their land. Their 'explicit right to pass' at the border, enshrined in the Jay Treaty of 1794, she explains, is both temporally located in specific juridical processes, and contingent on the often contradictory legal interpretations of two different settler governments – that in the nineteenth century became a question of 25 per cent blood quantum in the States and static distinctions of cultural continuity in Canada. The Indigenous border-crosser is, in other words, caught in a complicated web of recognition – a tension between de facto and de jure understandings of border crossing – that renders the right to cross only ever a *claim*, 'implicitly leav[ing] the legal regimes of Canada and the United States with the power to define ... how that right to pass shall be rendered and respected'.[4] For Simpson, the articulation of rights at the border amounts to a necessary refusal of that power.

I offer the preceding synopsis of Simpson's experience because, at one level, this chapter concerns a certain kind of optimism embedded in border theory's slips and evasions, hybridities and coalescences – in the gap, perhaps, between the rejection of discursive categories and the political hard edges of lived experience. It is an optimism that runs repeatedly up against the reality of border crossing – or not border crossing itself, per se, so much as what the Indigenous experience of border crossing as articulated by Simpson and countless others says about the assertion and maintenance of Indigenous sovereignty. It is worth noting that many Indigenous border crossings go far more smoothly – that the anecdote is no empirical evidence of impossibility, not least because safe, easy border crossings do not generally make good stories. In this sense, this chapter does not insist on a political impasse, though examples such as that of the lacrosse team above do demonstrate the continued and often thwarted negotiation of sovereign recognition (nation-to-nation rather than state-down recognition) staged at the Medicine Line. Nor does it, taking the invocation of that medicine, perform a disavowal of the ways in which the border has operated as sanctuary; has been consistently and successfully 'disrupted or even erased by the lived experiences of First Nations people'; or has been toyed with, evaded, undermined and neutralised conceptually and discursively by numerous Indigenous writers.[5] Rather, the chapter presents a selective review of the emergence of an 'American Indian' border theory before noting the key terms of its rejection – an invitation to further elaboration rather than an exhaustive scouring of the scholarship. Following that, it will suggest that rather than presenting a dichotomy in which borders are either present or absent, these positions identify nodes on a spectrum of resistance and return: resistance to the power of settler-colonial regimes and return to Indigenous centres through the re-marking of borders.

In doing so, the chapter considers the tensions at the boundaries of the discipline – characterised here as North American Indigenous studies broadly and Native North American literary studies more specifically. It will relate those tensions to the real-world tensions in Indigenous and settler-colonial relations which are most explicitly reflected, as Wallace Coffey and Rebecca Tsosie elucidate, in the relationship between conceptual notions of cultural sovereignty and the material claims of political sovereignty – or, in other words, between the figurative turns border theory has taken and the literal border site.[6] Consideration of border theory in the context of Native North American literary studies, then, speaks urgently to the issue that John Gamber describes as the 'single most critical issue in Native American studies today' as it is 'throughout Indian country: tribal sovereignty'.[7]

Thinking about sovereignty in the context of the border invariably emphasises Indigenous sovereignty's concern with tribal nationhood, self-governance and citizenship. As Kevin Bruyneel asserts, 'The literal and explicit practice of boundary-crossing represents the political position of those indigenous people who do not accept the notion that the presence of settler-states and nations deprives them of their rights of citizenship in their own nations.'[8] It also marks the shift from a 1990s emphasis on identity politics variously calibrated by grammars of authenticity, postmodernity and cosmopolitanism to the twenty-first century prioritisation of tribal nationalist and tribal literary nationalist concerns. This movement simultaneously points to the sameness-and-difference inherent in the United States' two borders, which demands consideration of both, reminds us that the conceptual models produced at the Mexico–US border do not necessarily translate to the Canada–US border, and implicitly decentres the US in the process.

Recalling Thomas King's powerful insistence that the border *is* 'a figment of someone else's imagination', Joshua Miner rightly notes that even figments bear 'real-world sociopolitical, cultural, and psychic consequences'.[9] While fiction can unsettle those consequences, as Miner argues, those disruptions are, themselves, symptomatic of that 'optimism' to which I allude above. This chapter, then, addresses the gap between border studies and Indigenous studies – a gap that resounds in Simpson's refusals. It has its conception in questions about the fit between border theory and 'American Indian studies', posed by a young Native American writer in conversation. As an obvious starting point, Paula Gunn Allen's *Off the Reservation: Reflections of a Boundary Busting, Border Crossing Loose Cannon*, 'La Frontera Na(rr)atives' channels Gloria Anzaldúa's work.[10] The book as a whole, however, does not so much theorise the border as situate its observations of hegemonic culture at the margins. The logical follow-up query – why isn't border theory more fully engaged with in American Indian studies? – presents its own set of sub-questions, not least around its territorial implications. There is a whole other chapter to be written on the nationally bound nature of such terminology. At first order level, King's truism that the Canada–US border is a 'figment of someone else's imagination' may have been uncritically adopted by way of justifying the fact that 'scholars south of the border, even Native American literary scholars, rarely paid attention to Canadian Aboriginal issues'.[11]

A recent short article by Cherokee and Quapaw/Chickasaw scholar Geary Hobson confirms that this tendency is finally being directly confronted 'down south'. Recognising 'a growing distance between US and Canadian Native writers and scholars' Hobson seeks in 'Borders Be Damned!' to 'break down some fences' in relation to the outcomes of the postponed 2019 Returning the Gift literary circle's annual prizes, originally planned to take place in Calgary.[12] Listing Indigenous writers in all genres who hail from territories north of the Medicine Line, Hobson notes with dismay that the RTG had come to be seen as a 'States thing' before announcing that the 2019 lifetime achievement award would have an all-Canadian shortlist. An addendum reveals that the deserved honour went to Métis author Maria Campbell.[13] I have written elsewhere about the paucity of 'Canadian' coverage in the early establishing surveys of Native North American literature.[14] More recently, efforts have been made at literary engagement across the border without necessarily always acknowledging the different challenges effected *by* the border. The barriers to, and the problems with, this kind of work are precisely the dangers of elision and occlusion that limit pan-Indian and pan-Indigenous frameworks – the common ground of colonised experience produces what Gillian Roberts refers to as the 'sameness and difference' of the settler states themselves, wherein different legal, political and cultural histories dictate the necessity of nuance and attention to localised detail.[15]

Real World Refusals and Literary Evasions

The border confrontation Audra Simpson recalls reflects two things deep at the heart of her refusals. The first is that, from the start, border theory in Native American Literary scholarship developed, perhaps inevitably, in direct relation/resistance to the construction of racialised codes – full and mixedblood/pure and hybrid – and their cultural corollaries the grammars of tradition and authenticity. And, secondly, perhaps self-evidently, that border theory seeks to produce a form of imaginative liberation from any connection between culture and territory as an inherently imperial designation and from externally imposed definitions of who and what Native people could be. Notwithstanding Simpson's point about gain, demobilisation joins pacification and containment at the heart of the 'colonial dream of fixity, control, visibility, productivity, and . . . docility'.[16] Both border theory and its opposition, then, emerge in North American Indigenous studies in direct resistance to the state mechanisms by which such dreams may be achieved.

The degree to which the development of Indigenous literary theory has maintained a conceptual distance from border theory formulations is perhaps best illustrated when I asked Gerald Vizenor himself to speak at a Canada–US border conference in 2009. He responded quite characteristically – teasingly – by asking how I connected the theme of the conference to his work. It is intriguing, at the level of the anecdote at least, that he asked this question, not least because, since Kimberly Blaeser's work in the early 1990s, many critics *have* equated his emphasis on fluidity and resistance to containment, on liberatory linguistic play and the rejection of essential delimiters of identity, and on the status of the liminal, to various iterations of border theory and nominally allied paradigms such as hybridity, cosmopolitanism and latterly transnationalism.

As Chris LaLonde notes in this volume, 'Vizenor situates scenes and characters in liminal situations and ... borders figure prominently in his work, no matter the genre' (p. 116). In another recent – and explicit – iteration of thinking-with-Vizenor, Zalfa Feghali notes that the parallels between Anzaldúa's mestiza and Vizenor's discursive trickster are 'unmistakable, which is not to say that the two figures are the same'.[17] That Anzaldúa's border-crossing subject is generally absent from recent Indigenous theorising – although she does appear in early 1990s journal articles on Native American literature – and 'the figure of the trickster is rarely, if ever, used in border studies, though it fits into the border-crosser paradigm at least as well as Anzaldúa's new *mestiza*', constitutes a curious lacuna in both fields.[18]

José David Saldívar's description of the US–Mexico border in his 1997 book *Border Matters* as a 'paradigm of crossing, circulation, material mixing, and resistance' has clear application in long-standing discussions of cultural encounter and transcultural exchange in Native American and First Nations literary studies and in Native studies more broadly.[19] Blaeser, for example, was writing as early as 1993 about the ways in which Native literatures implicitly acknowledge the contact zones in which Indigenous people circulate.[20] Blaeser's invocation of the border paradigm within a discussion of the challenge to theorisation that Native American literatures posed was followed by her book-length study of Vizenor's work, *Writing in the Oral Tradition*, in which she delineates Vizenor's theoretical deployment of figures of evasion and liberation that, as she more recently reiterated, 'repeatedly [call] up images of borders and border crossings, [and] of the possibility of transformation'.[21] In 'The Language of Borders, the Borders of Language', she observes that 'Vizenor writes to disrupt the idea of difference that fortifies frontiers, to dissolve false frames of separation, and to liberate both meaning and the marginalized inhabitants of all "other" edges of these Americas', not unlike Anzaldúa, perhaps, and certainly in keeping with the poststructuralists Vizenor so frequently engages.[22] Blaeser thus positions Vizenor, specifically, within the same conceptual frames invoked by border theories – his approach to signification analogous to Anzaldua's 'vague and undetermined' border 'created by the residue of an unnatural boundary' – aligning his linguistic and discursive play to his indictment of political and legislative frameworks as 'boundaries' designed to limit freedom.[23]

The semantic and paradigmatic manoeuvres of border theory, then, infuse early interventions.

At the turn of the twenty-first century, Robin Riley Fast, in her turn, illustrated this sense of theoretical utility most explicitly, where she argues,

> Contemporary Indian poetry itself suggests that, with important modifications, the terms *border*, *borderland*, and *border writing*, used most frequently in discussions of Chicano/a culture, can help to elucidate these diverse and variously contested spaces and the responses they incite. Revised to acknowledge the differing realities of Native American experience, some elements of border theory are well suited to serve a poetry often defined by its commitment to political struggle.[24]

Fast's and Blaeser's formulations bookend a formative decade for Native-centred literary criticism, by presenting the application of a modified border theory to the themes and concerns of Native North Americans as commonsensical and self-evident. They are joined, mid-decade, by Louis Owens' articulation of the frontier, which stands, he argues, 'in neat opposition to the concept of "territory"' as territory is imagined and given form by the colonial enterprise in America. 'Whereas frontier is always unstable, multidirectional, hybridized, characterized by heteroglossia, and indeterminate', he asserts, 'territory is clearly mapped, fully imagined as a place of containment'.[25] Like Vizenor, we might see Owens' theorising as border theory-'adjacent' – capturing the spirit, if not the lexicon, of the latter.

With the exception of readings of Owens' and Vizenor's work, or readings of other people through Owens' and Vizenor's near parallel theoretical apparatus, therefore, border theory has been *largely* conspicuous by its absence in published scholarship. Border crossing between Canadian and US and US and Mexican contexts within Indigenous studies remits has been minimal at best. More recently, Matthew Herman has briefly elucidated Laura Furlan's 'broadened' use of borderlands theory in tracing crossings and exchange in Louise Erdrich's fiction.[26] Given Herman's 2010 text's subtitle – the full title is *Politics and Aesthetics in Contemporary Native American Literature: Across Every Border* – the relative absence of border theory from his own argument, however, is telling.

Herman's primary purpose – to assess 'the status in theory of contemporary Native American literature in relation to the recent political turn in Native American literary studies' – attests to the systemic nature of that absence, while his submission of a shift from 'resistance theory to hybridity theory' offers us a possible understanding of the general reluctance to deploy border theory, to which I will return shortly.[27] Furlan's essay, in turn, asserts that border studies' critical project has valuable application for theorising the movements between reservation and urban spaces.[28] Even so, while in the abstract it offers useful insight into the fluid and mobile nature of culturally (and biologically) mixed identities, it skims over the political implications and arguably reinforces a view of Indigenous nations as marginal rather than centre. Moreover, despite the brief invocation of Saldívar, its engagement with border theory more broadly is limited.

The general thrust of these approaches prioritises the discursive arena – a liberatory drive that simultaneously renders borders, and particularly the international boundary itself, increasingly abstract. Maintaining this course while also asserting a sovereign-nationalist dimension to the texts he scrutinises, Joshua Miner demonstrates the ways in which narrative has long been a mechanism by which Indigenous writers have subverted the oppressive containment of the cadastral boundary: invoking Owens, Miner notes that Native writers refuse logics of containment to 'insist upon the freedom to reimagine themselves within a fluid, always shifting [border] space'.[29] In making these moves, Miner attempts to navigate the tension between forms of cultural and intellectual sovereignty free to imagine themselves into what James Cox calls the 'transborder imaginary' and a political sovereignty in which the material contest over land and borders is not so easily – or imaginatively – resolved.[30]

Equally productively, Feghali turns to Vizenor's trickster discourse where, as noted earlier, she finds a border-crosser somewhat consonant with Anzaldúa's mestizaje, an 'irresistible' comparison that allows her to make the claim that 'it becomes clear that what Anzaldúa prescribes can be accurately described as [Vizenorian] *survivance*'.[31] As Claudia Sadowski-Smith has done previously, Feghali bemoans not simply the lack of border theory in Native literary studies, but also the sidelining of the Canada–US border and, therefore, the '"complications" cross-border First Peoples pose' to our understanding of that border.[32] Like Chris LaLonde in this volume,

Feghali finds in Vizenor's theoretical manoeuvrings groups of 'exiles [who have] set forth to confound the border in the name of natural reason and continental liberty' (p. 125).

As is clear, then, Owens' frontier theory – itself influenced by Vizenorian thought – and Vizenor's trickster hermeneutics have long offered affinitive tropes for border crossing and mestizaje for those who would seek out this terrain in Native literary studies. Trickster territory is a seductive space – Indigenous-centred and yet elusive, liberatory and resistant to logics of containment.[33] So the question of why, beyond this relatively limited scope, border theory has failed to proliferate becomes almost harder to understand than the absence of the specificity of the border itself.

Literary Nationalism and Tribal Centres

The rise of tribal literary nationalism, accompanied by vociferous resistance to the dominance of Eurowestern theory, suggests perhaps one major reason. Many, including Simon Ortiz, Elizabeth Cook-Lynn and Blaeser, were calling for and producing Indigenous-centred theorising well before the falsely binary 'debate' between nationalism and cosmopolitanism broke in the early 2000s, and Blaeser is far from alone in having identified the Anishinaabe-ness of Vizenor's own theoretical standpoint.[34] One early foray into this terrain, Blaeser's 'Native Literature: Seeking a Critical Centre', established readings of Vizenor as located in his own situated sense of Anishinaabeakiing: Indigenous-centred, and formative of a means of engagement beyond tribal nation and nation state borders that she would go on to call 'Inter–Indigenous–Nationalism'. Inter–Indigenous–nationalism, in turn, resounds in contemporary claims that tribal nationalism has at its foundation an incipient transnationalism.[35] Nevertheless, many of the arguments around what came to be known as American Indian literary nationalism at the turn of the twenty-first century pushed back against Vizenorian theory – its apparent Eurocentricity, its obfuscating difficulty, the seemingly endless play of deconstruction which has led many critics to echo Craig Womack's complaint that Vizenor, as progenitor and major theoretical influence on the field, 'has traded tropes for reality'.[36]

In his own considered critique of Vizenorian play, Cherokee scholar Sean Teuton argues that 'In this trickster space, where race and colonialism continue to operate but have been rendered invisible, scholars, in the end, cannot explain crucial differences in social and political power, nor lay claim to a distinct tribal history and hold it up to the world.'[37] More significantly, perhaps, he insists that 'self-identified mixedblood critics, writing in this zone of the trickster, have been left with little theoretical recourse but subversion ... to remain epistemologically consistent, they cannot justify their own normative claims to American Indian identity or history'.[38] Kelli Lyon Johnson similarly insists that '"Mixed-blood" discourses resonate with (often European) theories of cultural exchange and hybridity, which ... risks rendering invisible the very elements that comprise what is hybrid.'[39] Echoing Teuton, Christopher Taylor insists that very few characters in Native fiction 'actually understand themselves as syncretic cultural subjects'. Rather, even those characters who are of mixed descent are more often described as 'Indians with ancestors who intermarried with white settlers':[40] not so much mestizaje figures as individuals centring particular identities that nevertheless acknowledge the complex legacies of colonialism.

The sparsity of border theory, in other words, is bound up in the same anxieties that underpinned what Taylor calls the 'metacritical debate' that emerged at the turn of the twenty-first century and became 'polarized between theorists favoring an inward-facing nationalism and those insisting on an outward-facing cosmopolitanism'.[41] Characterised as a contest between 'nationalists and hybridists', the polarisation in these debates has often been overstated, its nuances lost.[42] Many of the assertions against Vizenor, for instance, become problematic in light of Vizenor's work on the constitution of the White Earth Anishinaabe Nation – particularly given Teuton's secondary claim that trickster theory is 'disconnected from a distinct culture and land' and 'cannot support a coherent Native identity nor protect actual Native territories', which both Vizenor and Blaeser at least might contest.[43]

Nevertheless, Vizenor's proposal – as Teuton formulates – that 'American Indians ... inhabit the interstitial space between the colonies and the nations, the white and the Indian, and thus subvert the demands of each cultural register' posits an in-between that is simultaneously both coherent in the terms of border theory, and readily understandable as a problem to those for whom such theorising 'actually undermine[s] the ground on which Indian people recover culture and demand redress'.[44] More to the point for Teuton, and as Simpson's earlier anecdote demonstrates: 'Those American Indians who actually travel across and are often detained at colonial borders might not find this cross-blood cultural margin so liberating.'[45] Taylor, meanwhile, notes that Owens' 'emphasis on continuous flux suggests a zone that is almost unknowable in any precise historical way'.[46] Such positions very clearly recall critiques of border theory by critics who *have* focused on Indigenous articulations of the border: 'many of the pioneering border theorists . . . avoid borders altogether by . . . transforming the divisions between races, sexualities, languages, and political geographies', the danger of which being that 'border writing and border studies become utopian spaces where "in-betweenness" has no political impact or relevance'.[47] The critique of hybridity theories, trickster hermeneutics and the fugitive paradigm of border studies (notwithstanding the compelling readings of, say, the betwixt and betweenness of Louise Erdrich's characters so common in the 1990s and early 2000s) seem ever more consonant.

Andrea Smith also contests the hybridity discourse central to much border theory on the grounds that it posits a dichotomy between borderlands as 'the place of change, indeterminacy, and flux' and Indigeneity 'as static, unchanging and inflexible', as a form of culture '"with no tolerance for deviance"'.[48] Notwithstanding her own dissembling, Smith remains one of very few scholars to have presented an Indigenous Studies-specific argument against Anzaldúa. Mestizaje, she argues, celebrates a 'tolerance for ambiguity' that paradoxically validates the very racialised distinctions it seeks to dissolve, and she echoes Sonia Saldivar-Hull's critique that, in enacting a passage from '"marginalized other to whole woman"', mestizaje implies not only an essential incompleteness in Indigeneity, but also that 'indigenous identity in and of itself is incapable of addressing the challenges and complexity of contemporary life'.[49]

If the ideological inferences of mestizaje are unconscionable for Smith, as they were for Jack Forbes, who invested in a de facto border studies agenda in work in the late 1950s and early 1960s and who infamously read Anzaldúa's mestiza as indicative of a desire for Indigenous erasure, so too are the juridico-political connotations of border theory's border crossings for Audra Simpson.[50] She writes:

> The study of borders within North America is dominated by and imagined almost exclusively within the Chicano studies literature. In that literature the act of crossing borders is an occasion for transgression . . . *Unlike Chicanos, who move through juridical identities and designations as they cross the border, for Iroquois peoples the border acts as a site not of transgression but for the activation and articulation of their rights as members of reserve nations. . . .*[51]

Despite his claims for sovereign-nationalist interpretations of border crossing, then, Miner's border-crossers are still transgressors, caught in limbo, hovering in the in-between wherein their rhetorical liberation in either utopian space or as inveterate transgressives risks emptying the border encounter of its political import. They illustrate, per Simpson, the erasures of discursively abstract borders, their 'strategy of resistance by evasion' contrasting starkly with Simpson's strategy of resistance by confrontation; she, in turn, refuses the opposition of colonial agents and 'fugitive objects' at the border site itself.[52]

The hegemonic recuperability of such a state 'by those with an interest in denying the validity of a coherent discourse of resistance', to quote Gerry Smyth, is palpable.[53] In implicitly validating the colonial logic of race and racial mixing, it risks the subsumption of the 'mixedblood' into the hegemonic order of the settler-colonial regime. For Simpson, inversely, the physical fact of confrontation at the border, the refusal of the ways it seeks to codify the Indigenous border-crosser, and the risk implicit in that refusal of *de*mobilisation, remains a more potent means of reasserting Haudenosaunee ways of being and knowing. Thus, for Mishuana Goeman, confronting the border rather than evading it renders the site 'a place of deep power struggle and enunciation'.[54] It is most powerfully so because Simpson does not engage the terms of the settler state but refuses designation by race. Furthermore, she declares, 'When I stand at the border guard's counter and present myself in terms that are *not* cadastral, I am pulling up . . . histories into this critical moment of translation, and possibility.'[55] Among these histories is the knowledge of pre-colonial Haudenosaunee conceptions of space, land and 'territory'. Again, the encounter between border studies and Indigenous studies occurs not at the symbolic site of abstract borders, but within the parameters of specific, historic, territorial organisation that long predate European map-making on the continent.

Indigenous Space(s) and Nation State(s)

In the final third of this discussion I want to come back to several iterations of Indigenous space in relation to nation state and other borders that effect some kind of resolution. Firstly, they do so by acknowledging the border without reifying it, recognising that it has material political, cultural and psychological impacts on the status and community well-being of Indigenous peoples in North America. Secondly, that recognition refuses the totalising containment that the hardest of borders enact – the diametric opposite of border theory's borderlands – while maintaining a distinctness in which multiple identities do not simply fold into one another in the ways those opponents of hybridity theories decry. The irrefutable common ground, then, between the cultural theory and the political theory and ethnography cited in this chapter, remains: colonial boundaries have been artificially imposed on Indigenous peoples who continue, by virtue of their movement across those borders, to confront and reveal the lie of those borders' naturalness, resisting submission to the binate logics of the settler state. Their key difference, all other factors stripped away, is arguably one of emphasis: metaphor versus reality; individual versus the collective – accountability to community.

Padraig Kirwan's *Sovereign Stories* addresses the presence and function of boundaries in Native American literary studies. Analysing the purpose of boundary construction in a number of contemporary texts, Kirwan argues that 'Scholars working in the area of Native American Literary Studies have much to gain from an examination of the relationship between "boundary making" and the "discernible discourse" through which such acts of territorialisation are "made visible."'[56] He does so, however, without recourse to border theory per se and always with central attention on the 're-evaluation of sovereignty, separatism, and self-determination'.[57] That focus, in turn, serves to examine 'the ways in which borders "separat[e] an inside from an outside" – thereby protecting the welfare of communities and writers – while *also* "linking" exterior and interior territories' that, while not outright rejecting them, seems to move away from the major gestures of border and borderlands thinking.[58]

Similarly but differently, in an example of the ways in which movement across the border – in literary texts at least – connotes mobility in more than one sense, Gillian Roberts writes in a compelling reading of works by Jeannette Armstrong, Thomas King and Drew Hayden Taylor that,

> For many Indigenous peoples, particularly those whose territories straddle the international boundary, the Canada–US border is both arbitrary and invalid, given these peoples' 'original occupancy of nation-state lands and alternative notions of nation'. But at times in these narratives, particularly when encountering white Americans who pose some kind of physical threat, Indigenous characters strategically perform and insist upon Canadian identity, inserting the border as a buffer between themselves and American aggressors.[59]

Shifting the discussion from identity to citizenship, Roberts' argument also turns from the apparently transgressive to the decisively strategic. Somewhere between those two categories of being, the border site itself resists its role in the in-between as either utopian space or inveterate transgressive zone – both of which risk emptying the border encounter of its political import. That sense of strategic performance of plural citizenships echoes in what Stuart Christie calls the pluralisation of contemporary Indigenous sovereignty, arguing that while 'the contemporary uses to which indigenous sovereigns and Anglo-Europeans, respectively, put nation and nationality are fundamentally different . . . both kinds of sovereignty may be put to effective use in the indigenous interest'.[60] Pushing gently away from the discursive towards the 'autonomy of actual indigenous peoples, places, and the material worlds they inhabit', or pointing towards the 'difference in emphasis between the power of words and the power of worlds', Christie himself seeks some kind of rapprochement between 'constructivist' and 'materialist' or sovereigntist and hybridist approaches of Indigenous literary production.[61]

Just a year after Christie's book appeared in 2009, Christopher Taylor labelled the object of a similar argument 'overlapping sovereignties', seeking said rapprochement in Mary Louise Pratt's contact zones. In both iterations – and to some degree in Roberts' formulation, too – we evince a sense of play and performativity, a strategic articulation of, rather than fugitive subversion in the gaps between, sovereignties. While this notion proposes a viability of movement between sovereign spaces and political categories, it somewhat resists the notional fluidity of identity inherent in hybridity discourse.

Although it offers a somewhat different geometric metaphor and a shift to geopolitical rather than cultural or identity-focused frames of reference, Simpson's own use of the phrase 'nested sovereignty' conjures an equally similar sense of complex polity, of autonomy even under the imposition of external jurisdiction.[62] Somewhat harder edged than Christie's pluralisms, which he describes as a 'shared horizon' that implicates settlers and Indigenous nations in a parallel (if not combined) project, Simpson insists on understanding nested sovereignty thus: 'Like Indigenous bodies, Indigenous sovereignties and Indigenous political orders prevail *within and apart* from settler governance.'[63] In this iteration, the border does not dissolve in the crossing: the supposed borderlands are not margins but centres of sovereign exercise that span two colonial entities. While border theory efficiently exposes the fallacy of binate structures, of either/or, in/out, it also, as Russ Castronovo asserts, potentially reinforces such dichotomies: at the level of the individual, the in/out confrontation of many Haudenosaunee as performed by Simpson, then, enacts an honest attack on the logics that prove ready to interpellate Native travellers as either citizens *or* fugitives into national narratives of containment.[64] At the level of the community, that confrontation communicates the integrity of a prior sovereignty, within and across settler state claims.

This latter suggestion resounds in the final of these types of iteration of sovereignty-at-the-border that I wish to recall here. Kevin Bruyneel's 'third space' of sovereignty presents perhaps the most direct challenge to the discursive manoeuvres of border theory, even as it draws on parallel pretexts in post-colonial theory. Using language redolent of border theory, Adam Barker writes in a review of *Third Space* that Bruyneel 'reveals the ways that Indigenous resistance confounds colonial thought by transgressing borders and boundaries. Instead of static and contained polities, to be regarded with "colonial ambivalence", Indigenous nations in resistance instead assert themselves as dynamic, surprising, flexible, and fundamentally challenging to political thought in America.'[65] This is irrefutably so. But more importantly, in his invocation of third space theory, Bruyneel describes 'a location inassimilable to the liberal democratic settler-state, and as such it problematizes the boundaries of colonial rule but does not seek to capture or erase these boundaries'.⁶⁶ Bruyneel's third space, in other words, offers a location for the articulation of political sovereignty that is resolutely unconcerned with the cultural melange of Owens' frontier or the fugitive evasion of Vizenor's cadastral boundaries. Citing Bruyneel's third space, though – 'neither simply inside nor outside the American political system' – Joshua Miner concludes that 'borderlands, then, are a contiguous "out there." They are political and legal and economic limbo.'⁶⁷ That word 'limbo' perhaps blunts his argument, even as it reflects the reality of that tension between de facto and de jure crossing, rendering Indigenous space entirely contingent on American political (and geographical) will, sublimated to the margins of the nation state. Missing the significance of Bruyneel's 'simply' ironically nullifies the dynamic nature of Indigenous sovereignties as they move across, between and within spaces. Indeed, far from being in limbo and rather than being sites solely for disruption, distortion, erasure or subversion, boundaries function as active sites of Indigenous agency, or 'active locations for the expression of forms of sovereignty and political identity that do not conform to the seemingly unambiguous binary choices set out by the liberal democratic settler-state': not fugitive or liminal sites, again, so much as strategic centres.⁶⁸

The various positions covered in this chapter have arguably less distance between them than posing them as opposite sides of a debate might otherwise imply. Since the early 2010s, for instance, those apparently fluid notions of identity inherent to the trickster discourse celebrated by Vizenor and others have increasingly been drawn back into the Indigenous centres (and even nation-centred locations) of Anishinaabeg Studies. As Niigaanwewidam James Sinclair explains, 'Although critics like to cite Vizenor's point that his concept of "native transmotion is survivance, a reciprocal use of nature, not a monotheistic, territorial sovereignty," this does not mean that he envisions land claims, borders, and tribal citizenship as irrelevant.'⁶⁹ Rather, Sinclair continues, he posits alternatives based in tribal values to those that 'colonial agents in the West have created ... using principles of individualism, capitalism, and colonialism'.⁷⁰ That might perhaps constitute a kind of refusal. And there is another refusal in the words of Sinclair's compatriot,

Leanne Betasamosake Simpson who gives Vizenor a metaphorical nudge when she agrees with him that Nishnaabeg sovereignty was *sui generis*. 'Nishnaabeg sovereignty was *sui generis*', she avers; but 'it was also territorial ... there *was* a territory that was defined by Nishnaabeg language, philosophy, way of life, and political culture' – a political authority alternative to the European conception of territory it refuses.[71] Just as 'The explicit and literal practice of boundary-crossing represents the political position of those indigenous people who do not accept the notion that the presence of settler-states and nations deprives them of their rights of citizenship in their own nations', so too its figurative parallel – that which Coffey and Tsosie designate as cultural as opposed to political sovereignty – affirms what Matt Herman designates a 'transcendent territoriality'.[72]

The contexts of Anishinaabeg and Haudenosaunee citizenship and sovereignty are, self-evidently, markedly different, highlighting the continuous need for specificity in the development of Indigenous-centred theories of belonging in and between the settler states of Canada and the USA and the challenge in transporting site- and culture-specific ideas. For these assorted scholars and activists, though, the border figures not as an abstract site of erasure in the imaginative enactment of cultural identity but as a locus of contest in the sovereign claims to both Indigeneity and mobility. Thus, the act of crossing becomes central, in Bruyneel's words, to the attempt to 'reclaim or re-mark' the boundaries through and against which sovereignty is articulated.[73] These examples demonstrate, however, the degree to which neither hard nor soft borders preclude either the fluidity of self-identity or the spatio-temporal arrangement of relations and networks commonly designated as territory. LeAnne Simpson, indeed, already knows what that terrain looks like. It is a profoundly ethical space and one worth pointing to for the way in which it unsettles all of the preceding discussion for, arguably, proceeding from the wrong perception of bounded space: for '"boundaries," in an Indigenous sense, are about relationships'. She writes,

> As someone moves away from the centre of their territory – the place they have the strongest and most familiar bonds and relationships – their knowledge and relationship to the land weakens. This is a boundary, a zone of decreasing Nishnaabeg presence as you move out from the centre of the territory. This

is a place where one needs to practise good relations with neighbouring nations. Presence is required to maintain those good relationships. Communication is required to jointly care-take this region, which is much wider than a line.[74]

This relational reframing of borders and bordered space effectively disrupts the hierarchical nature of margins and centres inherent in binary conceptions of inside/outside, illustrating Taylor's overlapping sovereignties in spatial terms. It resists, too, the ways in which border sites become points of conflict, stressing that boundaries are not so much locations that organise territories as spaces that contribute to the structuring of relationships. But it does not refuse the idea of the border or the idea of territory or the idea of collective relation to land per se. It is a useful nuance to the assumptions that borders, somehow, are an intrinsically colonial imposition, asking us not to erase them but to reconceptualise both their form and function, contra Anzaldúa's definition of a border as 'set up to . . . distinguish *us* from *them* . . . a dividing line, a narrow strip along a steep edge'.[75] In her refusal, Audra Simpson highlights the 'perception of Mohawk mobility as already a crime, a contravention of the fixity of place, borders, and settled states'.[76] The impasse definitely presents an occasion for the condemning of settler state boundaries for their containment of Indigenous bodies; but they also represent opportunities. If, as Amilhat Szary argues, 'what is made visible at places where international boundaries are performed can be considered a sovereign exercise of power', Audra Simpson's refusal and LeAnne Simpson's concentricity both – if differently – perform an exercise of alternative political authority. To return to the original question about the sparsity of border theory, we might suggest that the key difference between the positions this chapter has articulated is that one emphasises subversion and resistance while the other emphasises the exercise of sovereignty at the site at which that sovereignty is denied. That gap, itself, is small – a matter of framing rather than intent. Ultimately, Audra Simpson's encounter with the border site – an encounter quite explicitly between Indigenous agency and an agent of the state – furnishes the proof to Russ Castronovo's insistence that 'negotiations along the border [can] have the unintended counterpurpose of solidifying and extending racial and national boundaries';[77] but in articulating a sovereignty that is not, by her own insistence, cadastral, Simpson also refuses the state's logic.

In the context of Haudenosaunee resistance in particular, most clearly embodied by Clinton Rickard's 'fight for the line' through the formation of the Indian Defense League of America, embodied action at the physical border bears essential decolonial witness not to the host of false binaries undercut in conventional border theory but to the competing political sovereignties of the Indigenous/settler-colonial boundary.[78] Audra Simpson readily concedes the asymmetries at work at the boundaries of the settler nation state whereby the 'colonial fiction' simultaneously constructs the inherent right of Indigenous people to pass as itself a colonial fiction. Then, those acts of border crossing also illuminate the impasse at the heart of sovereignty, or, in Audra Simpson's words again, the double-bind whereby 'autonomy is exercisable only because recognition is conferred upon those peoples to exercise this autonomy'.[79] In saying this, she echoes her Kahnawake mentor Gerald Taiaiake Alfred's 'suspicion of sovereignty as a location dependent on colonial law'. As Simpson clarifies, 'that explicit right to pass' – the very terms of the Jay Treaty through which legions of commentators have discarded the international boundary as 'irrelevant' to Native peoples – 'implicitly leaves the legal regimes of Canada and the United States with the power to define who those Indian nations are and how that right to pass shall be rendered and respected. As well, and very critically, the regimes of the United States and Canada were bequeathed the power to choose whom they would recognize as members of these communities.'[80]

In the face of such an impasse, a return to the evasive gambles of trickster discourse has immense appeal. But the kind of dichotomy presented here between a soft and hard border is itself another false choice. Just as commentators have worked hard to refuse the false distinction between cosmopolitanism and nationalism in Native literary studies, Indigenous sovereignty itself is not a closed category in which recognition of borders produces a discourse that simply replicates Eurowestern notions of the same. Indeed, on the one hand, the articulation of Indigenous sovereignty itself exposes, in Bruyneel's terms, the 'impossibility of [settler] sovereignty as a totalizing claim to supreme, legitimate authority'.[81] On the other, as Simpson implies, her claim to the specific right to pass is itself cultural rather than explicitly territorial, relational rather than absolute, and worth repeating: 'When I stand at the border guard's counter and present myself in terms that are *not* cadastral', she writes, 'I am pulling up these histories' – of culturally continuous mobility for trade, ceremony and kinship – 'into this critical moment of translation, and possibility'.[82]

Notes

1. Audra Simpson, *Mohawk Interruptus: Political Life Across the Borders of Settler States* (Durham, NC: Duke University Press, 2014), 117.
2. Ibid., 119.
3. Ibid., 183.
4. Quoted in Mishuana Goeman, 'Disrupting a Settler-Colonial Grammar of Place: The Visual Memoir of Hulleah Tsinhnahjinnie', in *Theorizing Native Studies*, ed. A. Simpson and A. Smith (Durham, NC: Duke University Press, 2014), 254.
5. See Beth LaDow, 'Sanctuary: Native Border Crossings and the North American West', *American Review of Canadian Studies* 31 (2001): 25–42; and Karl Hele, *Lines Drawn Upon the Water: The First nations Experience in the Great Lakes' Borderlands* (Waterloo, ON: Wilfrid Laurier University Press, 2008), ix.
6. See Wallace Coffey and Rebecca A. Tsosie, 'Rethinking the Tribal Sovereignty Doctrine: Cultural Sovereignty and the Collective Future of Indian Nations', *Stanford Law & Policy Review* 12 (2001): 191–222.
7. John Gamber, 'Native American Studies', in *A Concise Companion to American Studies*, ed. John Carlos Rowe (Oxford: Blackwell, 2010), 172.
8. Kevin Bruyneel, *The Third Space of Sovereignty: The Postcolonial Politics of U.S.-Indigenous Relations* (Minneapolis: University of Minnesota Press, 2007), 119.
9. Joshua Miner, 'Navigating the "Erotic Conversion": Transgression and Sovereignty in Native Literatures of the Northern Plains', in *Beyond the Border: Tensions across the Forty-Ninth Parallel in the Great Plains and Prairies*, ed. Kyle Conway and Timothy Pasch (Montreal: McGill-Queens University Press, 2013), 171. In addition to for example Beth LaDow's work on the sanctuary quality of the Medicine Line, it is also well worth bearing in mind Benjamin Hoy's observations that, in the nineteenth century in particular, some Indigenous nations actively supported the border survey and even sought to make the border more 'meaningful' in pursuit of protection of their own lands. Benjamin Hoy, *A Line of Blood and Dirt: Creating the Canada-United States Border across Indigenous Lands* (Oxford: Oxford University Press, 2021).

10. Paula Gunn Allen, *Off the Reservation: Reflections on Boundary-Busting, Border-Crossing Loose Cannons* (Boston, MA: Beacon Press, 1999).
11. Paul DePasquale, Renate Eigenbrod and Emma LaRoque, *Across Cultures/Across Borders: Canadian Aboriginal and Native American Literatures* (Peterborough, ON: Broadview Press, 2010), 11. Such complaints are commonplace and have only very partially been addressed by, for example, Robert Warrior's reframing of the transnational turn for Indigenous Studies: Robert Warrior, 'Native American Scholarship and the Transnational Turn', *Cultural Studies Review* 15.2 (2009): 119–30.
12. Geary Hobson, 'Borders Be Damned!', *English Language Notes* 58.1 (2020): 40.
13. Ibid., 61.
14. David Stirrup, 'Reading Around the Dotted Line: From the Contact Zones to the Heartlands of First Nations Literatures', in *The Native American Renaissance: Literary Imagination and Achievement*, ed. A Robert Lee and Alan Velie (Norman: University of Oklahoma Press, 2013), 307–29.
15. See, for example, Gillian Roberts, 'Sameness and Difference: Border Crossings in *The Stone Diaries* and *Larry's Party*', *Canadian Literature* 191 (2006): 86–102.
16. Philip J. Deloria, *Indians in Unexpected Places* (Lawrence: University of Kansas Press, 2004), 27.
17. Zalfa Feghali, 'Border Studies and Indigenous Peoples: Reconsidering our Approach', in *Beyond the Border: Tensions across the Forty-Ninth Parallel in the Great Plains and Prairies*, ed. Kyle Conway and Timothy Pasch (Montreal: McGill-Queens University Press, 2013), 164.
18. Ibid.
19. José David Saldívar, *Border Matters: Remapping American Cultural Studies* (Berkeley: University of California Press, 1997), 13.
20. Kimberly M. Blaeser, 'Native Literature: Seeking A Critical Centre', in *Looking At The Words of Our People: First Nations Analysis of Literature*, ed. Jeannette Armstrong (Penticton, BC: Theytus, 1993), 56.
21. Quoted in Robin Riley Fast, *The Heart as a Drum: Continuance and Resistance in American Indian Poetry* (Ann Arbor: University of Michigan Press, 2000), 9; Kimberly M. Blaeser, *Gerald Vizenor: Writing in the Oral Tradition* (Norman: University of Oklahoma Press, 1996); Kimberly M. Blaeser, 'The Language of Borders, the Borders of Language in Gerald Vizenor's Poetry', in *The Poetry and Poetics of Gerald Vizenor*, ed. Deborah Madsen (Albuquerque: University of New Mexico Press, 2012), 1.

22. Blaeser, 'The Language of Borders', 1.
23. Ibid.
24. Fast, *The Heart as a Drum*, 9, 5.
25. Louis Owens, *Mixedblood Messages: Literature, Film, Family, Place* (Norman: University of Oklahoma Press, 2001), 26.
26. Matthew Herman, *Politics and Aesthetics in Contemporary Native American Literature: Across Every Border* (New York: Routledge, 2010), 57.
27. Ibid., 1.
28. Laura M. Furlan, 'Remapping Indian Country in LouiseErdrich's *The Antelope Wife*', *Studies in American Indian Literatures* 19.4 (2007): 55.
29. Miner, 'Navigating the "Erotic Conversion"', 173.
30. James Cox, *Red Land to the South: American Indian Writers and Indigenous Mexico* (Minneapolis: University of Minnesota Press, 2012), 19.
31. Ibid.
32. Ibid., 165.
33. See, though, Reder and Morra's *Troubling Tricksters* for important critiques of the deterritorialisation of trickster in much literary use of the figure. Deanna Reder and Linda M. Morra, ed. *Troubling Tricksters: Revisioning Critical Conversations* (Waterloo, ON: Wilfred Laurier University Press, 2010).
34. See for instance Jace Weaver, Robert Warrior and Craig Womack's *American Indian Literary Nationalism* (Albuquerque: University of New Mexico Press, 2006).
35. See, for example, Robert Warrior, 'Native American Scholarship and the Transnational Turn', *Cultural Studies Review* 15.2 (2009): 119–30.
36. Craig S Womack, 'A Single Decade: Book-Length Native Literary Criticism between 1986 and 1997', in *Reasoning Together: The Native Critics Collective*, ed. Craig Womack, Daniel Heath Justice and Christopher B. Teuton (Norman: University of Oklahoma Press, 2008), 68.
37. Sean Kicummah Teuton, *Red Land, Red Power: Grounding Knowledge in the American Indian Novel* (Durham, NC: Duke University Press, 2008), 14.
38. Ibid.
39. Kelli Lyon Johnson, 'Writing Deeper Maps: Mapmaking, Local Indigenous Knowledges, and Literary Nationalism in Native Women's Writing', *Studies in American Indian Literatures* 19.4 (2007): 107.
40. Christopher Taylor, 'North America as Contact Zone: Native American Literary Nationalism and the Cross-Cultural Dilemma', *Studies in American Indian Literatures* 22.3 (2010): 31.

41. Ibid., 26.
42. Ibid., 28.
43. Teuton, *Red Land, Red Power*, 14.
44. Ibid., 84.
45. Ibid., 85.
46. Taylor, 'North America as Contact Zone', 39.
47. See Arnold E. Davidson, Priscilla L. Walton and Jennifer Andrews, *Border Crossings: Thomas King's Cultural Inversions* (Toronto: University of Toronto Press, 2003).
48. Andrea Smith, 'Against the Law: Indigenous Feminism and the Nation-State', *Affinities* 5.1 (2011): 56–69. https://ojs.library.queensu.ca/index.php/affinities/article/view/6123, 62; quoting Anzaldúa.
49. Ibid., 62, 63.
50. There is, perhaps, no small irony in the fact that both Smith and Forbes themselves claimed Indigenous identities that have since been demonstrated to be false.
51. Simpson, *Mohawk Interruptus*, 116. Italics added.
52. Miner, 'Navigating the "Erotic Conversion"', 175.
53. Gerry Smyth, 'The Politics of Hybridity: Some Problems with Crossing the Border', in *Comparing Postcolonial Literatures: Dislocations*, ed. Ashok Bery and Patricia Murray (New York: St. Martin's, 2000), 43.
54. Mishuana Goeman, 'Disrupting a Settler-Colonial Grammar of Place', 254.
55. Simpson, *Mohawk Interruptus*, 143.
56. Padraig Kirwan, *Sovereign Stories: Aesthetics, Autonomy, and Contemporary Native American Writing* (Oxford and New York: Peter Lang, 2013), 27. Quoting Juliet Fall, *Drawing the Line: Nature, Hybridity, and Politics in Transboundary Spaces* (London: Ashgate, 2005).
57. Ibid., 28.
58. Ibid. Quoting Henk Van Houtum, Olivier Kramsch and Wolfgang Zierhofer, *B/ordering Space* (London: Ashgate, 2005).
59. Gillian Roberts, *Discrepant Parallels: Cultural Implications of the Canada–US Border* (Montreal: McGill-Queen's University Press, 2015), 125.
60. Stuart Christie, *Plural Sovereignties and Contemporary Indigenous Literature* (New York: Palgrave Macmillan, 2009), 2.
61. Ibid., 4.
62. Simpson, *Mohawk Interruptus*, 12.
63. Christie, *Plural Sovereignties*, 11; Simpson, *Mohawk Interruptus*, 11.
64. See Russ Castronovo, 'Compromised Narratives along the Border: The Mason-Dixon Line, Resistance, and Hegemony', in *Border Theory: The Limits of Cultural Politics*, ed. Scott Michaelson and David E.

Johnson (Minneapolis: University of Minnesota Press, 1997), 195–220.
65. Adam J Barker, Review of *The Third Space of Sovereignty*, in *Settler Colonial Studies* 5.1 (2015): 103.
66. Bruyneel, *The Third Space of Sovereignty*, 21.
67. Miner, 'Navigating the "Erotic Conversion"', 174.
68. Bruyneel, *Third Space of Sovereignty*, 21.
69. Niigaanwewidam (Niigonwedom) James Sinclair, *Nindoodemag Bagijiganan: A History of Anishinaabeg Narrative* (PhD thesis, University of British Columbia, 2013), 257.
70. Ibid., 257–8.
71. Leanne Betasamosake Simpson, *Dancing on Our Turtle's Back: Stories of Nishnaabeg Re-Creation* (Winnipeg, MB: ARP Books, 2011), 89.
72. Bruyneel, *Third Space of Sovereignty*, 119; Herman, *Politics and Aesthetics*.
73. Bruyneel, *Third Space of Sovereignty*, xix.
74. Simpson, *Dancing on Our Turtle's Back*, 89.
75. Gloria Anzaldúa, *Borderlands/La Frontera: The New Mestiza* (San Francisco, CA: Aunt Lute Books, 1987), 3.
76. Simpson, *Mohawk Interruptus*, 144.
77. Castronovo, 'Compromised Narratives', 196.
78. Goeman, 'Disrupting a Settler-Colonial Grammar', 254.
79. Audra Simpson, 'Under the Sign of Sovereignty: Certainty, Ambivalence, and Law in Native North America and Indigenous Australia', *Wicazo Sa Review* 25.2 (2010): 108.
80. Quoted in Goeman, 'Disrupting a Settler-Colonial Grammar', 254.
81. Bruyneel, *Third Space of Sovereignty*, 221.
82. Simpson, *Mohawk Interruptus*, 143.

Bibliography

Anzaldúa, Gloria. *Borderlands/La Frontera: The New Mestiza*. San Francisco, CA: Aunt Lute Books, 1987.
Barker, Adam J. Review of *The Third Space of Sovereignty*. *Settler Colonial Studies* 5:1 (2015): 103–8.
Blaeser, Kimberly M. *Gerald Vizenor: Writing in the Oral Tradition*. Norman: University of Oklahoma Press, 1996.
Blaeser, Kimberly M. 'Like "Reeds Through the Ribs of a Basket": Native Women Weaving Stories'. *American Indian Quarterly* 21:4 (1997): 555–65.
Blaeser, Kimberly M. 'Native Literature: Seeking A Critical Centre' in *Looking At The Words of Our People: First Nations Analysis of*

Literature. Ed. Jeannette Armstrong. Penticton: Theytus Press, 1993. 51–62.
Blaeser, Kimberly M. 'The Language of Borders, the Borders of Language in Gerald Vizenor's Poetry' in *The Poetry and Poetics of Gerald Vizenor*. Ed. Deborah Madsen. Albuquerque: University of New Mexico Press, 2012. 1–22.
Bruyneel, Kevin. *The Third Space of Sovereignty: The Postcolonial Politics of U.S.-Indigenous Relations*. Minneapolis: University of Minnesota Press, 2007.
Carlson, David J. 'Trickster Hermeneutics and the Postindian Reader: Gerald Vizenor's Constitutional Praxis'. *Studies in American Indian Literatures* 23:4 (2011): 13–47.
Castronovo, Russ. 'Compromised Narratives along the Border: The Mason-Dixon Line, Resistance, and Hegemony' in *Border Theory: The Limits of Cultural Politics*. Ed. Scott Michaelson and David E. Johnson. Minneapolis: University of Minnesota Press, 1997. 195–220.
Christie, Stuart. *Plural Sovereignties and Contemporary Indigenous Literature*. New York: Palgrave Macmillan, 2009.
Coffey, Wallace and Rebecca A. Tsosie. 'Rethinking the Tribal Sovereignty Doctrine: Cultural Sovereignty and the Collective Future of Indian Nations'. *Stanford Law & Policy Review* 12 (2001): 191–222.
Coulthard, Glen. *Red Skin, White Masks: Rejecting the Colonial Politics of Recognition*. Minneapolis: University of Minnesota Press, 2014.
Cox, James. *Red Land to the South: American Indian Writers and Indigenous Mexico*. Minneapolis: University of Minnesota Press, 2012.
Davidson, Arnold E., Priscilla L. Walton and Jennifer Andrews. *Border Crossings: Thomas King's Cultural Inversions*. Toronto: University of Toronto Press, 2003.
Deloria, Philip J. *Indians in Unexpected Places*. Lawrence: University of Kansas Press, 2004.
DePasquale, Paul, Renate Eigenbrod and Emma LaRoque. *Across Cultures/Across Borders: Canadian Aboriginal and Native American Literatures*. Peterborough, ON: Broadview Press, 2010.
Fall, Juliet, *Drawing the Line: Nature, Hybridity, and Politics in Transboundary Spaces*. London: Ashgate, 2005.
Fast, Robin Riley. *The Heart as a Drum: Continuance and Resistance in American Indian Poetry*. Ann Arbor: University of Michigan Press, 2000.
Feghali, Zalfa. 'Border Studies and Indigenous Peoples: Reconsidering our Approach' in *Beyond the Border: Tensions across the Forty-Ninth Parallel in the Great Plains and Prairies*. Ed. Kyle Conway and Timothy Pasch. Montreal: McGill-Queens University Press, 2013. 153–69.

Forbes, Jack D. *Frontiers in American History and the Role of the Frontier Historian*. Reno, NV: Desert Research Institute, 1966.

Furlan, Laura M. 'Remapping Indian Country in LouiseErdrich's *The Antelope Wife*'. *Studies in American Indian Literatures* 19:4 (2007): 54–76.

Gamber, John. 'Native American Studies' in *A Concise Companion to American Studies*. Ed. John Carlos Rowe, Oxford: Blackwell, 2010. 172.

Goeman, Mishuana. 'Disrupting a Settler-Colonial Grammar of Place: The Visual Memoir of Hulleah Tsinhnahjinnie' in *Theorizing Native Studies*. Ed. Audra Simpson and Andrea Smith. Durham, NC: Duke University Press, 2014. 235–65.

Gunn Allen, Paula. *Off the Reservation: Reflections on Boundary-Busting, Border-Crossing Loose Cannons*. Boston, MA: Beacon Press, 1999.

Hele, Karl. *Lines Drawn Upon the Water: The First Nations Experience in the Great Lakes' Borderlands*. Waterloo, ON: Wilfrid Laurier University Press, 2008.

Herman, Matthew. *Politics and Aesthetics in Contemporary Native American Literature: Across Every Border*. New York: Routledge, 2010.

Hobson, Geary. 'Borders Be Damned!' *English Language Notes* 58:1 (2020): 40–62.

Hoy, Benjamin. *A Line of Blood and Dirt: Creating the Canada-United States Border across Indigenous Lands*. Oxford: Oxford University Press, 2021.

Johnson, Kelli Lyon. 'Writing Deeper Maps: Mapmaking, Local Indigenous Knowledges, and Literary Nationalism in Native Women's Writing'. *Studies in American Indian Literatures* 19:4 (2007): 103–20.

King, Thomas. *One Good Story, That One*. New York: HarperPerennial, 1993.

Kirwan, Padraig. *Sovereign Stories: Aesthetics, Autonomy, and Contemporary Native American Writing*. Oxford and New York: Peter Lang, 2013.

LaDow, Beth. 'Sanctuary: Native Border Crossings and the North American West'. *American Review of Canadian Studies* 31 (2001): 25–42.

Miner, Joshua. 'Navigating the "Erotic Conversion": Transgression and Sovereignty in Native Literatures of the Northern Plains' in *Beyond the Border: Tensions across the Forty-Ninth Parallel in the Great Plains and Prairies*. Ed. Kyle Conway and Timothy Pasch. Montreal: McGill-Queens University Press, 2013. 170–98.

Owens, Louis. *Mixedblood Messages: Literature, Film, Family, Place*. Norman: University of Oklahoma Press, 2001.

Owens, Louis. *Other Destinies: Understanding the American Indian Novel*. Norman: University of Oklahoma Press, 1993.

Reder, Deanna and Linda M. Morra, ed. *Troubling Tricksters: Revisioning*

Critical Conversations. Waterloo, ON: Wilfrid Laurier University Press, 2010.

Roberts, Gillian. *Discrepant Parallels: Cultural Implications of the Canada–US Border*. Montreal: McGill-Queen's University Press, 2015.

Roberts, Gillian. 'Sameness and Difference: Border Crossings in *The Stone Diaries* and *Larry's Party*'. *Canadian Literature* 191 (2006): 86–102.

Saldívar, José David. *Border Matters: Remapping American Cultural Studies*. Berkeley: University of California Press, 1997.

Simpson, Audra. *Mohawk Interruptus: Political Life Across the Borders of Settler States*. Durham, NC: Duke University Press, 2014.

Simpson, Audra. 'Under the Sign of Sovereignty: Certainty, Ambivalence, and Law in Native North America and Indigenous Australia'. *Wicazo Sa Review* 25:2 (2010): 107–24.

Simpson, Leanne Betasamosake. *Dancing on Our Turtle's Back: Stories of Nishnaabeg Re-Creation*. Winnipeg, MB: ARP Books, 2011.

Sinclair, Niigaanwewidam (Niigonwedom) James. *Nindoodemag Bagijiganan: A History of Anishinaabeg Narrative*. PhD thesis, University of British Columbia, 2013.

Smith, Andrea. 'Against the Law: Indigenous Feminism and the Nation-State'. *Affinities* 5:1 (2011) 56–69. https://ojs.library.queensu.ca/index.php/ affinities/article/view/6123

Smyth, Gerry. 'The Politics of Hybridity: Some Problems with Crossing the Border' in *Comparing Postcolonial Literatures: Dislocations*. Ed Ashok Bery and Patricia Murray. New York: St. Martin's Press, 2000. 43–55.

Stirrup, David. 'Reading Around the Dotted Line: From the Contact Zones to the Heartlands of First Nations Literatures' in *The Native American Renaissance: Literary Imagination and Achievement*. Ed. A. Robert Lee and Alan Velie. Norman: University of Oklahoma Press, 2013. 307–29.

Taylor, Christopher. 'North America as Contact Zone: Native American Literary Nationalism and the Cross-Cultural Dilemma'. *Studies in American Indian Literatures* 22:3 (2010): 26–44.

Teuton, Sean Kicummah. *Red Land, Red Power: Grounding Knowledge in the American Indian Novel*. Durham, NC: Duke University Press, 2008.

Van Houtum, Henk, Olivier Kramsch and Wolfgang Zierhofer. *B/ordering Space*. London: Ashgate, 2005.

Warrior, Robert. 'Native American Scholarship and the Transnational Turn'. *Cultural Studies Review* 15:2 (2009): 119–30.

Weaver, Jace, Robert Warrior and Craig Womack. *American Indian Literary Nationalism*. Albuquerque: University of New Mexico Press, 2006.

Womack, Craig S. 'A Single Decade: Book-Length Native Literary Criticism between 1986 and 1997' in *Reasoning Together: The Native Critics Collective*. Ed. Craig Womack, Daniel Heath Justice and Christopher B. Teuton. Norman: University of Oklahoma Press, 2008. 1–104.

CHAPTER 6

Grit and Grief: Wayde Compton's *49th Parallel Psalm* as borderblur elegy

Tanis MacDonald

Heather Smyth has noted that British Columbian poet Wayde Compton has been 'archiving and generating what can productively be called a Black Pacific node of the black diaspora' since the publication of Compton's first book, *49th Parallel Psalm*, in 1999.[1] That book establishes Compton's poetics as a signature blend of history and genre-b(l)ending, working in an experimental, musical, rhetorical and lyrical style that Compton calls 'turntablism'. In his website notes on the development of the collaborative sound poetry project for 'The Reinventing Wheel', Compton observes that 'the written word is the sixth element of hip-hop', so it should come as no surprise that bpNichol's avant-garde term 'borderblur' applies well to Compton's poetics.[2] Nichol used the term to connote his practice of genre-mixing in a single project, blending lyric and experimental modes, sound and visual poetry, short fiction and cartoons, photographic satires and critical essays. Compton's oeuvre also offers a serious commitment to blending fiction with poetry, literary criticism with history, archives with fiction, and sound recording with lyric and experimental poetries, and he has spoken about forging 'turntablism' partly in reaction to his frustration with the limitations of a single style of discourse and with the whiteness of the Canadian literary canon in particular.[3]

Wayde Compton has, over the course of fifteen years and five books, become a go-to author about Canadian border discourse. (Gillian Roberts' chapter in this volume discusses Compton's prose fiction via his 2014 short story collection, *The Outer Harbour*.)

Compton's *49th Parallel Psalm*, while working the rich ground between literary genres, takes its central metaphor and its primary narrative from two border-crossing stories: a retelling of the Biblical story of enslaved people's exodus from Egypt, and a historical account of 600 Black American settlers who emigrated from San Francisco to Victoria, BC, in 1858 (see the section 'Chronology of the Canada–US Border' at the end of the book). The border, in Compton's blend of the two stories, is more than a physical or psychological barrier, and also more than a metaphor for transformation; the subjectivity of both groups – terrorised by utopia as they are – is predicated in part by a liminality that can almost, but not quite, serve them in transformation. In contradistinction with narratives of Black Canadian history that laud the border crossing as the road to freedom and citizenship, Compton's work with the border is more about questioning where the border is and what it may grant those who can find it in order to cross it. Liminality is often construed as a playful perpetual dwelling in possibility, but in *49th Parallel Psalm*, Compton explores possibility via the wit of imbedded protest, the acerbic bite of 'forty mays and /forty mights', the phrase full of Biblical echo and refusal, critiquing Enlightenment promises of selfhood.

Distrustful of borders not just for their placement but also for their promotion of a transcendental philosophy and an even more transformative citizenship, Compton brings asperity to historical and contemporary sorrow in his work, in which melancholy can be viewed as a tool of oppression. In a poem voiced by the editor of the first Black newspaper in California, *The Mirror of the Times*, Compton notes that Black citizens are not only required to 'read be/tween' what the paper can print and what it wishes to print, but they must also dwell there, 'be be/tween//the lines':

> my tongue. my byline. the aching cant. this labyrinth. the typeset. the moveable. nothing but moveable. all we got is moveable. the way the wind blows. my hands at the end of the day. all I got. not even my letters.[4]

The state of being between the lines is absolutely a visual pun on border crossing, but it is also a warning of how lines, letters and literature have repeatedly failed Black people in general, and the migrating Black citizens of 1858 San Francisco as a historical case in point. In *49th Parallel Psalm*, this also functions as foreshadowing. The trip north to British North America on the boat named the *Commodore* will not be a cure for that 'aching cant', which is also an 'aching can't': what can't be held, pronounced, written, proven, sustained, and what is always already lost for people who are disallowed citizenship.

Not much has been written to date about the elegiac drive of Compton's work or the ways that grieving after a citizenship denied functions in border-crossing poetics as an occasion for grief that manifests as grit as often as sorrow. Bringing elegy studies to border discourse may seem an unlikely pairing, but since the seventeenth century the elegy has been a genre that thrives on the paradoxical dimensions of its own conventions and its extreme malleability, and it is especially suited to meet the challenges of speaking to and through shifts in social constructs of power. Contemporary elegy theory stretches towards exploration of profound ambivalence that attends shifts in subjectivity predicated by loss, and sometimes, by 'finding' a much-desired object or condition. Compton's work can be situated in a contemporary elegiac mode played out on a national and global scale, especially in context with other necropolitical elegies by writers who interrogate Canada's historical positions in global politics, with special emphasis on the politics of migration: Dionne Brand's *Ossuaries* (2010); Erín Moure's *The Unmemntioable* (2012); and René Sarojini Saklikar's *children of air india* (2012), among others. Each of these works engages in border crossings and often fractious negotiations of citizenship between Canada and other nations.

These necropolitical elegies, with their shifting emphases upon speaking and silence, might also be called elegies of shibboleth history: poems in which the pronunciation of memory carves out an enunciation of a grieving public, and the enunciation of that public reappropriates a history that has been effaced by ideological forces. Compton's invocation of the exodus from Egypt as a parallel for the 1858 voyage of the *Commodore* north to Vancouver and Salt Spring islands embeds Biblical narrative in the text, and though Compton does not allude to the shibboleth story from chapter 12 of the Book of Judges, that story is absolutely a border-crossing story, and a deadly one. Following a rout by the forces of Gilead against the Ephraimites, anyone who wished to cross the River Jordan was asked to pronounce the word 'shibboleth', an agricultural term meaning (depending on the context), an ear of corn or a flood. The regional dialect of the Ephraimites did not include the phoneme 'sh' so the Gileadites had the impunity to kill anyone who pronounced the word as 'sibboleth'. Mispronunciation meant death for 'forty and two thousand' people; Judges 12:6 shows us border patrol, Old Testament style.

The shibboleth, as an utterance that displays one's heritage – especially a heritage that includes migration or diasporic shifts in citizenship – constitutes the very work of mourning that the elegy shapes. Such a pronunciation of memory is never enough, and the way the elegy can never be enough to satisfy the demands of grief, but rather operates as an artefact of mourning: a declaration of affect that cannot be answered. If we consider *49th Parallel Psalm* as a book-length necropolitical elegy, we must note that Compton is writing poems about the enunciation of a nineteenth-century Black Canadian public, and the enunciation of that public re-turns a history that has been haunted by a narrative that designates the border as a mechanism of transformation: from American to Canadian, from slave to citizen, from impoverished refugee to prosperous landowner. 'The aching cant' of *49th Parallel Psalm*, the moveable type – so often a sign for modernity – that moves nothing politically, the hands full of wind at the end of the day: all are metaphors for a language that will not bring freedom but instead invites further oppression by the state. Elegiac politics are set in high relief by this enunciation of the empty language, reinvoking history that has been effaced, erased, blurred, assimilated or ignored by the nation state, or in this case, by the legacies of two nation states, each arguing for its own version of sovereignty. If we undertake a reading of *49th Parallel Psalm* as an elegiac text that regards the history of border crossing with a jaded eye, then we can return to Achille Mbembe's injunction to read necropolitically and to recall that biopower is fundamentally about who lives and who dies, and the political and social conditions that dictate these dire divisions: the 'instrumentalization of human existence and the material destruction of human bodies and populations'.[5]

Dashing All the Way: 'a people of the dash'

In the 'Xanada' section of *49th Parallel Psalm*, Compton examines the ambivalently figured journey of 600 Black Americans to

British Columbia in 1858 and offers a critical history of the mechanisms of this immigration and aftermath, calling these Black settlers 'a people of the dash'.⁶ The phrase puns on the contemporary expression 'hyphenated Canadians', or Canadians whose cultural heritage is foregrounded as part of their citizenship: African–Canadian, Caribbean–Canadian, Indo–Canadian. While the practice of hyphenating citizenship may be well-meaning, it is also part of a marginalising discourse that tears down hybridity and dualism as much as it supports them.⁷ The simultaneous inclusiveness and estrangement of the dash is reflected in the visual elements called up by Compton's term: a map's depiction of a border as a perforated line of dashes that demarcate separate nations, and the pun on the 'dash across the line' into Canada made by many Black people prior to (and after) 1865 in search of civil and legal emancipation. This phenomenon of double-dashing – that is, dashing across the dash – suggests a history that is both past and perpetual; in Canadian parlance, and to extend the pun, going, we could call it 'the beginning of the long dash', alluding to the many years of negotiating borders and subjectivities that the border crossing accrues, and also the audio beep used by the Canadian Broadcasting Corporation as a time-zone indicator: wherever you are in Canada at the beginning of the long dash, you know that what time it is. In *49th Parallel Psalm*, the mutabilities of time and space act as melancholic slides that power the work. The wit – and sometimes the anger – of this wordplay honours the constitutive state of 'the inbetween', what Compton calls the Canadian 'Halfrican Nation' whose generational heritage crosses borders that are both national and generic, and whose affective legacy of historical border crossing performs a profound ambivalence that troubles Canada's trope of the 'grateful migrant' in the cultural narrative of nation.⁸

Additionally, the dash has violent implications, especially as the narratives of Biblical exodus and journey north intersect. Psalm 137, a constant intertext in *49th Parallel Psalm*, begins with 'By the rivers of Babylon, there we sat down, yea, we wept, when we remembered Zion' (KJV) but that same Psalm ends with the grief-stricken people voicing the violent revenge fantasy of killing their oppressors' infants:

> O daughter of Babylon, who art to be destroyed; happy shall he be, that rewardeth thee as thou hast served us.

Happy shall he be, that taketh and dasheth thy little ones
   against the stones.⁹

Using 'dash' as a verb indicating a killing blow underscores the possibility that grief is not always enervating, but can be righteously and violently motivating. The movement between grief and violence is short and swift in Psalm 137, and Compton, in the poem 'Company', echoes this movement even as he revises what is dashed against the rocks in his description of Black settlers' lives in a mining town run by the Hudson's Bay Company. The speaker notes the rock is simultaneously hard foundation and breakable substance, commodity and community:

> founded on the dashing stones. whichever
> pieces make it through the sluice gates shining
> enough
> to gather and wash and sell and melt and mould¹⁰

The disciple Peter's promises that Christ is the rock upon which he will build his church is ironically invoked in this poem, as is the longed-for return of the Black settlers to the oppressors' land. This deep ambivalence is part of the elegy's historical engagement with paradox, what W. David Shaw has productively analysed as 'an open war of opposites: an insurrection of the self, a civil strife' that powers the modern elegy.¹¹ The 'people of the dash', those who dashed across the line, save the remnants of what is dashed against the rocks and separated by the sluice gate in order to pay for a journey 'home'. Despite the threat of violence in the nation from which they were exiled, they work to earn enough for the passage back to America, and the phrase on which Compton ends the poem, 'all the way back where we came from' intentionally echoes the xenophobic taunt from which no immigrant or refugee escapes: that if someone doesn't like it in Canada, they should go back where they came from.

Compton notes that his archival milieu and his poetics are 'Afroperipheral' rather than 'Afrocentric', considering the role of positionality in geographies of identity along with the dissemination of a wry and productively cynical citizenship wrought from a perpetuity of displacement, resonating through Compton's work as 'the appendix of the epic and the echo of the odyssey'.¹² Thinking about this Afroperipheralism and its relationship to border crossings, negotiated citizenship and cultural subjectivities offers another take on borderblur that involves Compton's use of literary subgenres, like speculative fiction in his 2014 book *The Outer Harbour* and elegy in *49th Parallel Psalm*. Gillian Roberts, in her chapter in this volume, rightly asserts that Compton fashions a Derridean hauntology from the spectrality of border crossing and negotiated citizenship: being in two places at once while 'present' in neither. The borders between literary subgenres may not be as rhetorically and geographically emphatic as the borders between nations, but Compton's delight in blurring boundaries – sometimes suggesting that borders are a trick of the mind that dissolve you if you look straight at them – extends to his work with affect, troubling the national narrative of transformation via border crossing.

Heaven Lies

49th Parallel Psalm problematises the ways that traditional slave narratives are often taught or read as narratives of unalloyed gratitude, a reading position that conveniently ignores the politics of arrival with its displacements, xenophobia and alliances to the home place. Compton is certainly not the only Black Canadian poet to do so; George Elliott Clarke's Governor General's award-winning 2001 collection *Execution Poems* undoes Canada as the safe place of (perpetual) arrival for Black Empire Loyalists and their descendants. Halifax poet El Jones, in her 2013 poem '1812: Be Loyal, Be Strong, Get Free', asserts that the work of 'getting free' may have begun for Black Empire Loyalists in 1812, but that the labour of maintaining freedom remains constant and requires fierce and ongoing political activism. Compton's 'Afroperipheralism' locates itself in a space occupied (and theorised) by inheritants with complex identity positions: those who are of mixed racial heritage; those who have mixed citizenship and/or nationalities; those who must parse a convoluted nature-and-nurture narrative of adoption; and those who negotiate the balancing act of growing up peripheral to a culture.

Blurred geographical and national borders suggest that Compton's borderblur grows from material circumstance as well as challenge to genre. For instance, in 'Where Heaven Lies', one of the later poems in *49th Parallel Psalm*, the speaker, one of the Black citizens of Victoria, reads a newspaper headline in 1865 about the American emancipation of the slaves. Far from being overjoyed, he is wry about the sudden turnabout in American politics and his own 'flight to freedom' across the border:

> on the Brit side of the border, freer
> as of 1833, 49thdegree, norther, nearer
> to God and the top
> of the world. Lord
> been here seven years.[13]

The bitterness of surveying his past – that he 'left everything' only to end up with a 'handful of "magic beens"' (a pun scored by incredulous disappointment) is magnified by the irony of the speaker's emancipatory journey: renunciation of one nation state only to see that country achieve a longed-for tolerance which the speaker can no longer access. 'Where Heaven Lies' is an apt title, one presaged by the earlier poem 'O' that retells the resurrection of the Egyptian god Osiris, and reacquaints the reader with the idea that 'the west . . . is where heaven lies'.[14] The plays on 'lies' as falsehoods is important. The story of the Black settlers' journey up the coast from San Francisco to the then tiny settlement of Victoria, emigrating from pre-Civil War America to a British colony that would not become Canada for another nine years, is a story with a legacy that is deeply ambivalent in Compton's text, most markedly so for the ways it deviates from standard historical accounts of that journey.

Fil Fraser, in his text *How the Blacks Created Canada*, tells the story of the Black settlers who came north on the *Commodore* as a cornerstone of nation-building. In his opening chapter 'Saving British Columbia for Canada', Fraser emphasises that the Hudson's Bay Company factor James Douglas' Scots–Guyanese heritage was openly acknowledged when his contemporaries referred to him as a 'Scotch West Indian'.[15] He goes on to note Douglas' marriage to a Métis woman, his probity as the governor of the Colony, his steadfastness as a Hudson's Bay 'company man', and his proven success as the chief factor of Fort Victoria: all, for Fraser, evidence of Douglas' fair dealing as a 'no-nonsense autocrat' who welcomed the Black San Franciscans for the business opportunities they brought to the settlement as well as his kinship with them as people of colour.[16] In a similar vein, Natasha L. Henry's book *Emancipation*

Day unequivocally names Douglas as 'an abolitionist and a man who detested intolerance' and lauds Douglas as a man who worked to uphold the abolition of the slavery of First Nations people in Fort Victoria, as well as someone who championed financial and landowning opportunities for the Black settlers from America (see the section 'Chronology of the Canada–US Border' at the end of the book).[17] Henry suggests that racism in Victoria grew despite Douglas' best efforts, but Compton's view – obstreperously borderblurred – is less generous and less forgiving. For Compton, while Douglas undoubtedly made the journey north possible for the Black settlers, an immigration that would have nearly doubled the population of Victoria at the time, Douglas had feet of clay, ultimately betraying the Black colonists when he 'coolly withdrew support for them upon their arrival'.[18] To add social insult to political injury, for Compton, Douglas never publicly acknowledged his own mixed racial heritage even as he facilitated the immigration. Compton goes on to wonder what it might mean for Douglas' legacy as a liberator of Black Americans to be subject to a historical critique, addressing Douglas as:

> our own quadroon Moses,
> should I place a violet on your grave
> or hawk a little spit
> for your betraying ways?[19]

Compton goes on to characterise Douglas as not quite a race traitor, but as someone whose historical legacy was ambiguous at best, calling Douglas a 'company // man. on the winning team. / backing the right horse. the best telegony'.[20] Civil War-era America and the British colony of Canada West ultimately became equally culpable in the systemic racism that Black Americans faced on both sides of the border. Perhaps the best evidence of Compton's interrogation of this political vicissitude can be seen in 'Where Heaven Lies'; the speaker does not refuse to return to America after the Civil War is over and the emancipation of slaves is declared, but comically, and sadly, declares what the headline *ought* to read, rendered in large bold font in the poem: 'Hell freezes over; white people discover empathy'.[21] Should we be hearing a decades-long echo of Dennis Lee's admonition about Canadian history in *Civil Elegies* in 'Where Heaven Lies'?

> never at
> home in native space and not yet
> citizens of a human body of kind. And it is Canada
> that specializes in this deprivation.²²

While Lee is writing at the end of the 1960s and will go on to allude to a history of 'losers and quislings', the notion of Canada as 'a specialist in deprivation' of citizenship is useful to read against the border-crossing narrative as one of transformative freedom. Sharon A. Roger Hepburn notes in her 2007 text, *Crossing the Border: A Free Black Community in Canada*, that this narrative was strong and motivating enough that not even rumours (promoted by anti-abolitionists) that Canada's climate would be unaccommodating dissuaded Black settlers from coming to Canada. But given the reception, we must wonder how psychologically accurate Hepburn's quotations from S. G. Howe's 1864 *Report to the Freedman's Inquiry Commission* were for some of the Black settlers in British North America. Was the social and political climate 'a freezing sort of Hell'?²³ Was the hyperbole that spoke of weather 'so cold that men going mowing had to break the ice with their scythes' reflected in the xenophobic coldness of white communities? Were the rumours of 'wild geese so numerous and ferocious that they would scratch a man's eyes out' played out in lynchings and other violence? Certainly disappointment in Canada as a place of freedom that is not *quite* freedom is layered into the pun Compton makes on iron pyrite (or fool's gold) with the 'Pyrrhic victory' of the emigration north:

> landed at
> Victoria, haven
>
> where we was jumped in
> to a gang called Brit in,
> then Canada. in
>
> tensionally, we shipped out²⁴

The tension and intention of shipping out becomes even more pointed when the border dissolves beneath the feet of the border-crossers, as it does in the prose-poem 'Emancipation Day' from Compton's 2004 book *Performance Bond*:

The Canada, the Canaan land, would not be their dreams of difference. Maybe once, for some, but no more: all had been sold. The perimeter had been liquidated ... The border had waded into the river back there with them, going the other way, fleeing. It had passed them. They had missed it.[25]

Psalms and Parallels

The mourning arc of Compton's poetry parallels the 'loss and bitter laughter' that Jahan Ramazani notes as integral to the African–American elegy led by Langston Hughes' 'Weary Blues'.[26] However, Compton's historical borderblur questions the ambivalence of the contemporary elegy and its vexed position in postmodern life, interrogating the impulse 'to amen in / to Psalm 137', wondering how to grieve by the waters of Babylon after an immigration that was a 'Pyrrhic victory'.[27] The poem 'Crucial Blues' dismantles the fabled journey north that shapes the narratives of many former enslaved and free peoples seeking a different freedom in Canada as Canaan.[28] The Black San Franciscans could not remain where their civil rights were whittled away by Californian laws designed to make the 'beautiful west' of freedom and landowning into another American South where Black citizenship was undermined via the same exclusionary and legislated violence. But as Compton notes in 'Habeas Corpus', the Black settlers who came north to Canada could not find an easy peace with yet another emigration.[29] The choice between nations seems to be no choice at all as the Black San Franciscans 'measure out our prospects ... Panama / Sonora. / Vancouver's Island'.[30] Far from offering an unalloyed joy of following the North Star to freedom, Compton writes a much more nuanced portrait of bordercrossers whose hope has been seriously eroded by the failure of California to uphold its promises to freed people:

> The Pioneer Committee will un
> earth us in some new some
> where: settlement. sediment. coast. I notice
> no one uses the word *home*[31]

The divisions between nation states and states of affect are blurred but not necessarily comforting for all their ambiguities. Like the 'dash', the parallel is an exemplary metaphor for Compton's borderblur, and in this book no parallel is blurrier than the eponymous 49th. In the poem 'Jump Rope Rhyme of the 49er Daughters', Compton strategically conflates the term 'forty-niners' as a doubled allusion to the people who trekked north along the West Coast to northern BC and the Yukon for the Gold Rush in 1849, and those who negotiated crossing the 49th parallel for purposes of citizenship. The latitudinal border that seems so logically situated as the *'entre nous'* zone between Canada and the United States, the world's famed 'longest undefended border', was a hot-point negotiation, established as the British North American–United States border, extending west from Lake Superior to the Pacific as late as the Treaty of Washington in 1846. If President James Polk had his way, the border between the States and what became Canada would have been at the 54th parallel and forty minutes, as indicated by Polk's campaign slogan '54–40 or fight!', making Canada a much more northerly nation.[32]

But there is another kind of forty-nine in this text: the 49th Psalm. While this Psalm, like the previously discussed and more widely-read Psalm 137, is about exile and the Promised Land, it is less mournful and less violent, warning against misinterpreting worldly wealth as security: 'their inward thought is that their houses shall continue forever and their dwelling places to all generations; they call their lands after their own names'.[33] Far from promoting the Manifest Destiny of settlement and western expansion, the words of this Psalm warn that the dream of owning land or passing it down through generations is a false supposition. There can be no doubt that Compton's text is Biblical in its tone and its critique, but the myth extends to Canada as 'Xanada', a riff on Coleridge's Xanadu with an extra caution. By substituting the X, we lose the 'can': the possibility of Canada. It may help to remember that Xanadu is a lost kingdom, ripped away from Coleridge by the interruption of the visitor from Porlock, never to be captured again: a dream not so much deferred as never written. Or is the 'X' a reference to Malcolm X's political placeholder name, a rejection of the violent colonial past? Is what is 'crossed out' in Canada something fundamental to our narrative of nation?

In 'The Blue Road', a prose fiction piece in *49th Parallel Psalm*, Compton features a character called Lacuna who is travelling to 'the Northern Kingdom', and in 'O' he suggests that British Columbia is 'the beautiful west' of Egyptian belief: the place of the afterlife.[34]

As Isis says initially and several other characters echo throughout the text, British Columbia as landing place and ambivalently figured 'safe haven', is all blue – even figured as a rainbow in different shades of blue.[35] Given Compton's blend of musical and poetic soundscapes in turntablism, the pun on the 'blues', be they as weary as Hughes' or otherwise, is absolutely intentional:

> I
> dance these Pyrrhic feet, these broken be
> ats, this miner quay, homing in on a place called
> From.[36]

Since the 1990s, elegy studies have grown suspicious of consolation, and while Jahan Ramazani notes the modern elegy's 'fierce resistance to solace' is a result of the waning of faith in the twentieth century, a more political view is worth considering.[37] There is no question that the forces of right-wing ideology in the corporate bodies of the patriarchy, the military-industrial complex, and the capitalist system are very invested in the Freudian cycle of pathologised melancholia and psychologically balanced consolation as it will smooth out the embarrassing snarls in a narrative of nation. The calcification of a grief narrative (or in Compton's case, a grit narrative) into an official history of grateful immigration suggests that grief itself is a body manipulated by national rhetoric. In an interview with Donna Bailey Nurse in 2011, Compton notes that his work explores the 'sad hyperbole' of nineteenth-century Black settlers to Canada, whose 'isolation [was] made worse by the absence of institutions to deal with it'.[38] In this same interview, though Nurse refers to Compton as a 'traditional poet-critic', Compton presents himself as something different: not as a historian purely interested in the critical presence of border crossing, freedom-searching, ambivalently received immigrants, but as a writer interested in 'editorializing' a history and experimenting with how grief and the peripheral may be spoken.[39] Ramazani's study of the blues and the elegy notes that both traditions are antiphonal, and Compton's line breaks suggest one side of that exchange, an elegiac voice in search of a reply.[40]

Poet Erín Moure has noted (in her groundbreaking 1988 book *Furious*) that the quest for a language that challenges the limitations of memory with its articulation of grief and anger is language that exists as 'a stutter at the edge of', that seemingly truncated phrase with its final preposition acting as a hook into the unspeakable.[41] Compton's 'Where Heaven Lies' ends with this kind of despair and hope as stutter, both articulated and unspoken, as a borderblurred elegiac sign for people who were welcomed and unwelcomed to Canada:

> we ain't even one step forward here. our moment
> nothing but a stutt
>
> er
> he
> re.[42]

That stutter, a speech act testifying to being, returns us to Compton's turntablism with its critique on the necessity of repeating the desire for freedom *ad infinitum*. But that stutter is also aligned with Erín Moure's open-handed language-play in their dual determination to enunciate presence in whatever language is necessary, to fashion borderblur as an act of defiance and to record the speaking – throughout history – of the unspeakable. He/re.

Notes

1. Heather Smyth, 'The Black Atlantic Meets the Black Pacific: Multimodality in Kamau Brathwaite and Wayde Compton', *Callaloo* 37.3 (2014): 390.
2. Wayde Compton, 'The Contact Zone Crew'. Accessed 16 January 2016: waydecompton.com
3. Wayde Compton, 'The Diaspora's Upper Left Hand: *Octopus* and *Callaloo*', *Callaloo* 30.3 (Summer 2007): 794.
4. Wayde Compton, *49th Parallel Psalm* (Vancouver, BC: Arsenal Pulp Press, 1999), 35.
5. Achille Mbembe, 'Necropolitics', trans. Libby Meintjes, *Public Culture* 15.1 (2003): 11–40, 14.
6. Compton, *49th*, 56.
7. Cf. Fred Wah, *Faking It: Poetics and Hybridity* (Edmonton, AB: NeWest Press, 2000).
8. Wayde Compton, *Performance Bond* (Vancouver, BC: Arsenal Pulp Press, 2004) 15.
9. The Holy Bible: King James Version, Psalm 137:8–9.
10. Compton, *49th*, 56.

11. David W. Shaw, *Elegy and Paradox: Testing the Conventions* (Baltimore, MD: Johns Hopkins University Press, 1994), 5.
12. Wayde Compton, *After Canaan: Essays on Race, Writing and Region* (Vancouver, BC: Arsenal Pulp Press, 2010), 16–17.
13. Compton, *49th*, 73.
14. Ibid., 17.
15. Fil Fraser, *How the Blacks Created Canada* (Edmonton, AB: Dragon Hill, 2009), 27.
16. Ibid., 27, 26–8.
17. Natasha L. Henry, *Emancipation Day: Celebrating Freedom in Canada* (Toronto: Dundurn, 2010), 187.
18. Compton, *49th*, 18.
19. Ibid.
20. Ibid., 18–19.
21. Ibid., 73.
22. Dennis Lee, *Civil Elegies and Other Poems* (Toronto: House of Anansi, 1994), 27.
23. S. G. Howe, *Report to the Freedman's Inquiry Commission 1864: The Refugees from Slavery in Canada West*, (Reprint. New York: Arno Press, 1969), 11; quoted in Sharon A. Roger Hepburn, *Crossing the Border: A Free Black Community in Canada*, (Urbana and Chicago: University of Illinois Press, 2007), 12.
24. Compton, *49th*, 74.
25. Compton, *Performance*, 41.
26. Jahan Ramazani, *Poetry of Mourning: The Modern Elegy from Hardy to Heaney* (Chicago: University of Chicago, 1994), 175.
27. Compton, *49th*, 55, 75.
28. Ibid., 40–1.
29. Ibid., 37.
30. Ibid., 41.
31. Ibid.
32. Fraser, *How*, 22–3.
33. The Holy Bible: King James Version, *Psalms* 49:11.
34. Compton, *49th*, 85.
35. Ibid., 17.
36. Ibid., 75.
37. Ramazani, *Poetry*, 4.
38. Donna Bailey Nurse, interview with Wayde Compton, *What's a Black Critic to Do? II: Interviews, Profiles and Reviews of Black Writers* (London: Insomniac Press, 2011), 182.
39. Ibid., 181.
40. Ramazani, *Poetry*, 139.
41. Erín Moure, *Furious* (Toronto: House of Anansi Press, 1988), 91.
42. Compton, *49th*, 73.

Bibliography

Clarke, George Elliott. *Execution Poems*. Wolfville, NS: Gaspereau Press, 2001.

Compton, Wayde. *49th Parallel Psalm*. Vancouver, BC: Arsenal Pulp Press, 1999.

Compton, Wayde. *After Caanan: Essays on Race, Writing and Region*. Vancouver, BC: Arsenal Pulp Press, 2010.

Compton, Wayde. *Performance Bond*. Vancouver, BC: Arsenal Pulp Press, 2004.

Compton, Wayde. 'The Contact Zone Crew'. waydecompton.com. Accessed 16 January 2016.

Compton, Wayde. 'The Diaspora's Upper Left Hand: *Octopus* and *Callaloo*'. *Callaloo* 30.3 (Summer 2007): 793–4, 953.

Fraser, Fil. *How the Blacks Created Canada*. Edmonton, AB: Dragon Hill, 2009.

Henry, Natasha L. *Emancipation Day: Celebrating Freedom in Canada*. Toronto: Dundurn, 2010.

Hepburn, Sharon A. Roger. *Crossing the Border: A Free Black Community in Canada*. Urbana and Chicago: University of Illinois Press, 2007.

Howe, S. G. *Report to the Freedman's Inquiry Commission 1864: The Refugees from Slavery in Canada West*. New York: Arno Press, 1969 (reprint).

Jones, El. '1812 Poem: Get Free'. YouTube. www.youtube.com. Accessed 8 April 2013.

Lee, Dennis. *Civil Elegies and Other Poems*. Toronto: House of Anansi, 1994 [1972].

Mbembe, Achille. 'Necropolitics'. Trans. Libby Meintjes. *Public Culture* 15.1 (2003): 11–40.

Moure, Erín. *Furious*. Toronto: House of Anansi Press, 1988.

Nurse, Donna Bailey. Interview with Wayde Compton. *What's a Black Critic to Do? II: Interviews, Profiles and Reviews of Black Writers*. London: Insomniac Press, 2011. 179–86.

Ramazani, Jahan. *Poetry of Mourning: The Modern Elegy from Hardy to Heaney*. Chicago: University of Chicago, 1994.

Shaw, W. David. *Elegy and Paradox: Testing the Conventions*. Baltimore, MD: Johns Hopkins University Press, 1994.

Smyth, Heather. 'The Black Atlantic Meets the Black Pacific: Multimodality in Kamau Brathwaite and Wayde Compton'. *Callaloo* 37.3 (2014): 389–403.

Wah, Fred. *Faking It: Poetics and Hybridity*. Edmonton, AB: NeWest Press, 2000.

CHAPTER 7

Border Hypotheses: Speculations on Territory and Sovereignty in Wayde Compton's *The Outer Harbour*

Gillian Roberts

Black British Columbian poet Wayde Compton's work has consistently returned to questions of border crossings, particularly those involving Black North Americans across the Canada–US border. Compton's poetry has focused on the Black Californian pioneers who came to British Columbia in the nineteenth century (in *49th Parallel Psalm*, 1999) and the Black Vancouver community located in Hogan's Alley (in *Performance Bond*, 2004), destroyed in 1970 as part of an urban renewal project. Compton's writing has both sought to write these forgotten histories back into visibility and to do so through an inventive poetics (discussed in Tanis MacDonald's treatment of Compton's 'borderblur' in this volume), disrupting official histories through form as well as content. In *The Outer Harbour: Stories* (2014), his first collection of short fiction, Compton continues to invoke Black North American border crossing, but also implicitly reworks the ontology of the Canada–US border as a hauntology through his deployment of a speculative fiction in which spectrality features heavily. Whereas Compton's previous creative texts have tended to focus on history, *The Outer Harbour* projects a future in which a new island – named Pauline Johnson Island – appears in Vancouver's outer harbour and is subject to twenty-first-century methods of colonisation. Further, crowd-control holograms at a G25 protest and mysterious migrants who blink in and out of visibility populate this future Vancouver, the presence of the former enabled and the presence of the latter policed by the state.

The Outer Harbour implicates borders in dispossession, primarily that of Indigenous peoples and migrants, as Compton imagines a struggle between the government, capital and the land itself. Attention to the spectral as it appears in the collection and as it has been theorised emphasises the border as a site of both violence and haunting, at the same time as it produce inheritors: children of the border. As Jacques Derrida writes, 'the specter is the future, it is always to come, it presents itself only as that which could come or come back'.[1] If Compton's previous work has focused on uncovering Black North American – especially Black British Columbian – pasts, his engagement with spectrality in his speculative fiction enables us to read, project and contest not only past injustices situated at or pushed to the nation state's threshold but also the injustices of the future that Compton extrapolates from history and its legacies in the present.

Situating the Canada–US border in a hemispheric context can offer useful comparisons of borders as haunted spaces, at the same time as Canada's own particular history and status cannot be conflated with those of countries even more subject to US political and economic dominance. Focusing on the Western hemisphere in general, but on Mexico's relationship to the United States in particular, Jesse Alemán argues that '"in-ter" Americanism understands that the nations of the western hemisphere already contain *within* ("intra") their borders national others whose formative presence is subsequently buried (interred) but nonetheless felt and often expressed through gothic discourse'.[2] For Alemán, Spanish colonialism is responsible for 'hemispheric horrors': 'difference maintains the borders across the Americas that distinguish one nation from the other, but sameness produces an inter-American gothic hemisphere'.[3] In the context of this Gothic hemisphere, the relationship between the United States and Mexico constitutes 'a familial relation that vexes citizenship as much as it troubles their national literary histories, for their confluences indicate how one country is already embedded within the history of the other, perhaps because the borders across the Americas are so porous'.[4]

Further north, the Canada–US relationship might also be described as 'a familial relation that vexes citizenship', although as a result of French and British, rather than Spanish, imperial projects. The much-vaunted status of the Canada–US border as the longest undefended border in the world, a reputation that waned following 9/11, certainly bears out the intra-American porosity Alemán identifies, yet whereas the US–Mexico border is also the border between 'America and América',[5] the Anglo dominance in both Canada and the United States has brought them together in opposition to the rest of the hemisphere. As Bryce Traister writes, the Mexico–US and Canada–US borders 'presen[t] a different set of problems to be negotiated and articulated as a critical borderlands practice'.[6] If Canadian nationalism has long looked to the Canada–US border as a kind of buffer for Canadian sovereignty, or indeed, a symptom – in its lack of defence – of that sovereignty's fragility, the comparison with Mexico and its dispossession offers a rather stark contrast.

Whereas the Mexico–US border, with its 'haunted past and ongoing present', figures as the scar of Mexico's dispossession, simultaneously standing in for Mexico–US difference (military conquest and an acute imbalance of power) and Mexico–US sameness (because of the US territory that used to be Mexico and 'Mexicans remaining within the boundaries of the new United States territories' as 'a conquered people'), the Canada–US border's own negotiation of sameness and difference diverges from *la frontera*.[7] If, in Alemán's terms, 'Mexico is a strangely familiar place that troubles the US's trans-American imaginary', we might say that Canada is a strangely familiar place that, on the whole, does *not* trouble the United States.[8] As Lorraine Code writes, Canada–US differences range from 'mere variations in cultural *timbre*, inflection, intonation' to 'deep divisions in the histories that have made each of these two nations what they are, both locally and globally', while observers often 'impatient[ly] insis[t] that the similarities are so overwhelming as to erase the differences'; indeed, as Jody Berland claims, 'every Canadian has heard a visiting American saying that Canada is "just like home", congratulating his or her listeners for their apparent sameness on the basis of a half-day of profound ethnographic experience involving cars, billboards, hotel menus, and conference programs'.[9] The 'just like home' assessment constitutes 'a friendly, patronizing gift', one that asserts sameness as it simultaneously raises an imbalance of cultural power between Canada and the United States.[10] But the Canada–US border's relationship to sameness becomes most apparent in a deep historical sense in its own status as a scar of dispossession: not of Canada by the United States but by Canada *and* the United States of Indigenous peoples. If the border constitutes a site of asserting Canadian sovereignty in relation to the United States, it also a site where Indigenous nations whose territory lies along the division imposed by the two settler-colonial nation states 'deploy their own sovereignty in ways that refuse the absolute sovereignty' of both Canada and the United States.[11]

In Compton's *The Outer Harbour*, the action of the collection's linked stories takes place just north of the Canada–US border, in Vancouver and elsewhere in British Columbia's Lower Mainland, on Coast Salish territories.[12] But the border is invoked through historical context, characters' personal histories, and the ways in which the nation state seeks to police the bodies of Others. If Code's Canada–US 'inflections' of difference appear in elements of Compton's stories, so do the deep histories of colonial dispossession that straddle the border just as Indigenous territories do. In *The Outer Harbour*, the Canada–US border first appears as a kind of window, or perhaps more specifically a screen, through which the lives of Canadian characters appear against the backdrop of US-focused political events. The first story in the collection, entitled '1,360ft^3 (38.5m^3)', orients the reader temporally and spatially. In temporal terms, we are told that the characters 'savour the last days of the first summer of the next one thousand years'; there are references to a bird flying into a window, to 'plummeting bodies in motion' before TV coverage of what can only be 9/11 – 'Oh my God, you've got to look at this' – confirms that the collection begins in September 2001.[13] While the details of 9/11 itself go unmentioned in the collection, the orientation of the reader in relation to this particular date subtly invokes the context of how Western nation states identify, construct and respond to Others from within and without their borders in the twenty-first century in the fallout of these attacks.

This initial story introduces the character of Riel, who will resurface later in the collection. Riel 'has no Native ancestry', despite the fact that 'he was named after the Métis revolutionary', Louis Riel: 'why, exactly, Riel does not know' (12). His Cree roommate, Frances, 'makes her scepticism of the great man's misinvocation known' by hailing Riel with the song 'Louie, Louie' instead (12). Riel knows of his father only that 'he is black, he is from San Francisco, and he is long gone' (12). Riel is the collection's first, but by no means last, cross-border baby, making literal Alemán's notion of the relationship between nations as 'a familial relation'. The children of the border in *The Outer Harbour* also include the Indigenous activist Fletcher

Sylvester, in 'The Lost Island', who 'had a Snohomish mother from the US, and a local father from a band unknown to Fletcher or anyone else' (34), and Donald and Albert, the conjoined twins whose Black jazz musician father is originally from Sacramento, attracted to their white mother, she speculates later, because of her Canadianness: 'I think he had an idea to go away with me to Canada right from the get–go ... like I was there to take him away from the States' (63), suggesting an echo of historical moments when Canada has been looked to for cross-border sanctuary, such as the Underground Railroad prior to the abolition of slavery in the United States and the Vietnam War, during which many draft resisters headed north. The centrality of cross-border existence in the collection is also underscored through the first story's title, its simultaneous use of imperial and metric measurements, a feature repeated in a later story in the collection, '400ft^3 (11.33 m^3)', providing an example of 'inflection' in Canada–US difference through the Canadian measurement's presence, even if as a parenthetical afterthought. Again, the 9/11 context introduced in the first story furnishes a juxtaposition of Canada and the United States that is borne out – even in this domesticated fashion – in the signalling of national difference through measurement as well as the apparent downgrading of Canada by marginalising the metric measurements through the parentheses.

The invocation of measurements also reflects the collection's concerns with both occupation and the art movement of 'Rentalism'. In 'The Front: A Reverse-Chronological Annotated Bibliography of the Vancouver Art Movement Known as "Rentalism", 2011–1984', the commentary on the manifesto of the Storefront Liberation Front (SFLF) acknowledges that 'the movement was born in the most expensive property market in Canada. However, the SFLF also express their hope that the form will spread to the United States in the wake of the global financial crisis. But there's no analysis of why Rentalism seems unable to budge from its city of origin, half a decade after its birth' (78–9). Thus, where Compton's collection features the movement of people primarily from the United States to Canada, giving birth to cross-border children, 'The Front' demonstrates a lack of movement in the other direction in the case of Rentalism's objectives, possibly implying that Canadian political and aesthetic movements are ignored south of the border, but also suggesting a site-specificity to Rentalism and the economic conditions particular to Vancouver's real estate market.

The Outer Harbour treats the subject of occupation – in both its colonial and domestic forms – in relation to the phenomenon of Pauline Johnson Island. If, as Laurie Ricou writes, the Canada–US border, once it arrives at Vancouver, is 'an unwavering linear and visible border dissolv[ing] into a meandering hypothesis traced in water' (23), Compton's deployment of speculative fiction allows the collection to test the hypothesis of what might result from the emergence of a new piece of land in Vancouver's outer harbour. The outer harbour may not be very far from the Canada–US border, but the naming of Pauline Johnson Island, which is not at the site of the border itself, nevertheless has clear implications for the role the border plays, as well as for Indigenous/non-Indigenous relations. 'The Lost Island' explains that after the island, a volcano, 'first bubbled up out of the water', 'Parliament declared the island a restricted ecological reserve, and named it after the Mohawk poet who had chosen Vancouver as her adopted home' (36). Johnson – Tekahionwake – moved to Vancouver in 1909, where she lived until her death four years later. In 1922, a monument to the poet was erected in Stanley Park. As Joanne Leow observes, Compton's story is 'clearly written with one literary ghost in mind: Tekahionwake's short story' of the same title, collected in *The Legends of Vancouver* (1911).[14] In this story, the lost island is introduced as Indigenous territory that has disappeared: 'It is there somewhere, up some lost channel, but we cannot find it. When we do, we will get back all the courage and bravery we had before the white man came.'[15] Thus, Compton's projection of the island and its naming has both historical and literary precedents, given Tekahionwake's work and the city's memorialising of the poet.

The details of the life, work and politics of Tekahionwake, 'a complex and contradictory figure', resonate in the government's choice of name for the island.[16] As Veronica Strong-Boag and Carole Gerson note, Tekahionwake, daughter of a Mohawk father and an English mother, was both 'often a fervent imperialist' and an advocate for Indigenous peoples.[17] Just as Canadian nationalism during Tekahionwake's lifetime 'sometimes constituted itself as both heir to and critic of British imperialism', so too Tekahionwake's praise for Canada coexisted with a hope for a 'fairer future' in which Canada 'could embrace the difference of the First Nations'.[18] For Tekahionwake, with her 'dual loyalty' to imperial and Indigenous contexts, 'both the Dominion and the Empire, like Britain before them, were great because of, not despite, their mixture of races'.[19] The Mohawk are a nation whose territory straddles the colonially imposed Canada–US border, as well as other colonially imposed borders in the form of provincial and state demarcations; thus, the Mohawk 'confron[t] the competing claims to sovereignty of materially dominant state(s) that sit atop their land and administer their populations'.[20] Although Tekahionwake herself asserted both her own Canadianness and Canada's difference from the United States, and as such 'could not escape the temptation to credit the Dominion with a better record in its treatment of Indians' as she maintained a faith in 'a more inclusive Canada' for the Mohawk today who 'refuse the "gifts" of American and Canadian citizenship', the Canada–US border is 'an international border that cuts through their historical and contemporary territory and is, simply, in their space and in their way'.[21]

In *The Outer Harbour*, some 4,300 km (2,700 mi) from Mohawk territory, the Indigenous activist, Fletcher Sylvester, claims that 'when the island coughs up its vapours . . . it is speaking Mohawk' (36). He and his fellow activists occupy the island for the sake of 'Liberation of the New Pan-Indigenous Territory' (40), understanding that, in British Columbia, a province almost entirely without treaty, 'brand new land' equals 'brand new colonization' (34). Fletcher thus makes the naming of Pauline Johnson Island more meaningful than the government that appropriates both the island and the poet. Tekahionwake's friendship with Chief Sa7plek of the Skwxwú7mesh nation in what is now southern British Columbia – who told Tekahionwake the stories comprising *Legends of Vancouver* – in the early twentieth century, a friendship that 'linked two of Canada's most active Native groups, the Iroquois and the Squamish', formed part of her own 'growing pan-Indian sensibility'; indeed, as Deena Rymhs argues, in *Legends of Vancouver*, Tekahionwake produces a 'mediation of Squamish and Mohawk tribal cultures'.[22] A century later, Fletcher explicitly articulates inter-Indigenous allegiances through the claiming of a pan-Indigenous territory that will encompass both Coast Salish peoples and the Mohawk. Further, his own personal history, coupled with Tekahionwake's Mohawk identity, encompasses Canada–US border crossings as well as multiple Indigenous nations.

Through the inclusion of Fletcher's activism, the collection suggests that the government's naming of the island after Pauline

Johnson is not intended to acknowledge properly the land as Indigenous land, but rather a 'colonial usurpation ... made only more blatant by the choice of Pauline Johnson's English name ... instead of her Mohawk one'.[23] At best, the naming is simply a cosmetic measure (perhaps one facilitated by Tekahionwake's assertions of her ties to Canada and the British Empire), belied by its status first as a 'protected zone' (34) where only government-approved scientists have access. The government's response is consistent with a North American Gothic whose 'colonial project [seeks to] establis[h] order in the wilderness'.[24] As a new island – and an active volcano at that – Pauline Johnson Island harks back to early North American Gothic texts in its representation of 'the threats and dangers of the natural world'.[25] In *The Outer Harbour*, scientists working on Pauline Johnson Island use the discourse of 'colonization' (37) to discuss new forms of plant and animal life on the island, but the government does not acknowledge its own colonisation. It is Fletcher and his fellow activists who, on the island, are in a 'place that makes them illegal by being there – standing, walking, waiting, thinking, peopling it. Being people where they shouldn't be' (43). Fletcher's companions consist of other Indigenous activists and Jean, who is Black and pregnant with Fletcher's child, their collective rendering as illegal revealing the settler-colonial state's simultaneous policing of Indigenous and diasporic people.

Not until later in the collection, in a series of posters, do we discover what results from the occupation: 'The Boom' features a poster arguing for 'justice for Fletcher Sylvester!' and advertising a 'rally to protest the killing of an Indigenous political activist' during the 'pro-sovereignty occupation of Pauline Johnson Island' (103). Other posters advertise a 'demonstration against the re-zoning of Pauline Johnson Island' following the government's 'outrageou[s] rescind[ing] [of] Pauline Johnson Island's status as an ecological reserve, green-lighting its official incorporation into the City of Vancouver' for the purposes of 'private development' (107), a development confirmed by the advertising brochure that follows, which unashamedly mimics the historical colonisation of what is now Canada:

> ARRIVAL is a 10-storey residential tower built on Vancouver's newest waterfront. On Pauline Johnson Island, a '99% safe and dormant volcanic site',* at the gateway of beautiful Burrard

Inlet, ARRIVAL boldly blends the pioneer spirit of Canada's heritage with 21st century bravado.

BE BRAVE. BE THERE. BEGIN. (109)

This advertisement for the private housing development promotes a re-enactment of Euro-colonial arrival, suggesting through the reference to 'the pioneer spirit of Canada's heritage' that these arrivals constitute the beginning of the nation, the island *terra nullius* there for the Euro-Canadian taking – a far cry from the 'UNCEDED NATIVE LAND' (44) banner unfurled by Fletcher and his activist companions. The myth of Canada's European so-called 'founding nations' persists in its erasure of the First Nations. That the government should have chosen to name the island after an Indigenous poet only to allow private development that writes over Indigenous presence in its advertising campaign emphasises the strategic amnesia and discursive violence of the settler-colonial nation state, even as the state's physical violence has been manifest on this very site through the killing of Fletcher Sylvester.

We discover nothing further about the fate of Pauline Johnson Island until the final piece in the collection, 'The Outer Harbour', which reveals that a 'conversion of the residential tower into detention housing' (168) has taken place, the latest phase in the island's status as 'a laboratory for several forms of social and economic experimentation'.[26] Pauline Johnson Island, both despite and because of the government's intentions, constitutes a space of the *unheimlich*, 'which can also be translated as un-home-y, or, more gracefully, as unsettling'.[27] If, 'quite literally, the uncanny is the unsettled, the not-yet-colonized, the unsuccessfully colonized, or the decolonized', as Renée Bergland argues in the context of US American literature, *The Outer Harbour*'s conjuring of Pauline Johnson Island demonstrates that the settler is always already unsettled.[28] After its incarnation as the ecological reserve, the island, turned over to private capital, is then intended to become an elite residential space. The fact that it then fails to do so reveals its 'un-home-y' status, a status that itself effects the transformation of the residential buildings into the 'Pauline Johnson Island Special Detention Facility' (167). Here, the detainees, lodged in the former residential tower, are now 'in a prison, of sorts . . . the lobby ha[ving] been converted into a security centre' (168). The detainees are referred to as ICDP – Individual and Collective Displacement Phenomenon – as well as, simply, 'the migrants' (168). Discovered aboard a vessel called *Ocean Star* (170), these migrants 'blink-out' and back into visibility, resembling Derrida's description of the spectre: 'it is flesh and phenomenality that give to the spirit its spectral apparition, but which disappear right away in the apparition, in the very coming of the *revenant* or the return of the spectre. There is something disappeared, departed in the apparition itself as reapparition of the departed.'[29] Previous attempts to detain the ICDP on the mainland have failed, given that the migrants have proven 'uncontainable at the Burnaby Facility' and the government has feared the possibility of their 'disappearing, one by one, into the general population' (172).

On the one hand, these 'disappearing' migrants echo, in a hemispheric context, the analogy drawn between 'the border-disappeared' at the Mexico–US boundary and the 'kidnapping, torturing and murdering thousands of ... citizens' in South and Central America from the 1970s to the 1990s, with the disappearance of Mexico–US border-crossers compared to other acts of state violence.[30] On the other hand, in *The Outer Harbour* the state wants to keep these migrants in view, the better to surveil them and to *prevent* their invisibility amongst the citizenry. The ICDP migrants resemble spectres through 'their liminal positions between visibility and invisibility, life and death, materiality and immateriality'.[31] This liminality also extends to questions of the migrants' geographical origin and government attempts to identify it. Whereas Pauline Johnson Island was first zoned by the government for the purposes of scientific research, now research teams are once again present, but this time to study the phenomenon of the migrants, whose location of origin 'no one has yet determined', and whose language 'has not been identified' (173) – the implication being that there is no clear location to which the migrants can be deported.

The government's expropriation of Indigenous territory and the sequestering of the migrants suggest Pauline Johnson Island as a kind of reserve, albeit for migrants rather than Indigenous people. However, the status of the mysterious 'migrants' is hinted at through other narratives in the collection to do with migration, performance, and technology. The first story, '1,360ft^3 (38.5m^3)', features Riel's jettisoning of his previous life, walking out of his apartment and his relationship – barefoot – having been jarred by, first, two years previously, the event of 'hundreds of Chinese nationals arriv[ing] on the coast illegally from Fujian Province, packed onto rickety fishing vessels, and then ... Riel watched a media circus develop around their incarceration and deportation' (16); secondly, the event that prompts the memory of the Chinese migrants, a 'mystery migrant' is discovered in a shipping container – presumably measuring 1,360 ft^3 (38.5 m^3), as in the story's title – whose identity and language cannot be determined by officials. It is later revealed that the migrant, named Verŝajna, is a performance artist 'born in Canada ... making all the calls to deport her fully ironic' (23). Riel meets Verŝajna at a panel discussion of her performance, and they begin a relationship, as the final story, 'The Outer Harbour', indicates. If in the United States, following 9/11, 'the new discourse of the homeland' intersected with an increased scrutiny of borders and 'revivifie[d] an isolationist discourse that elides the imperialist dimensions of drawing such borders', it is crucial that *The Outer Harbour* locates its temporality in precise terms, underscoring Canadian anti-immigration sentiment and a border policing that both precede 9/11 and are heightened after this event, as the collection's projection in the future indicates.[32]

The title story includes a piece by Verŝajna that explains a protest performance in relation to a G25 summit held in Vancouver, in which a collective called Counter Clockwise staged a *'pre-enactment* of the G25 riot we all assumed would happen' (185). This event, a 'fore-echo of the real thing we believed would likely come' (185), contrasts with 'the real G25 riot', a 'massive and prolonged' event, 'covering most of downtown Vancouver' (186). The Counter Clockwise pre–enactment is simulated (with papier-mâché bricks thrown at individuals posing as police, for instance), but so, it turns out, are elements of the real riot, which features 'the most surprising and bizarre weapon[:] a new non-lethal crowd-control device called the Multiple Perception Immobilization Device (or the MPID)' (186). MPID creates 'three-dimensional holographic "bodies"' (188) designed to 'caus[e] the instinctive immobilization and/or slowing of subjects, who believe their movements are restricted. By inflating their numbers artificially, the rioters become distracted, slowed, and ultimately vulnerable to other pacification measures' (181). Crucially, as Verŝajna points out, the G25 riot in Vancouver constitutes the first time MPID is deployed in Canada, despite the fact that it was 'developed in the private sector by the Canadian company Waking Dream Entertainment Services', a company that 'crossed over from primarily marketing multimedia "live action role-playing" supplies to providing security solutions for law enforcement and military purposes' (180) after being acquired by another company. Prior to its use on Canadian soil, MPID was 'previewed overseas, though details on those outcomes are currently unavailable' (181).

It seems possible, therefore, that the mystery migrants, the ICDP, are in some way connected to MPID, and in particular, its outsourced testing, away from Canada, as 'these speculative and transgressive alter-realities [are] grounded in local yet also transnational circumstances'.[33] Just as Veršajna has played the role of a mystery migrant herself, only to reveal herself as a Canadian citizen, so too the ICDP migrants may also be Canadian in origin, products of the Canadian company that has done its testing elsewhere (likely the majority world, exploited by this first world country's corporate interests). In this scenario, the spectral ICDP, blinking in and out of visibility, are indeed revenants in Derrida's sense: 'a specter is always a *revenant*. One cannot control its comings and goings because it *begins by coming back*'; the ICDP's mysterious arrival, uninvited and unauthorised, is actually a return. Analogous to 'ghosts [that] are characteristically attached to the events, things, and places that produced them in the first place', the migrants are already Canadian, spat out by their corporate creator but arrived back at the nation state's border only to find themselves in a detention centre, haunting the country that struggles to police them.[34]

If the outsourced testing of MPID suggests an inherently racist capitalism that seeks out economically vulnerable nations in order to conduct experiments for the benefit of first world enterprise, the collection has also made clear the racist legacy of Waking Dream Entertainment Services. In 'The Secret Commonwealth', Donald, one of the formerly conjoined twins, attends a role-play event, where he and his girlfriend, May, seem incongruously positioned as 'a black man and woman among . . . creatures' (122). According to May, the event is supposed to 'fee[l] like it could be a thousand years ago' (121). 'It's always a thousand years ago', Donald replies, cryptically. Yet this statement is essential in relation to the location – outside Vancouver – of the event and the fact that its staging 'is certainly medieval, with various Eurocentric shadings', including a 'Middle English language pavilion' (122). A thousand years ago, for the role-play company, only exists in a Eurocentric incarnation, the staging of the 'the secret commonwealth' clashing with the territory on which it takes place but also working to naturalise European presence. Donald and May should, in fact, be less incongruous than the 'blond, braided Viking' (122), given the latter's anachronistic presence in the twenty-first century. But the role-play framing replicates Euro-colonialism, effacing Indigenous history while insisting upon a simulation of medieval Europe.

Further, a group called the 'Spectres' appear in blackface (124), the role-play therefore not only reifying European presence in the Americas but also perpetuating explicitly racist practices. We later discover that 'holographic antagonists' (162) have been used at the secret commonwealth event, bridging the company's entertainment and security interests and exposing the fact that 'the pastoral innocence of play may always share an uneasy border with the castle-keep of force, security, and an armed peace' (163), one that depends particularly on the policing of Othered people. These spectres (both those in blackface and the 'holographic antagonists') have been manufactured – figuratively and literally – by the company; but the inclusion of spectres in blackface in the secret commonwealth event nevertheless exposes the nation's racist legacies, regardless of the company's intentions or what versions of the history or the future it is trying to sell.

Given the provenance of MPID and ICDP, then, the fate of Pauline Johnson Island continues to be circumscribed by white supremacy. 'The Outer Harbour', the collection's final story, comprises various fragments of different texts: a review; a radio interview transcript; an excerpt from a report on MPID; an excerpt from Verŝajna's piece; and assorted images, including several hand-drawn maps of Vancouver's outer harbour, and different versions of details from a larger image entitled *Expropriatus* by Suhaima Sylvester Martin – presumably the daughter of Fletcher Sylvester and Jean Martin – which resembles a hand-drawn blueprint featuring domestic consumer goods, many copies of which appear photographed on the side of a building (potentially the detention centre itself). These verbal and visual texts are interspersed with a narrative that features three figures: a girl, who is the ghost of a dead ICDP migrant and the creator of the outer harbour maps (200); an 'insurgent', who, though unnamed, is clearly Fletcher Sylvester, given the references to the circumstances of his death on Pauline Johnson Island; and a 'composite' (184). This 'composite' is likely the result of MPID, for, as Veršajna's account of the G25 summit makes clear, MPID creates holographic progeny:

> I saw a particular 'person' in the crowd and immediately felt a sense of recognition, seeing some of my own facial features as it passed; but in its face I also saw Riel's – his eyes, my brow, his cheekbones, my chin, and our clothes patchworked into one outfit ... Our holographic 'child' (as I think of it now) was walking in the opposite direction ... I eventually lost sight of it in the crowd. (188–9)

The dead migrant girl claims that the composite is 'one of us', potentially underscoring the relationship between ICDP and MPID but also including Fletcher, since she claims the composite is 'like you and me' (178). Significantly, then, the collection closes with a focus on three figures who represent different relationships to the territory of the Lower Mainland in general and to Pauline Johnson Island in particular, but who also form a community of spectres who 'will make plans to rendezvous with those yet to come. They will discuss what it means to regroup' (194). This 'regrouping' indicates an ongoing haunting, 'producing a something-to-be-done'[35] that exceeds the boundaries of the collection.

The final three figures relate differently to the Lower Mainland, extending Compton's engagement with what Tanis MacDonald describes in this volume as 'inheritants with complex identity positions' (p. 164). The lineages embedded in the personal histories of *The Outer Harbour*'s final three figures resonate significantly in terms of inheritance in the Derridean sense. For Derrida, the inheritor, 'a necessarily second generation', is both 'originarily late' and a 'redresser of wrongs'.[36] At the same time, 'one never inherits without coming to terms with ... some specter'.[37] As the spectre 'haunts *like a ghost* and by way of this haunting, demands justice',[38] the inheritor becomes a point of intersection for both haunting and redressing that injustice. If the Canada–US border throughout the collection has featured as a site to be crossed, generating the births of several characters (Riel, Fletcher, Donald and Albert), that border means different things in the personal but politicised contexts of these characters' histories: Fletcher was raised by white adoptive parents in Victoria, but his birth parents were Indigenous, from either side of the colonial border imposed on both land and sea; for how, as the

Canadian poet David McFadden humorously suggests, can 'the dots and dashes of the international boundary gliste[n] in the waves'?[39] The border is indeed just a Euro–North American 'hypothesis' on both soil and water.[40] The centrality in *The Outer Harbour* of the new (or newly visible) Pauline Johnson Island attests to the government saying more than it knows – it is, as Fletcher insists, 'Indian land' (34) – when it comes to territory and sovereignty.

That the government should invoke Pauline Johnson in a province almost entirely without treaties between settler-invaders and Indigenous peoples perhaps deflects from the need to acknowledge the Coast Salish nations of the Lower Mainland. Bergland writes in the US American context of Indigenous peoples being rendered as ghosts in the national literature: 'By discursively emptying physical territory of Indians and by removing those Indians into white imaginative spaces, spectralization claims the physical landscape as American territory.'[41] Similarly, Jennifer Andrews observes that 'Indigenous people in Canada have been historically rendered as ghostly in order to legitimate their colonization and assimilation.'[42] In the twenty-first-century Canadian context imagined by *The Outer Harbour*, however, the government discursively indigenises the island while simultaneously attempting to claim it as a neocolonial space: a recognition, through the island's naming, that no doubt seems politically necessary or at least expedient in the twenty-first century, but one that nevertheless doubles as erasure.

Yet Fletcher, a child of the border, and more particularly a child of the border that shouldn't be in Indigenous terms, clearly haunts the island after his murder at that site, part of a growing collective of those discarded by the nation state, 'people who are meant to be invisible show[ing] up without any sign of leaving'.[43] The composite and dead ICDP girl who are Fletcher's companions at the end of the book are children of the border in another sense, given MPID's provenance through outsourced testing and the ICDP girl's status as a revenant. In this way, Compton bears out Cynthia Sugars and Gerry Turcotte's observation that 'Canadian writers have been led to conjure, and indeed channel, the crowded landscape of ghosts ... that circulate above, around, and within the parameters of the Canadian nationalist project', with *The Outer Harbour*'s own 'crowded landscape' comprising the spectral MPID, ICDP and the dead activist Fletcher Sylvester in 'the complex contact zone that is twenty-first-century Vancouver'.[44] As Derrida writes,

> No justice ... seems possible or thinkable without the principle of some *responsibility*, beyond all living present, within that which disjoins the living present, before the ghosts of those who are not yet born or who are already dead, be they victims of wars, political or other kinds of violence, nationalist, racist, colonialist, sexist or other kinds of exterminations, victims of the oppressions of capitalist imperialism or any of the forms of totalitarianism.[45]

Compton's text addresses a number of these 'exterminations' through the circumscription and policing of Pauline Johnson Island and the role of border-crossers in challenging not simply the geographical margins of the nation state but also its coercive marginalising of Others who unsettle its authority.

In *The Outer Harbour*'s speculative fiction, then, Compton reworks the border's figuring in his writing, which has consistently acknowledged Indigenous presence but has previously focused more on the recovery of cross-border Black North American histories, evidence of Compton's significant and increasing 'non–Afrocentrist interest in other minorities and coalition-building'.[46] Compton's use of speculative fiction marks a departure from his previous dissemination of overlooked Black North American histories to hypotheses about ongoing and future colonialisms, borders that continue to be drawn and violently policed by the nation state in order to exclude its designated Others: the Indigenous peoples whose land it occupies, and the migrants it seeks to contain and expel. The Canada–US border's dominant historical association with sanctuary, as invoked by Donald and Albert's mother in this collection, elides the Canadian state's acts of violence at its threshold, as testified to in our political present with the perpetuation of the Safe Third Country agreement – itself a product of 9/11's fallout – which precludes Canada's acceptance of asylum seekers who have first arrived in the United States. Justice, Derrida claims, requires 'this *non-contemporaneity with itself of the living present* ... that which secretly unhinges it ... this responsibility and this respect for justice concerning those who *are not there*, of those who are no longer or who are not yet *present and living*'.[47] Compton's deployment of spectral beings haunting the borders of the nation state produces a constellation of inheritances that undermine those borders in the agitation for a justice that will be responsible to both the past and the future.

Acknowledgements

Thank you to my students on Q43342 Contemporary Canadian Literature at the University of Nottingham, 2015–16, for our discussion of Compton's work; to audiences at the Culture and the Canada–US Border network's Theorising the Canada-US Border symposium in Paris, May 2015 and the Association for Canadian and Québécois Literatures conference in Ottawa, May 2015; and to my colleagues in the Print, Visual and Musical Culture research cluster in the Department of American and Canadian Studies at the University of Nottingham for their engagement with this material. Thanks also to Joanne Leow who generously shared the script of her Mikinaakominis/TransCanadas conference paper, a version of which was later published in *University of Toronto Quarterly*, while I was drafting this chapter.

Notes

1. Jacques Derrida, *Specters of Marx*, trans. Peggy Kamuf (London: Routledge, 2006 [1994]), 48.
2. Jesse Alemán, 'The Other Country: Mexico, the United States, and the Gothic History of Conquest', in *The Spectralities Reader: Ghosts and Haunting in Contemporary Cultural Theory*, ed. María del Pilar Blanco and Esther Peeren (London: Bloomsbury, 2013), 510–11.
3. Ibid., 516, 519.
4. Ibid., 511.
5. Ibid., 510.
6. Bryce Traister, 'Border Shopping: American Studies and the Anti-Nation', in *Globalization on the Line: Culture, Capital, and Citizenship at U.S. Borders*, ed. Claudia Sadowski-Smith (New York: Palgrave, 2002), 34.
7. María del Pilar Blanco, *Ghost-Watching American Modernity: Haunting, Landscape, and the Hemispheric Imagination* (New York: Fordham University Press, 2012), 180; Rodolfo Acuna, *Occupied America: A History of Chicanos* (New York: Harper & Row, 1981, 2nd edn), 3.
8. Alemán, 'The Other Country', 510.
9. Lorraine Code, 'How to Think Globally: Stretching the Limits of Imagination', *Hypatia* 13.2 (1998): 82; Jody Berland, 'Writing the Border', in *Canadian Cultural Studies: A Reader*, ed. Sourayan Mookerjea, Imre Szeman and Gail Faurschou (Durham, NC: Duke University Press, 2009), 476.

10. Ibid., 476.
11. Audra Simpson, *Mohawk Interruptus: Political Life across the Borders of Settler States* (Durham, NC: Duke University Press, 2014), 115.
12. Vancouver is located in the overlapping territories of the Musqueam, Skwxwú7mesh (Squamish) and Tsleil-Waututh.
13. Wayde Compton, *The Outer Harbour: Stories* (Vancouver: Arsenal Pulp Press, 2014), 15, 26, 27, 29. All further references in the chapter to this text will appear in parentheses.
14. Joanne Leow, 'Lost Islands, Future Islands: Reading Wayde Compton's *The Outer Harbour* Relationally', *University of Toronto Quarterly* 89.1 (2020): 150.
15. E. Pauline Johnson (Tekahionwake), *Legends of Vancouver* (Toronto: McClelland & Stewart, 1961 [1911]), 94–5.
16. Veronica Strong-Boag and Carole Gerson, *Paddling Her Own Canoe: The Times and Texts of E. Pauline Johnson (Tekahionwake)* (Toronto: University of Toronto Press, 2000), 180.
17. Ibid., 10.
18. Ibid., 184, 217, 11.
19. Ibid., 200, 199.
20. Simpson, *Mohawk Interruptus*, 39.
21. Strong-Boag and Gerson, *Padding Her Own Canoe*, 209, 212; Simpson, *Mohawk Interruptus*, 7, 115.
22. Strong-Boag and Gerson, *Paddling Her Own Canoe*, 29, 181; Deena Rhyms, 'But the Shadow of Her Story: Narrative Unsettlement, Self-Inscription, and Translation in Pauline Johnson's *Legends of Vancouver*', *Studies in American Indian Literatures* 13.4 (2001): 53.
23. Ana María Fraile-Marcos, 'Afroperipheralism and the Transposition of Black Diasporic Culture in the Canadian Global City: Compton's *The Outer Harbour* and Brand's *Love Enough*', *African American Review* 51.3 (2018): 184.
24. Jennifer Henderson, '"Something not Unlike Enjoyment": Gothicism, Catholicism, and Sexuality in Thomson Highway's *Kiss of the Fur Queen*', in *Unsettled Remains: Canadian Literature and the Postcolonial Gothic*, ed. Cynthia Sugars and Gerry Turcotte (Waterloo, ON: Wilfrid Laurier University Press, 2009), 175.
25. Ibid.
26. Pilar Cuder-Domínguez, '*A mari usque ad mare*: Wayde Compton's British Columbian Afroperiphery', *Atlantic Studies* 15.2 (2018): 212.
27. Renée Bergland, *The National Uncanny: Indian Ghosts and American Subjects* (Hanover: Dartmouth College, University Press of New England, 2000), 11.
28. Ibid., 381.

29. Derrida, *Specters of Marx*, 5.
30. Marta Caminero-Santangelo, 'The Lost Ones: Post-gatekeeper Border Fictions and the Construction of Cultural Trauma', *Latino Studies* 8.3 (2010): 306.
31. María del Pilar Blanco and Esther Peeren, 'Introduction: Conceptualizing Spectralities', in *The Spectralities Reader: Ghosts and Haunting in Contemporary Cultural Theory*, ed. (London: Bloomsbury, 2013), 2.
32. Aaron DeRosa, 'The End of Futurity: Proleptic Nostalgia and the War on Terror', *Literature Interpretation Theory* 25 (2014): 93.
33. Winfried Siemerling, *The Black Atlantic Reconsidered: Black Canadian Writing, Cultural History, and the Presence of the Past* (Montreal and Kingston: McGill-Queen's University Press, 2015), 351.
34. Derrida, *Specters of Marx*, 11; Avery Gordon, *Ghostly Matters: Haunting and the Sociological Imagination* (Minneapolis: University of Minnesota Press, 2008, 2nd edn), xix.
35. Gordon, *Ghostly Matters*, xvi.
36. Derrida, *Specters of Marx*, 24, 25.
37. Ibid., 24.
38. Blanco and Peeren, 'Introduction', 9.
39. David W. McFadden, *Great Lakes Suite* (Vancouver, BC: Talonbooks, 1997), 192.
40. Laurie Ricou, *The Arbutus/Madrone Files: Reading the Pacific Northwest* (Edmonton, AB: NeWest, 2002), 23.
41. Bergland, *The National Uncanny*, 5.
42. Jennifer Andrews, 'Rethinking the Canadian Gothic: Reading Eden Robinson's *Monkey Beach*', in *Unsettled Remains: Canadian Literature and the Postcolonial Gothic*, ed. Cynthia Sugars and Gerry Turcotte (Waterloo, ON: Wilfrid Laurier University Press, 2009), 210.
43. Gordon, *Ghostly Matters*, xvi.
44. Cynthia Sugars and Gerry Turcotte, 'Introduction: Canadian Literature and the Postcolonial Gothic', in *Unsettled Remains: Canadian Literature and the Postcolonial Gothic*, ed. Cynthia Sugars and Gerry Turcotte (Waterloo, ON: Wilfrid Laurier University Press, 2009), xiii; Leow, 'Lost Islands, Future Islands', 146.
45. Derrida, *Specters of Marx*, xviii.
46. Winfried Siemerling, 'New Ecologies of the Real: Nonsimultaneity and Canadian Literature(s)', *Studies in Canadian Literature* 41.1 (2016): 135.
47. Derrida, *Specters of Marx*, xviii. Italics in the original.

References

Acuna, Rodolfo. *Occupied America: A History of Chicanos*. New York: Harper & Row, 1981 (2nd edn).

Alemán, Jesse. 'The Other Country: Mexico, the United States, and the Gothic History of Conquest' in *The Spectralities Reader: Ghosts and Haunting in Contemporary Cultural Theory*. Ed. María del Pilar Blanco and Esther Peeren. London: Bloomsbury, 2013. 506–26.

Andrews, Jennifer. 'Rethinking the Canadian Gothic: Reading Eden Robinson's *Monkey Beach*' in *Unsettled Remains: Canadian Literature and the Postcolonial Gothic*. Ed. Cynthia Sugars and Gerry Turcotte. Waterloo, ON: Wilfrid Laurier University Press, 2009. 205–27.

Bergland, Renée L. *The National Uncanny: Indian Ghosts and American Subjects*. Hanover: Dartmouth College, University Press of New England, 2000.

Berland, Jody. 'Writing the Border' in *Canadian Cultural Studies: A Reader*. Ed. Sourayan Mookerjea, Imre Szeman and Gail Faurschou. Durham, NC: Duke University Press, 2009. 472–87.

Blanco, María del Pilar. *Ghost-Watching American Modernity: Haunting, Landscape, and the Hemispheric Imagination*. New York: Fordham University Press, 2012.

Blanco, María del Pilar and Esther Peeren. 'Introduction: Conceptualizing Spectralities' in *The Spectralities Reader: Ghosts and Haunting in Contemporary Cultural Theory*. London: Bloomsbury, 2013. 1–27.

Blanco, María del Pilar and Esther Peeren, ed. *The Spectralities Reader: Ghosts and Haunting in Contemporary Cultural Theory*. London: Bloomsbury, 2013.

Caminero-Santangelo, Marta. 'The Lost Ones: Post-gatekeeper Border Fictions and the Construction of Cultural Trauma'. *Latino Studies* 8.3 (2010): 304–27.

Code, Lorraine. 'How to Think Globally: Stretching the Limits of Imagination'. *Hypatia* 13.2 (1998): 73–85.

Compton, Wayde. *The Outer Harbour: Stories*. Vancouver: Arsenal Pulp, 2014.

Cuder-Domínguez, Pilar. '*A mari usque ad mare*: Wayde Compton's British Columbian Afroperiphery'. *Atlantic Studies* 15.2 (2018): 198–217.

DeRosa, Aaron. 'The End of Futurity: Proleptic Nostalgia and the War on Terror'. *Literature Interpretation Theory* 25 (2014): 88–107.

Derrida, Jacques. *Specters of Marx*. Trans. Peggy Kamuf. London: Routledge, 2006 [1994].

Fraile-Marcos, Ana María. 'Afroperipheralism and the Transposition of Black Diasporic Culture in the Canadian Global City: Compton's *The Outer Harbour* and Brand's *Love Enough*'. *African American Review* 51.3 (2018): 181–95.

Gordon, Avery F. *Ghostly Matters: Haunting and the Sociological Imagination*. Minneapolis: University of Minnesota Press, 2008 (2nd edn).

Henderson, Jennifer. '"Something not Unlike Enjoyment": Gothicism, Catholicism, and Sexuality in Thomson Highway's *Kiss of the Fur Queen*' in *Unsettled Remains: Canadian Literature and the Postcolonial Gothic*. Ed. Cynthia Sugars and Gerry Turcotte. Waterloo, ON: Wilfrid Laurier University Press, 2009. 175–204.

Johnson, E. Pauline (Tekahionwake). *Legends of Vancouver*. Toronto: McClelland & Stewart, 1961 [1911].

Leow, Joanne. 'Lost Islands, Future Islands: Reading Wayde Compton's *The Outer Harbour* Relationally'. *University of Toronto Quarterly* 89.1 (2020): 145–62.

McFadden, David W. *Great Lakes Suite*. Vancouver: Talonbooks, 1997.

Ricou, Laurie. *The Arbutus/Madrone Files: Reading the Pacific Northwest*. Edmonton, AB: NeWest, 2002.

Rymhs, Deena. 'But the Shadow of Her Story: Narrative Unsettlement, Self-Inscription, and Translation in Pauline Johnson's *Legends of Vancouver*'. *Studies in American Indian Literatures* 13.4 (2001): 51–78.

Siemerling, Winfried. 'New Ecologies of the Real: Nonsimultaneity and Canadian Literature(s)'. *Studies in Canadian Literature* 41.1 (2016): 125–42.

Siemerling, Winfried. *The Black Atlantic Reconsidered: Black Canadian Writing, Cultural History, and the Presence of the Past*. Montreal and Kingston: McGill-Queen's University Press, 2015.

Simpson, Audra. *Mohawk Interruptus: Political Life Across the Borders of Settler States*. Durham, NC: Duke University Press, 2014.

Strong-Boag, Veronica and Carole Gerson. *Paddling Her Own Canoe: The Times and Texts of E. Pauline Johnson (Tekahionwake)*. Toronto: University of Toronto Press, 2000.

Sugars, Cynthia and Gerry Turcotte. 'Introduction: Canadian Literature and the Postcolonial Gothic' in *Unsettled Remains: Canadian Literature and the Postcolonial Gothic*. Waterloo, ON: Wilfrid Laurier University Press, 2009. vii–xxvi.

Sugars, Cynthia and Gerry Turcotte, ed. *Unsettled Remains: Canadian Literature and the Postcolonial Gothic*. Waterloo, ON: Wilfrid Laurier University Press, 2009.

Traister, Bryce. 'Border Shopping: American Studies and the Anti-Nation' in *Globalization on the Line: Culture, Capital, and Citizenship at U.S. Borders*. Ed. Claudia Sadowski-Smith. New York: Palgrave, 2002. 31–52.

8

Afterword: Naming, Knowing and Negotiating Third Spaces of the Border

Victor Konrad

In the introduction to this book, Jeffrey Orr and David Stirrup confront the cliché that border studies is most closely associated with and steeped in the Mexico–US border. The Mexico–US borderland is theorised as a site that is conducive to cultural hybridity and transgressive cultural performance and practice. This border thinking has become portable, a means of understanding the state of mind as well as the boundary between nations, and the mental state of the permanent outsider. Yet, as Orr and Stirrup argue, in transposition of border thinking from the Mexico–US border to the Canada–US context, we lose nuances of class, linguistic, ethnic, economic, historical and environmental difference. A similar conclusion has been reached by other authors who have compared North American borders.[1] This leads to the question of what place does the Canada–US border site have in the sphere of border theory? This question is addressed in every chapter of the book, and I will extend the engagement in this afterword.

However, I wish to begin the afterword by confronting another cliché, namely that borders sift and sort crossings, thus populating a third space between Canada and the United States with residual people and ideas.[2] This cliché, I argue, has served to buttress border thinking in the US as a reactionary perspective, because most Canadians reside in a third space of in-betweenness, where nation, nation state, region and other aspects of cultural identity align with and live the border. As Orr and Stirrup observe, this condition tends to convey the Canada–US border as more metaphor than site, define

Canada more by what it is not than what it is (an anti-US), envision a non-space for Americans looking north, and sustain a nebulous but symbolic nation-building space for Canadians. We are then faced with the double-barrelled questions of not only what place does the Canada–US border site have in the sphere of border theory, but also how does the Canada–US border contribute to the advancement of border theory?

Although everyone is bordered in some way in a world consisting of layers of borders, and all people are border subjects, borders do not work for everyone in the same way.[3] As illustrated in this book, the Canada–US border has operated as a sieve or filter since it was established in successive sections across the North American continent and into the Arctic. Some people (and some goods, and ideas) cross the international boundary with ease, and they are expedited in their journeys, whereas others are delayed or blocked entirely because they do not conform to increasingly narrowed profiles of trusted and preferred border-crossers between two nation states growing further apart in a 'post-globalization' world.[4] The COVID-19 pandemic reinforced borderlines, and restricted human mobility and interaction between Canada and the United States to the extent that tourism, seasonal travel and community linkages across the border have all been impacted substantially.[5] Yet, *The Globe and Mail* reports that 'A highly contagious political virus is pouring over the Canada–US border' and it is influencing the Conservative Party in Canada.[6] According to the article, extreme conservative perspectives, honed in US politics, are now influencing conservative Canadians. Meanwhile, at the border, Canada's 'ArriveCan' online documentation requirement for Canadians and foreign crossers alike appears increasingly as a Canadian Border Services Agency (CBSA) personal data grab while it purports to help control the spread of the pandemic.[7] The border of constraint prevails to limit rather than enable crossing, or even mitigate border effects, despite the continued rhetoric of an open border. All the while, the border is transcended by seducing ideas and unseen pathogens, as well as those who 'Can-pass'.

The Canada–US border, quite simply, is not for everyone. It was not conceived for everyone. It has not evolved for the benefit of everyone, neither in the United States nor in Canada. And, in recent decades, the more sharply delineated boundaries of being in Canada, and in the United States of America, are reflected increasingly in the Canada–US border and how it works. The ontology of Canadian, and the ontology of American, both now are shaped by large data sets, re-grouped entities that span existence and becoming, extended realities and perceptions based on belief over truth, and the re-shuffled and re-positioned concepts and categories that define Canada and the United States. The Canada–US borderline remains in place, but the border has changed – metaphorically, metaphysically, existentially.[8]

This change in borders generally, according to border theorist Thomas Nail, reveals the border as a 'process of social division'.[9] The process, as portrayed in the chapters of this book, is one of bordering people constituted in nations but governed in federations, negotiating these borders, and resisting borderline inadequacies and injustices. The process is also, increasingly, one of making place for the third space of the border in an outdated and superceded framing of territory and sovereignty based on division and duality. In the following discussion, I draw from the observations and conclusions of each one of the chapters to illustrate how the border is imagined and portrayed, differentiated and labelled, defined and articulated, and, ultimately, branded and institutionalised, thus creating a place for third space of and at the border.

The Conundrum of Border Theory: Metaphysics of Being Bounded

Border theory has privileged nation states over nations and transnational constructs, yet we live in a world of resurgent nationalities and transnationalism. Although leading scholars in border studies have called for new approaches and insights and reframing of border thinking to accommodate process and globalisation, a general theory of border studies remains elusive.[10] An epistemological dilemma arises: Do humans construct borders in the process of creating societies and states? Does movement-oriented bordering create societies and states? Or, are both processes operating concurrently, and are borders in globalisation and post-globalisation contexts exemplary of the prevailing in-betweenness of the bordered world? In order to address these fundamental questions, it is necessary to clarify the philosophical underpinnings of border theory.

A philosophy of borders and bordering contains, like all philosophical constructs do, components of border logics, ethics, metaphysics and epistemology. Border logics govern the reasoning of border theory according to strict principles of validity. These logics may lead to abstract theory not necessarily based in border realities. Moral principles of border ethics govern human behaviour. Together, these components may eventually and ideally constitute an epistemology of borders, a theory of border knowledge justified by belief over opinion. Until now, however, border logics and border ethics have led mainly to some metaphysical comprehension of multi-scalarity motion and rhythm, structuration, agency, paradox, and liminality. Epistemological advances in framing dissensus, power, resource potential and belongingness associated with borders, and the nature of borderscapes and a-territoriality of borders remain works in progress.[11]

Border logics extend from the fundamental logic of separation of different entities, or the differentiation of two sides of a relatively consistent entity, as explained in the theory of 'parts and boundaries' (mereotopology) to explain connection relations (abutting, tangential, equality, overlaps) and axioms of ordering, composition and decomposition.[12]. Binary spatial relationships extend through time and space;[13] these boundaries may be *fiat* or *bona fide*.[14]

Border logics lead to the following inferences: borders may intersect and connect; they are mobile; borders may be scaled; they separate; and, borders may change over time and vary.

In a widely acclaimed article 'Beyond Borders: Towards the Ethics of Unbounded Inclusiveness', Finnish border studies scholar Jussi P. Laine seeks to balance the calls for the freedom of movement against the right to freedom of association, by advocating for unbounded inclusiveness and challenging the ingrained notion that the rights, duties and opportunities of people remain based in a territorially demarcated place.[15] Do moral principles govern behaviour surrounding borders?

> Ethics enter perceptions, reasoning, thought, and actions related to borders. A basic ethical position is that a border divides two entities which are potentially equal, and it follows that these entities hold or share equal rights and resources. Yet, this ideal

is not apparent, and borders characteristically separate different and unequal entities such as countries, social classes, races, and more. Bordering, by its very nature is othering. Others are considered not to belong. To define outside from inside is to render the outside exogenous, and to confirm the outside as unequal. With inequality established, bordering may be used to alienate Indigenous, hybrid, racially different and other distinct human populations. Critical border studies aim to re-centre ethical principles enshrined in social justice and civil society to question and assail bordering thought and practices that render precarious vast human populations.[16]

Abstract theories of borders and bordering, or border metaphysics, often derived from notions of boundaries in nature, have been applied to human-constructed borders and bordering. A prominent example is liminality which has been envisioned in ecology to characterise the layering and gradation of life zones, applies effectively in borderlands.[17] Liminality suggests that both human and non-human agents are intertwined in bordering, but the theory also implies that humans gain only a partial capacity to understand borders if our approaches remain anthropogenic.[18] Border metaphysics as developed in notions of liminality, the multi-scalar characteristics of borders, or motion and rhythm, for example, establish first principles of the being, change, necessity and possibility of borders.[19] These metaphysics, however, offer only partial explanations and differentiations of borders of nations as opposed to nation states, and borders of aggregates of nations and/or nation states as exemplified in empires, federations and other assemblages. Border metaphysics convey the 'order' of borders but fall short of representing the nuances of border life and experience. Nevertheless, border metaphysics underlie the epistemological ridges in our knowledge map of borders.[20] Among these ridges are the role of power in articulating borders, the conceptualisation of borderlands, the extension of engagement with border space and place through *dissensus* over consensus, and the operations of de-territorialisation and re-territorialisation in the space in-between.[21] 'Here, cultural, social and political identities are more fluid and belongingness may be plural.'[22] 'Our knowledge of borders, then, remains topographic – situated by epistemological ridges of awareness, yet incomplete in understanding of the interstitial components that, when combined with the prominences, will offer a framework for understanding borders more completely and effectively.'[23]

The editors of this book also use the notion of framing, in this instance more literally, to draw the frame around nations, and explicitly around nation states, in order to level the question of who is left out of the picture and excluded by the framing? The answer is both simple and complex. Simply stated, those associated with the people in power, often styled the majority, are within the frame, and those not associated with the majority are outside the frame. A more complex portrayal illustrates some minorities who are always outside the frame – Indigenous nations for example – whereas some minorities are in the process of becoming in the frame, some move in and out, and others remain at the margins. This begs the questions, what is being framed by borders, and why? Are contemporary borders merely a 'noisy hyphen'?[24] Orr and Stirrup argue that the process of framing borders has become a bordering of the theory, and that this has resulted in problems of homogenising, appropriating and taxonoming through theorisation. They argue that border theory grows from, and is linked to, the specific realities of the Canada–US border. The process is accretive, and the theory is organic and grounded, actually linking borders that are imagined, constructed and lived, and interlacing natural and conceptual borders. This accretive perspective on border theory enables us to move border theory beyond topographic epistemologies, to enhance the view across and through borders at the 'fatal intersection of time and space',[25] to convey the content and not only the result of geopolitics, to acknowledge the material, conceptual and geographical blind spots in the architecture of borders, and to enable a nuanced understanding of how borders are made and performed.

Metaphors of performance, filter and wall, for example, offer a focus on specific aspects of border use, but, according to Orr and Stirrup, the metaphors do not fully capture the dynamic and social aspects of interactions at the border. In fact, the metaphors of borders, like the borders themselves, normalise ways of speaking, acting and representing the self, thus creating a collection of facets, or multiplicities, that are difficult to account for in border theory. Furthermore, as expressed by Johan Schimanski, the border itself is also the product of the border crossing, or brought into being by border-crossers.[26] Schimanski cautions not to re-elide those lives and acts already elided by the political powers that impose and enforce the border. Border theory needs to be specific: borders operate as frames for nation states. As Orr and Stirrup summarise, the nation state border frame operates geographically, conceptually in terms of identity, politically in terms of policy imposition, and aesthetically in terms of representation of nationhood, citizenship and the collective arbitration of taste. To generalise beyond this nation state framework in a more extensive theory of borders is, indeed, possible and desirable, but this theorisation tips into another realm, much like crossing a border, and this requires recalibration of the border framework.[27]

Bordering Nations and the Creation of the Canada–United States Border

The Canada–US border evolved from a bordering of empires – mainly British, French, Spanish, Russian – to a bounding of a republic and a federation, with the diminution and disenfranchisement of nations in the space in-between. Nations that survived, both settler French and Indigenous, were relegated to marginalised and isolated spaces either at the border if they were military allies, or more often at a distance from the border. In the late eighteenth and early nineteenth centuries, both the United States and Great Britain moved their settler colonists close to the new boundary in north-eastern North America and the Great Lakes region to secure the borderlands. As Canada evolved into a federation, favoured 'nations' of immigrants from Europe were folded into the Canadian geographical and social fabric and situated near the border as it extended west along the 49th parallel. Even Americans, beyond Loyalists, were included, whereas visible minorities, Chinese and East Indian railroad construction workers for example, were relegated to marginal enclaves beyond the border. During the twentieth century, cross-border integration prevailed, and although settler colonial 'nations' dotted the borderlands, particularly in the Western Interior of the continent, Indigenous national territories continued to shrink, especially in the borderlands. The reinforcement of the Canada–US border in the twenty-first century has redefined and emphasised the presence of Indigenous and other minority nations in the borderlands.

These nations complicate at the very least, and often call into question the nation state's national project at the border. They create, as Jeffrey Orr describes in Chapter 1, a tension between formal and vernacular nationalisms through the uniformity, singularity, garrison mentality and simplification of one truth as espoused by the Canadian Border Services Agency (CBSA). Orr examines critically episodes of the short-lived TV series 'Border Security: Canada's Front Line' (2012–14) to show that rather than complicating and building nuance around identity and cultural difference, the producers of the show aim to reassure the audience that these difficult and troubling questions of ambivalence can and will be resolved. The goals of the TV show, and the nation state, in this instance Canada, are to require, and create if necessary, a coherent narrative to justify their existence. Yet, as Orr and Stirrup articulate in the Introduction, the quest for ontological security exists within, beyond and between nation state boundaries, and this search must be conducted within a space of the Canada–US border that both divides and connects geography, historical narratives, imagined pasts, possible futures and realities of the present. With all of these elements compressed and contorted at the border, small wonder that differentiation remains nebulous and that the border has become a critical site to identify 'safe citizens'.

The production and enforcement of national identity is accomplished through the creative representation of the border, but the recognition and acceptance of national identity, particularly by those who reside in borderlands, relies as well on accomplished differentiation and mediation of border space, a process Achille Mbembe refers to as 'borderization'.[28] The site of the border and the figure that the border portrays, according to Orr and Stirrup, are vital components to define the nation in context, to establish national identity and to relate national identities on an equal footing, steering away as it were from an overwhelming United States perspective, and dominant US, Canadian and Mexican national narratives. The border is too rich in insights about who we are for us to accept a distilled and packaged rendition of national identity. Expanded engagements with border discourse, artistic creation and media representation offer enhanced understanding of 'how we make the border, and how the border makes us', but these insights need to be grounded in the extensive and varied geography of borders and borderlands.

In the second and third chapters, Vincent Manzerolle and Pierre-Alexandre Beylier address, respectively, the infrastructural and settlement geography of the border. Both studies offer historical and contemporary perspectives, and focus on un-layering and theorising the spatial relationships inherent in the border zone of convergence. Whereas Beylier employs a comparison of twin cities on the Mexico–US and Canada–US borders to characterise settlement pairing and integration at the border, Manzerolle investigates the logistical dimensions of media that shape the circulation of products, people, information and capital. Both studies grapple with the inseparability of economic, political and cultural forces converged and materialised in the space in-between. Numerous border scholars have noted the messy integration that results from mediation of these forces.

Manzerolle offers to conceptualise borders as multi-media phenomena that act as interfaces of empire. Material 'grooves' of cross-border flows and 'distilled circulatory thresholds' reveal the binding of space-time in various bottlenecks and accelerants, in order to provide a 'synecdochic' view of the mediating function and the temporality of the Canada–US border along the Detroit River. The infrastructure of being, Manzerolle suggests, is enabled through infrastructural and logistical dimensions of media, media that extend from the geological template to the constructed and reconstructed logistical infrastructure. This non-linear depiction captures the circulatory nature of borders as liminal sites of mediation, whereas Beylier provides insight to the multifaceted dimension of integration. Twin cities are theorised as the epitome and apex of crossing the border: they convey functional integration; they are dynamic prosperous locations; they confirm cooperative initiatives; they exhibit an original socio-spatial system shaped by flows and interaction; they turn double-space into unique networked space. In effect, twin cities erase or, at least, transcend the border. The concentration of people at the borders between Canada and the United States and Mexico and the United States, Beylier relates, has evolved through religious origins, defensive, frontier, buffer, and north–south logics to form borderlands, and these borderlands have become the sites for twin city growth and prosperity. Although, the relationship between the development of borderlands and the fluorescence of twin cities at the border remains to be explored in greater depth, the complementarity and comparative advantage of these twin cities is well established. More studies are required, however, to assess the degree and nature of duplication, the essence of belonging together, and the formation of bicultural identity. Furthermore, as Beylier concedes, the securitisation of the post 9/11 era has mutated the twin city dynamic. Less apparent is the state of cross-border magnetism in twin cities. How does belonging together change as bicultural, and even bi-national, people in twin cities and other places in the borderlands alter relations? Although the answer remains elusive due to the continually evolving and fluid nature of borders, a constant is revealed in the prevailing human negotiation of borders and borderline resistance of 'others'.

Negotiation of Borders and Borderline Resistance: Indigenous//Colonial Settler//Black

How do you negotiate a border that does not exist for you? In order to address this problem, in Chapter 5 David Stirrup relates a story of Mohawk scholar Audra Simpson's encounter with a US border official intent on challenging her proclaimed right to cross the border as an Indigenous person. The right to cross is exposed as only a claim since nation states *hold* the right and the power to determine whether a person may cross or not. Simpson, on behalf of all Indigenous peoples, asserts the refusal of that power and questions the universal right of the nation state to decide who crosses the border.[29]

Rather than accept this impasse, and treat Indigenous peoples as residuals in border theory, Stirrup sees a 'certain kind of optimism embedded in border theory's slips and evasions, hybridities and coalescences, in the gap between rejection of discursive categories and political hard edges of lived experience'. He emphasises that this 'optimism runs repeatedly against the reality of border crossing'. This optimism, evident in the concepts and constructs of border theory – borderlands, borderscapes, liminality, for example – enables negotiation of borders and a 'spectrum of resistance and return'. Borders offer space for resistance. In fact, borders designate the space for resistance, making this space at once open for expression and yet open as well to surveillance. In this space, however, remains the prospect, as Stirrup states, of a 'return to Indigenous centres through the re-making of borders'. The nature and degree of remaking of borders remains speculative but some aims are evident in Indigenous scholarship, including resistance to construction of racialised codes such as blood quantum and measures of hybridity, and an imaginative liberation from culture territories designated by imperial powers and consistently imposed by the evolved nation states through definitions of who and what Indigenous peoples could be. Chapters 4 to 7 explore the imaginative liberation of border space, and they populate and colour this space with border people and places to create what Walter Mignolo calls 'sites of possibility'.[30] The contributing authors focus on Indigenous and Black resistance to borderlines, and the negotiation of borders by these people, borders espoused in what Stirrup refers to as 'colonial dreams of fixity, control, visibility, productivity, and docility'. The rich discussion in these four chapters draws from a growing literature and selected texts in order to challenge and enlarge border thinking. My aims in this afterword are to underline major points in the discussion and to connect these to a relational framing of border theory.[31]

Border people, generally, and visible minorities, specifically, both stand out and fit in-between as they resist and negotiate boundary lines.[32] This creates a sustained and visible, and sometimes abrasive, state of being between the lines. In order to achieve this apparent state of being, border people proclaim 'survivance' (vital survival outside basic survival), engage with transformation, alter resolution and extend justification. All of these generalised processes contribute to border resistance and negotiation, and each process is unpacked in varying degrees by David Stirrup, Chris LaLonde, Gillian Roberts and Tanis MacDonald.

Although survival is a recurrent theme in Canadian literature, Gerald Vizenor's articulation of 'survivance'[33] infuses the waning conceptualisation of survival with what LaLonde characterises as 'active repudiation of dominance, tragedy, victimry', and arms it with 'fundamental and foundational resistance'. Indigenous 'survivance' invokes continental liberty, that is, the natural opportunity and right of motion across the continent and hemisphere. Add to this the notion of natural reason that privileges creation over closure, and, according to LaLonde, in Chapter 4 we learn to 'disrupt the idea of difference that fortifies frontiers', 'dissolve false frames of separation' and 'liberate both meaning and marginalised inhabitants of the other edges of these Americas'.

This transformation, Stirrup explains in Chapter 5, would dissolve Eurowestern border theory if we could escape colonialism, but instead the transformation of border thought to an Indigenous perspective creates a border theory that is adjacent. Addressing Vizenor's vision, Stirrup summarises that 'American Indians inhabit interstitial space between colonies and nations, white and Indian, and thus subvert the demands of each cultural register's posits, an in-between that is simultaneously both coherent in terms of border theory, and readily understandable as a problem to those for whom such theorising actually undermines the ground on which Indian people recover culture and demand redress.' Transformation, then, is incomplete if it leads to in-betweenness that is utopian without political impact or relevance, or some form of ossified hybridity.

Resolution, suggests Stirrup, comes with the acknowledgement of the border without reifying it, and refusal to 'totalise' the continent with the belief that multiple identities simply fold into each other. We can agree with Stirrup's articulation of 'irrefutable common ground': 'Colonial boundaries were artificially imposed on Indigenous peoples who continue to confront and reveal the lie of the border's naturalness, resisting submission to binate logics.' In order to move on in our border thinking, LaLonde (after Mignolo) requires epistemological disobedience, that is thinking in exteriority, plurality, and with reference and reverence of place. We enter spaces inhabited by fugitives, for example the mid-nineteenth-century Black diaspora from San Francisco to Victoria addressed by Wayde Compton in his short stories and poetry. As both Tanis MacDonald and Gillian Roberts relate in the sixth and seventh chapters respectively, the Black state of being between the lines is one of dispossession as related similarly in Indigenous stories. The altered resolution for Wayde Compton's fugitives is populated by spirits and spectres, and the 'ontology of border', Roberts portrays as a 'hauntology'. The altered resolution for Vizenor is orchestrated by the trickster. LaLonde describes the multiple choreographies of the 'Trickster Plover of Liberty' whose dances on the shoreline (border) – broken wing, wobble with broken foot, erratic and acrobatic feigning – capture the experiences of the natives on Minnesota's White Earth Reservation.

Altered resolutions seek justification of what the border really is and what it does. This search for justice engages more extensive and inclusive rights, rights that acknowledge and represent citizenship denied and lands usurped. For Tanis MacDonald, the border is more than a physical and psychological barrier, more than a metaphor for transformation, and a space terrorised by utopia and predicated in liminality. MacDonald asks: Where is the border? What does it grant? What is possibility? Her inventive poetics of 'border-blur' foreground the limitations of a single style and whiteness of border discourse. Gillian Roberts explains Compton's achievement in *The Outer Harbour*: 'his engagement with spectrality in his speculative fiction enables us to read, project, and contest not only past injustices situated at or pushed to the nation state's threshold but also the injustices of the future that Compton extrapolates from history and its legacies in the present (2)'. We are left with border injustices revealed and to some degree mediated in theory. As Jussi Laine posits: 'In advocating for unbounded inclusiveness, I seek to challenge the widely accepted notion that people are from a certain territorially demarcated place, and their rights, duties – and opportunities in life, ought to remain based on their arbitrary fact.'[34] This level of justification and democratisation of border space remains elusive in our contemporary world, yet, having imagined and realised the space in-between, it is incumbent on us to make place for third space.

Making Place for Third Space: Territorial Opacity and Pluralist Sovereignty

Third space, as theorised by Edward Soja, is constituted with spaces that are both real and imagined.[35] Applied to border studies, third or in-between space emerges as the engagement space of two countries, the hybrid borderlands between them, the interaction zone, the stand-off location, the mediation place. Third space is a state of being – real or imagined – between the lines – real or imagined. My central argument in this is that theorising the space between nations, nations states, and different peoples generally, requires making place for third space by shifting our conceptions of territory and sovereignty from definitive notions sharpened by Eurocentric and Western ideals to more opaque, inclusive and extensive considerations. My effort has been to collect and distil the main conclusions of the studies in this book, and, hopefully, to convey these findings in a concise manner and with additional insight. I conclude with reflections on a potential, more ethical, third space of the Canada–US border, and borders more generally. This 'relational reframing', to use David Stirrup's term in Chapter 5, moves not only beyond the hierarchical nature of margins and centres, inside/outside binaries and border sites as points of conflict, as he intends, but also advances to interrogate the hardened edges of sovereignty and territory. These ideas are already implicit in the discussion throughout this book. My goals are to be more explicit and provocative.

Efforts by nation states, nations and federations, among other human associations, to define and bound territory remain at the heart of geopolitics even as processes of globalisation blur borderlines. The borders remain, particularly where they are strategically important. Territory remains in place as well, yet some of this territory is disputed, questioned, reimagined and even shared. Territory at the margins, in many instances has become more opaque, shared by some and guarded by others. Territorial opacity, ironically, reveals the aperture of third space. Often imagined at first, third space becomes more defined and shaped by resistance and negotiation, and it may finally emerge as discernable if not discrete territory. More likely, in our contemporary world of largely ossified borderlines, is the scenario, played out in many of the chapters in this book, of 'transcendent territoriality' in which border figures imagine and enact territory, and create third space. For Indigenous North Americans, this is territorial reclamation on a spectrum of realisation.

Third space enables a complex polity of different and overlapping sovereignties reflecting multiple allegiances, often at different scales. Audra Simpson forwards a concept of 'nested sovereignty' in which Mohawk sovereignty is realised within a third political space between US and Canadian sovereignties, and the additional allegiances and distinctions from Quebec, Ontario and New York.[36] The notion of pluralist sovereignty may appear counterintuitive, but as Kevin Bruyneel asserts in the conception of a third space of sovereignty for Indigenous peoples, and as Stirrup expands in his chapter, resistance has confounded colonial political thought about sovereignty, problematised imperial boundaries associated with the Eurocentric idea of borders, and forwarded the idea of multiple and potentially integrative sovereignties.[37] This is not a new idea, but it is an idea that needs a third space to grow.

Although it may appear that border hypotheses forwarded by all of the authors in this book, and specifically by Gillian Roberts in Chapter 7, are designated as 'Speculations on Territory and Sovereignty', a closer reading of Roberts' title and text reveals the multiple meaning of speculation as conjecture, supposition and theorising, and its relationship to spectrality which liberates us from dichotomous thinking and elevates (or levitates) thought to a broader perspective. In this book, the authors have shifted border thinking towards a more grounded yet imaginative relational reframing. The Canada–US border remains where it was established by colonial architects of empires and nation states. The power to articulate the border remains in the hands of the United States and Canada. Yet, cultures of and at the border are being renewed at time-honoured crossings and twin cities to form and enlarge these interstitial spaces. Indigenous resistance to borderlines has occasioned rethinking of the meaning of border, and now this thought is being extended to considerations of how Blacks and other minorities have engaged with the border. This book advances a sound theoretical framework and points to some exciting new directions for enquiry.

Notes

1. Guadalupe Correa Cabrera and Victor Konrad, ed. *North American Borders in Comparative Perspective* (Tucson: University of Arizona Press, 2020).
2. Edward Soja, 'Thirdspace: Journeys to Los Angeles and Other Real-and-Imagined Places', *Capital and Class* 22.1 (1998): 137–9; Kevin Bruyneel, *The Third Space of Sovereignty: The Postcolonial Politics of U.S.-Indigenous Relations* (Minneapolis: University of Minnesota Press, 2007).
3. Ila Nicole Sheren, *Portable Borders: Performance Art and Politics on the US Frontera Since 1984* (Austin: University of Texas Press, 2015).
4. Victor Konrad, 'New Directions at the Post-Globalization Border', *Journal of Borderlands Studies* 36.5 (2022): 713–26.
5. Border Policy Research Institute, 'COVID-19 and the US–Canada Border Report 3: Impacts on the Tourism Industry in Whatcom County', Fall 2020. cedar.wwu.edu/cgi/viewcontent/.cgi?article=1123&context=bpri_publications
6. David Dee Delgado, 'A Highly Contagious Political Virus is Pouring Over the Canada–US Border', *The Globe and Mail*, 17 August 2022. https://theglobeandmail.com/opinion/editorials/article-a-highly-contagious-political-virus-is-pouring-over-the-canada-us/
7. Laurie D. Trautman, 'The Impact of COVID-19 Test Requirements on Cross-Border Travel: A Case Study of Blaine WA', Winter 2022. cedar.wwu.edu/cgi/viewcontent.cgi?article=1129&context=bpri_publications

8. Victor Konrad and Melissa Kelly, ed. *Borders, Culture, and Globalization: A Canadian Perspective* (Ottawa: University of Ottawa Press, 2021).
9. Thomas Nail, *Theory of the Border* (New York: Oxford University Press, 2016).
10. For new considerations of border thinking, see David Newman, 'The Lines that Continue to Separate Us: Borders in our "Borderless" World', *Progress in Human Geography* 30.2 (2006): 143–61. On reframing the question of borders, see John Agnew, 'Borders on the Mind: Reframing Border Thinking', *Ethics and Global Politics* 1.4 (2008): 175–91. On general border theory questions, see Anssi Paasi, 'Bounded Spaces in a "Borderless World": Border Studies, Power, and the Anatomy of Territory', *Journal of Power* 2.2 (2009): 213–34, and 'A "Border Theory": An Unattainable Dream or a Realistic Aim for Border Scholars?', in *A Research Companion for Border Studies*, ed. D. Wastl-Walter (Aldershot: Ashgate, 2011), 11–31.
11. Victor Konrad, 'New Directions at the Post-Globalization Border', 715. On multi-scalarity and borders, see Jussi P. Laine's 'The Multiscalar Production of Borders', *Geopolitics* 21.3 (2016): 465–82. On motion and rhythm at the border, see Victor Konrad's 'Toward a Theory of Borders in Motion', *Journal of Borderlands Studies* 30.1 (2015): 1–18, and Nail, *Theory of the Border*. For a discussion of structuration, see M. A. Ferdoush, 'Seeing Borders Through the Lens of Structuration: A Theoretical Framework', *Geopolitics* 23.1 (2018): 180–200. On the matter of agency and interdisciplinary border work, see Emmanuel Brunet-Jailly, 'Theorizing Borders: An Interdisciplinary Perspective', *Geopolitics* 10 (2005): 633–49. Regarding paradox and border issues, see Randy Widdis, 'Looking Through the Mirror: A Historical Geographical View of the Canadian-American Borderlands', *Journal of Borderlands Studies* 30.2 (2015): 175–88. On liminality see Hastings Donnan and D. Haller, 'Liminal No More', *Ethnologia Europaea* 30.2 (2000): 7–22. On matters of dissensus, power and aesthetics, see Jacques Ranciere, *Dissensus: On Politics and Aesthetics* (London: Bloomsbury, 2015). For considerations of borders as a resource, see Christophe Sohn, 'Modelling Cross-Border Integration: The Role of Borders as a Resource', *Geopolitics* 19.4 (2014): 587–608. For issues of borders and belonging, see Giuseppina Marsico, 'Moving Between the Social Spaces: Conditions for Boundaries Crossing', in *Crossing Boundaries: Intercontextural Dynamics Between Family and School*, ed. G. Marsico, K. Komatsuand and A. Iannaccone (Charlotte, NC: Information Age, 2013), 361–74. Regarding borderscapes see Chiara Brambilla, 'Exploring the Critical Potential of the Borderscapes Concept', *Geopolitics* 20.1 (2015): 14–34. On the a-territorality of bor-

ders and borderlands, see Victor Konrad and Emmanuel Brunet-Jailly, 'Approaching Borders, Creating Borderland Spaces, and Exploring the Evolving Borders Between Canada and the United States', *The Canadian Geographer/Le geographe canadien* 63.1 (2019): 4–10.
12. Barry Smith, 'Mereotopology: A Theory of Parts and Boundaries', *Data and Knowledge Engineering* 20.3 (1996): 287–303.
13. Sandro Mezzandra and Brett Neilson, 'Between Inclusion and Exclusion: On the Topology of Global Space and Borders', *Theory, Culture and Society* 29.4–5 (2012): 58–75.
14. Barry Smith and Achille C. Varzi, 'Fiat and Bona Fide Boundaries', *Philosophy and Phenomenological Research* 60.2 (2000): 401–20.
15. Jussi P. Laine, 'Beyond Borders: Towards the Ethics of Unbounded Inclusiveness', *Journal of Borderlands Studies* 36.5 (2021): 745–63.
16. Konrad, 'New Directions at the Post-Globalization Border', 716. On bordering and the process of Othering, see Nira Yuval-Davis, Georgie Wemyss and Kathryn Cassidy, *Bordering* (New York: Wiley, 2019), as well as Henk Van Houtum and Ton Van Naerssen, 'Bordering, Ordering, and Othering', *Tijdschrift voor economischen sociale geographie* 93.2 (2002): 125–36. Also see Joshua W. Clegg, 'A Phenomenological Investigation of the Experience of Not Belonging', *Journal of Phenomenological Psychology* 37.1 (2006): 53–83. On bordering practices and identity, see Noel Parker and Nick Vaughan-Williams, *Critical Border Studies: Broadening and Deepening the 'Lines in the Sand' Agenda* (New York: Routledge, 2016). See also Mark B. Salter, 'Theory of the /: The Suture and Critical Border Studies', *Geopolitics* 17.4 (2012): 734–55.
17. Michel Agier, *Borderlands: Towards an Anthropology of the Cosmopolitan Condition* (New York: Wiley, 2016).
18. Thomas Nail, 'Kinopolitics: Borders in Motion', in *Posthuman Ecologies: Complexity and Process After Deleuze*, ed. R. Braidotti and S. Bignall (New York: Roman and Littlefield, 2019), 183–203.
19. Konrad, 'Toward a Theory of Borders in Motion'; Laine, 'The Multiscalar Production of Borders'.
20. Konrad, 'New Directions at the Post-Globalization Border', 716.
21. For more on the articulation and theorisation of borders, see Michael Dear, *Why Walls Won't Work: Repairing the US–Mexico Divide* (New York: Oxford University Press, 2013); David Newman, 'Borders and Power: A Theoretical Framework', *Journal of Borderlands Studies* 18.1 (2003): 13–25; Paasi, 'Bounded Spaces in a "Borderless World"'. For a seminal consideration of borderlands, see Gloria Anzaldua, *Borderlands/La Frontera: The New Mestiza* (San Francisco, CA: Aunt Lute Books [1987], 2012, 4th edn). On the matter of dissensus, see Ranciere, *Dissensus*.

22. Konrad, 'New Directions at the Post-Globalization Border', 717.
23. Ibid.
24. Fred Wah, *Diamond Grill* (Edmonton, AB: NeWest Press, 1996), 176.
25. Michel Foucault and Colin Gordon, 'Of Other Spaces: Utopias and Heterotopias', in *Rethinking Architecture: A Reader in Cultural Theory*, ed. Neil Leach (New York: Routledge, 1997), 330.
26. Johan Schimanski, 'Crossing and Reading: Notes Towards a Theory and Method', *Nordlit* 10.1 (2010), and 'Reading Borders and Reading as Crossing Borders', in *Borders and the Changing Boundaries of Knowledge*, ed. Inga Brandall, Marie Carlson and Onver A. Cetrez (Istanbul: Svenska forskningsinstitutet I Istanbul, 2015), 91–107.
27. Konrad, 'New Directions at the Post-Globalization Border', 717–20.
28. Achille Mbembe, *Necropolitics* (Durham, NC: Duke University Press, 2019).
29. Audra Simpson, *Mohawk Interruptus: Political Life Across the Borders of Settler States* (Durham, NC: Duke University Press, 2014), 117.
30. Walter Mignolo, 'Geopolitics of Sensing and Knowing: On (De) Coloniality, Border Thinking and Epistemic Disobedience', *Postcolonial Studies* 14.3 (2011): 273–83.
31. Thomas Ptak, Jussi P. Laine, Zhiding Hu, Yuli Liu, Victor Konrad and Martin van der Velde, 'Understanding Borders Through Dynamic Processes: Capturing Relational Motion from China's Radiation Center, Yunnan Province', *Territory, Politics, Governance* 10.2 (2022): 200–18.
32. Oscar Martinez, *Border People: Life and Society in the US–Mexico Borderlands* (Tucson: University of Arizona Press, 1994).
33. Gerald Vizenor, *Native Liberty: Natural Reason and Cultural Survivance* (Lincoln: University of Nebraska Press, 2009).
34. Laine, 'Beyond Borders', 745.
35. Soja, 'Third Space'.
36. Simpson, *Mohawk Interruptus*.
37. Bruyneel, 'The Third Space of Sovereignty'.

Bibliography

Agier, Michel. *Borderlands: Towards and Anthropology of the Cosmopolitan Condition*. New York: Wiley, 2016.
Agnew, John. 'Borders on the Mind: Reframing Border Thinking'. *Ethics and Global Politics* 1.4 (2008): 175–91.
Anzaldua, Gloria. *Borderlands/La Frontera: The New Mestiza*. San Francisco, CA: Aunt Lute Books, [1987] 2012 (4th edn).
Border Policy Research Institute. 'COVID-19 and the US–Canada Border

Report 3: Impacts on the Tourism Industry in Whatcom County', Fall 2020. cedar.wwu.edu/cgi/viewcontent/.cgi?article=1123&context=bpri_publications

Brambilla, Chiara. 'Exploring the Critical Potential of the Borderscapes Concept'. *Geopolitics* 20.1 (2015): 14–34.

Brunet-Jailly, Emmanuel. 'Theorizing Borders: An Interdisciplinary Perspective'. *Geopolitics* 10 (2005): 633–49.

Bruyneel, Kevin. *The Third Space of Sovereignty: The Postcolonial Politics of U.S.-Indigenous Relations*. Minneapolis: University of Minnesota Press, 2007.

Cabrera, Guadalupe Correa and Victor Konrad, ed. *North American Borders in Comparative Perspective*. Tucson: University of Arizona Press, 2020.

Clegg, Joshua W. 'A Phenomenological Investigation of the Experience of Not Belonging'. *Journal of Phenomenological Psychology* 37.1 (2006): 53–83.

Dear, Michael. *Why Walls Won't Work: Repairing the US–Mexico Divide*. New York: Oxford, 2013.

Delgado, David Dee. 'A Highly Contagious Political Virus is Pouring over the Canada–US Border'. *The Globe and Mail*, 17 August 2022. https://theglobeandmail.com/opinion/editorials/article-a-highly-contagious-political-virus-is-pouring-over-the-canada-us/

Donnan, Hastings and D. Haller. 'Liminal No More'. *Ethnologia Europaea* 30.2 (2000): 7–22.

Ferdoush, M. A. 'Seeing Borders Through the Lens of Structuration: A Theoretical Framework'. *Geopolitics* 23.1 (2018): 180–200.

Foucault, Michel and Colin Gordon. 'Of Other Spaces: Utopias and Heterotopias' in *Rethinking Architecture: A Reader in Cultural Theory*. Ed. Neil Leach. New York Routledge, 1997. 330.

Konrad, Victor. 'New Directions at the Post-Globalization Border'. *Journal of Borderlands Studies* 36.5 (2022): 713–26.

Konrad, Victor. 'Toward a Theory of Borders in Motion'. *Journal of Borderlands Studies* 30.1 (2015): 1–18.

Konrad, Victor and Emmanuel Brunet-Jailly. 'Approaching Borders, Creating Borderland Spaces, and Exploring the Evolving Borders Between Canada and the United States'. *The Canadian Geographer/Le geographe canadien* 63.1 (2019): 4–10.

Konrad, Victor and Melissa Kelly, ed. *Borders, Culture, and Globalization: A Canadian Perspective*. Ottawa: University of Ottawa Press, 2021.

Laine, Jussi P. 'Beyond Borders: Towards the Ethics of Unbounded Inclusiveness'. *Journal of Borderlands Studies* 36.5 (2021): 745–63.

Laine, Jussi P. 'The Multiscalar Production of Borders'. *Geopolitics* 21.3 (2016): 465–82.

Marsico, Giuseppina. 'Moving Between the Social Spaces: Conditions for Boundaries Crossing' in *Crossing Boundaries: Intercontextural Dynamics Between Family and School*. Ed. G. Marsico, K. Komatsuand and A. Iannaccone. Charlotte, NC: Information Age, 2013. 361–74.

Martinez, Oscar. *Border People: Life and Society in the US–Mexico Borderlands*. Tucson: University of Arizona Press, 1994.

Mbembe, Achille. *Necropolitics*. Durham, NC: Duke University Press, 2019.

Mezzandra, Sandro and Brett Neilson. 'Between Inclusion and Exclusion: On the Topology of Global Space and Borders'. *Theory, Culture and Society* 29.4–5 (2012): 58–75.

Mignolo, Walter. 'Geopolitics of Sensing and Knowing: On (De)Coloniality, Border Thinking and Epistemic Disobedience'. *Postcolonial Studies* 14.3 (2011): 273–83.

Nail, Thomas. 'Kinopolitics: Borders in Motion'. In *Posthuman Ecologies: Complexity and Process After Deleuze*. Ed. R. Braidotti and S. Bignall. New York: Roman and Littlefield, 2019. 183–203.

Nail, Thomas. *Theory of the Border*. New York: Oxford University Press, 2016.

Newman, David. 'Borders and Power: A Theoretical Framework'. *Journal of Borderlands Studies* 18.1 (2003): 13–25.

Newman, David. 'The Lines that Continue to Separate Us: Borders in our "Borderless" World'. *Progress in Human Geography* 30.2 (2006): 143–61.

Paasi, Anssi. 'A "Border Theory": An Unattainable Dream or a Realistic Aim for Border Scholars?' In *A Research Companion for Border Studies*. Ed. D. Wastl-Walter. Aldershot: Ashgate, 2011. 11–31.

Paasi, Anssi. 'Bounded Spaces in a "Borderless World": Border Studies, Power, and the Anatomy of Territory'. *Journal of Power* 2.2 (2009): 213–34.

Parker, Noel and Nick Vaughan-Williams. *Critical Border Studies: Broadening and Deepening the 'Lines in the Sand' Agenda*. New York: Routledge, 2016.

Ptak, Thomas, Jussi P. Laine, Zhiding Hu, Yuli Liu, Victor Konrad and Martin van der Velde. 'Understanding Borders Through Dynamic Processes: Capturing Relational Motion from China's Radiation Center, Yunnan Province'. *Territory, Politics, Governance* 10.2 (2022): 200–18.

Ranciere, Jacques. *Dissensus: On Politics and Aesthetics*. London: Bloomsbury, 2015.

Salter, Mark B. 'Theory of the /: The Suture and Critical Border Studies'. *Geopolitics* 17.4 (2012): 734–55.

Schimanski, Johan. 'Crossing and Reading: Notes Towards a Theory and Method'. *Nordlit* 10.1 (2010).

Schimanski, Johan. 'Reading Borders and Reading as Crossing Borders'. In *Borders and the Changing Boundaries of Knowledge*. Ed. Inga Brandall, Marie Carlson and Onver A Cetrez. Istanbul: Svenska forskningsinstitutet I Istanbul, 2015. 91–107.

Sheren, Ila Nicole. *Portable Borders: Performance Art and Politics on the US Frontera Since 1984*. Austin: University of Texas Press, 2015.

Simpson, Audra. *Mohawk Interruptus: Political Life Across the Borders of Settler States*. Durham, NC: Duke University Press, 2014. 117.

Smith, Barry. 'Mereotopology: A Theory of Parts and Boundaries'. *Data and Knowledge Engineering* 20.3 (1996): 287–303.

Smith, Barry and Achille C. Varzi. 'Fiat and Bona Fide Boundaries'. *Philosophy and Phenomenological Research* 60.2 (2000): 401–20.

Sohn, Christophe. 'Modelling Cross-Border Integration: The Role of Borders as a Resource'. *Geopolitics* 19.4 (2014): 587–608.

Soja, Edward. 'Thirdspace: Journeys to Los Angeles and Other Real-and-Imagined Places'. *Capital and Class* 22.1 (1998): 137–9.

Trautman, Laurie D. 'The Impact of COVID-19 Test Requirements on Cross-Border Travel: A case study of Blaine WA', Winter 2022. cedar.wwu.edu/cgi/viewcontent.cgi?article=1129&context=bpri_publications

Van Houtum, Henk and Ton Van Naerssen. 'Bordering, Ordering, and Othering'. *Tijdschrift voor economischen sociale geographie* 93.2 (2002): 125–36.

Vizenor, Gerald. *Native Liberty: Natural Reason and Cultural Survivance*. Lincoln: University of Nebraska Press, 2009.

Wah, Fred. *Diamond Grill*. Edmonton, AB: NeWest Press, 1996.

Widdis, Randy. 'Looking Through the Mirror: A Historical Geographical View of the Canadian-American Borderlands'. *Journal of Borderlands Studies* 30.2 (2015): 175–88.

Yuval-Davis, Nira, Georgie Wemyss and Kathryn Cassidy. *Bordering*. New York: Wiley, 2019.

Chronology of the Canada–US Border

Treaty of Albany, 1701

The Haudenosaunee Confederacy (the Iroquois League to the French, or the Iroquois Confederacy to the English) is one of the dominant Indigenous political organisations in the Great Lakes region. Because of France's alliance with the Huron, Algonquins, Montagnais and Abenaki, and the inability of the Haudenosaunee to access French trade, the Haudenosaunee initiate trade and alliances with Dutch merchants, and later with the British along the Hudson River (now in New York, USA). Through the Covenant Chain agreements, the Haudenosaunee and the British form a military alliance that lasts into the nineteenth century. This alliance assists Great Britain's colonial wars against the French and helps the Haudenosaunee to control much of the fur trade. With new weapons, the Iroquois set out to disrupt Huron control of the fur trade. These raids persist until 1701 when France, its Indigenous allies and the Haudenosaunee sign a treaty at Montreal known as the Great Peace. Through the agreement, the different Indigenous groups in the Great Lakes end attacks and share land, as if it were 'a dish with two spoons'. In a masterful stroke of colonial geopolitics, the Haudenosaunee Confederacy not only assures itself a stable peace with the other Indigenous people of the area, but it also secures British protection for those same lands and interests. Just prior to the conference at Montreal in 1701, Haudenosaunee leaders, who had gone to Albany, New York, agree to sell all the lands of the Great Lakes to the British in exchange for their protection and continued right to hunt and fish throughout the territory. Through two diplomatic manoeuvres, the Confederacy has gained protection from French attack, promises of British defence and access to the rich fur lands of the Great Lakes (Indigenous and Northern Affairs Canada).

The Formation of the Six Nations, 1720s

The five nations (Cayuga, Mohawk, Oneida, Onondaga and Seneca) of the Haudenosaunee accept the Tuscarora people of the south-east (present-day Ontario and New York), completing a political power structure that began in approximately 1142 and extends from north of the Great Lakes, east into the St. Lawrence valley, south to the Ohio valley and Allegheny mountains, and into New York. The six nations play a pivotal part in the British and French colonial wars that define the Canada–US border and continue to resist the imposition of colonial power structures over their traditional territories and rights (Indigenous and Northern Affairs Canada).

Execution of Marie-Josèphe (dite Angélique), 21 June 1734

Marie-Josèphe Angélique is convicted of setting fire to her owner's home in a failed escape attempt, resulting in the burning of much of what is now Old Montreal in modern-day Quebec. She is hanged for arson after being tortured for information and eventually confessing under duress. Born into slavery around 1700 in Madeira, she is brought to New England, and sold in 1725 to French businessman François Poulin de Francheville, whose house she is accused of burning. The circumstances of her trial and the evidence of her guilt are widely questioned. The early North American slave trade often includes transactions between colonies.

Settlement of Akwesasne, 1755 and Borderlands First Nations

From 1755, Mohawk families begin a new settlement at what the French called St. Regis, spanning the St. Lawrence River. Following the American Revolutionary War, this leaves them straddling the international boundary. Although the Mohawk still refer to the whole land base and community as Akwesasne, it is officially split into the Akwesasne Reserve in Quebec and Ontario and the St. Regis Mohawk Reservation in New York.

A number of other tribal nations are located on lands that straddle what becomes the Canada–US border, including the Ojibwe, Odawa, Lakota, the nations of the Wabanaki Confederacy, Colville, Salish, and others; and, on the Alaska–Canada border, the Haida, Tlingit and Tsimshian. While the Haudenosaunee are effectively placed on the border as a buffer, in the west the Blackfoot/Blackfeet are deliberately separated. The Blackfoot Indian Reservation in Montana is formed by treaty in 1855 on traditional territories, extending right up to the 49th parallel. Concerned about the vulnerabilities this posed to the international boundary, the Kainai/Blood (Blackfeet) reserve in Alberta, established under Treaty 7 (1877), has its southern boundary set in 1883, fourteen miles north of the Medicine Line.

The Royal Proclamation, 1763

After the Seven Year' War, Britain is the primary European power throughout much of North America and controls the fur trade. The British understand, however, that the success of their American colonies depends on stable and peaceful relations with First Nations people. In 1763, a Royal Proclamation is issued to announce how the colonies will be administered and establishes a firm western boundary for the colonies. All the lands to the west become the 'Indian Territories' where there can be no settlement nor trade without the permission of the Indian Department. It is strictly controlled by the British Military.

The Proclamation also establishes very strict protocols for all dealings with First Nations people. The Indian Department is to be the primary point of contact between First Nations people and the colonies. Furthermore, only the Crown can purchase land from First Nations people by officially sanctioned representatives meeting with the interested First Nations people in a public meeting. The Royal Proclamation becomes the first public recognition of First Nations rights to lands and title (Indigenous and Northern Affairs Canada).

The Treaty of Niagara, 1764

Although this treaty is not tied to the border explicitly, it signals the accession of twenty-four Indigenous nations to the principles of the Royal Proclamation and effectively settles the ongoing relationship between the Crown and those nations that were situated in the territories north of what will eventually be the border between Canada's eastern provinces and the USA's north-eastern and upper mid-western states.

Invasion of Montreal, 1775

American revolutionaries invade Montreal. They are defeated and pushed back at the Battle of Quebec one month later.

Southern Ontario Land Sales, 1781 onwards

Towards the end of the American Revolutionary War, the British begin purchasing tracts of land from the Mississaugas (Anishinaabeg people whose traditional lands were situated along the shores of Lake Superior and northern Lake Huron, and who later settled at the mouth of the Credit River/Lake Ontario). They intend to grant portions of this land to loyalists, including Indigenous loyalists such as Mohawk Chief Joseph Brant's Haudenosaunee followers. The remainder is crucial to settlement and new farming production.

The Treaty of Paris, 1783

This treaty ends the American War of Independence and defines the boundary between the newly established United States of America and the British colonies in North America from the 'mouth of the St. Croix River in the Bay of Fundy' to the north-westernmost point of Lake of the Woods, and thence due west to the Mississippi River and down that river. The British Crown cedes all its territories south of the Great Lakes to the United States. As the treaty makes no mention of Britain's Native American allies, the USA has to negotiate separate peace agreements with each of the nations. The important issues to be settled include not only peace, but also the ownership of vast tracts of land which the United States considers to be under its control by the British cession.

The Treaty of Fort Stanwix and The Haldimand Proclamation, 1784

The Treaty of Fort Stanwix is signed between delegates of the Six Nations Confederacy and the new American government as the British, effectively abandoning their Indigenous allies, cede their former lands in the Treaty of Paris and withdraw. (It should be noted that Canadian-based Haudenosaunee, though reforming their connections to the Confederacy during the war, remain neutral.) The treaty makes allowance for those Haudenosaunee who had either remained in or returned to their traditional lands and were now in conflict with settlers. The Haudenosaunee end up relinquishing all claims to the Ohio region as well as land along the banks of the Niagara River, and elsewhere. Although the Six Nations Council refuses to ratify the treaty, it significantly weakens the Confederacy in the US. In response, the Haldimand Proclamation, delivered three days later, is a decree issued by the Governor of the Province of Quebec, Frederic Haldimand, granting a tract of land to the Haudenosaunee who were loyal to the Crown during the American Revolutionary War and consequently find themselves unwelcome in the original thirteen colonies. Brant and others had secured a promise from the Crown to continued possession of the Mohawk Valley (in present-day New York State) in 1775, a promise that the Treaty of Fort Stanwix erases. Some eight years later, in 1783, they effectively choose this tract of land, which had to be purchased from the Mississauga.

Slave Trade Abolished in Upper Canada, 1793

The Parliament of Upper Canada (now Ontario) abolishes the slave trade, but not slavery, in its second legislative session, and decrees that all children born to female slaves would be freed at the age of twenty-five. (*An Act to Prevent the further Introduction of Slaves and to Limit the Term of Contracts for Servitude* (also known as the *Act to Limit Slavery in Upper Canada*).)

The Treaty of Amity, Commerce, and Navigation, Between His Britannic Majesty and the United States of America (The Jay Treaty), 1794

On 19 November 1794, the United States and Great Britain sign the Treaty of Amity, Commerce, and Navigation – the Jay Treaty – which establishes a Joint Commission to settle boundary disputes, re-establishes American trade with the West Indies, guarantees British evacuation of forts in the old north-west and recognises tribal rights vis-à-vis the border. Article three affirms that the border is to be non-existent for Indigenous nations:

> It is agreed that it shall at all times be free ... to the Indians dwelling on either side of the said boundary line, freely to pass and repass by land or inland navigation, into the respective territories and countries of the two parties, on the continent of America ... and freely to carry on trade and commerce with each other.
>
> [N]or shall the Indians passing or repassing with their own proper goods and effects of whatever nature, pay for the same any impost or duty whatever. But goods in bales, or other large packages, unusual among Indians, shall not be considered as goods belonging bona fide to Indians.

The rights of free passage guaranteed in the Jay Treaty are reaffirmed between the two countries two years later, although actual border-crossing problems and interpretive disagreements persist to the present day.

Louisiana Purchase, 1803

The United States purchases Louisiana from the French Crown. The watershed between the Hudson Bay and the Mississippi/Missouri Rivers is used to establish the northern border for the newly purchased lands.

The War of 1812, 1812–1814

The United States declares war on Great Britain and invades its nearest colonial holding, Upper Canada. US forces are defeated at the Siege of Detroit, aided by the forces of Tecumseh. British forces land near Washington DC, burning the US Capitol and the Presidential Palace (which is rebuilt, and the burn marks painted over, providing its nickname, The Whitehouse).

The Treaty of Ghent, 1814

This treaty ends the War of 1812 and provides that Commissioners should decide the sovereignty of the several islands in Passamoquoddy Bay, that they should determine the 'northwest angle of Nova Scotia' and the north-west head of Connecticut River, and that a map should be made depicting the boundary. Articles VI and VII provide that the Commissioners should decide the boundary from the 45th parallel to the north-westernmost point of Lake of the Woods. Under this treaty, an agreement is reached upon part of the boundary, but parts of the line through St. Mary's River and at the head of Lake Superior are not agreed upon. While the Treaty of Ghent supersedes the Jay Treaty for relations between the US and the British, the matter of its applicability to Indigenous peoples remains contested, in part because the Jay Treaty includes them in its negotiation and text, whereas the Treaty of Ghent does not.

Rush-Bagot Treaty, 1817

The Rush-Bagot Treaty of 1817 provides a plan for demilitarising the two combatant sides in the War of 1812, particularly by ending a naval arms race on the Great Lakes. It also sets down preliminary principles for border delineation between British North America (later Canada) and the United States.

London Convention, 1818

The 49th north parallel is established by the London Convention as the border that separates what will become, after 1867, the Canadian Provinces of Manitoba, Saskatchewan, Alberta and British Columbia, from the US states of Minnesota, North Dakota, Montana, Idaho and Washington. Westward expansion on both sides of the line sees the boundary extended long the 49th parallel under the Treaty of 1818 (from the North-west Angle to the Rocky

Mountains). British claims south of that latitude to the Red River Valley are extinguished.

Indian Removal Policy, 1830

The US government votes to remove Indigenous people east of the Mississippi Valley. The Anishinaabe in the Canada–US border regions are particularly affected by the legislation.

Abolition of Slavery in the British Empire, 1833

Parliament abolishes slavery in all territories of the British Empire except for Ceylon (modern Sri Lanka) and St Helena, which are controlled by the British East India Company. The Act marks the beginning of an effective break in territorial and legal approaches towards slavery between the Canadas and associated colonies, and the United States of America. In effect, the Canada–US border becomes an end point destination of the Underground Railroad for escaping American slaves.

1837–8 Patriot War

Two serious insurrections associated with political reform occur in Lower and Upper Canada, in 1837 and 1838. Many of the rebels, having been aided by US counterparts who saw an opportunity to annex the country, flee to the USA. These incidents lead to the British North America Act, 1840, which abolishes the legislatures of Lower and Upper Canada, replacing them with the unitary Province of Canada. During this period numerous raids by sympathisers and Canadian refugees, members of a secretive group known as The Hunter's Lodge, are made from the US into Canada along the border.

The Webster-Ashburton Treaty, 1842

The United States rejects several treaty attempts to settle the boundary of the north-eastern United States, and so it is not until the Webster-Ashburton Treaty of 1842 that an agreement is reached on the boundary from the source of the St. Croix River to the St. Lawrence River. The treaty also determines those sections of the boundary through the St. Mary's River to the north-westernmost point of Lake of the Woods, which had not been settled following the Treaty of Ghent.

The Oregon Treaty, 1846

This treaty extends the boundary from the summit of the Rockies westward along the 49th parallel to the Strait of Georgia and south and west through Juan de Fuca Strait to the Pacific. Disagreement as to part of the water boundary through the straits leads to arbitration and an award by the Emperor of Germany, which is formally accepted in the protocol of 1873.

1849 Montreal Annexation Manifesto

See entry below.

1850 Annexation Attempt

Around 1850 there is an attempt by the American-descended communities of Quebec's eastern townships to force union with the USA, not least in order to limit the growing power of the French Canadian polity. This is not intended to be an act of disloyalty to Britain but reflects a growing distance from the imperial heartlands and sympathy with the Annexation Association, formed in 1849 by British and French-Canadian participants in the 1837–8 rebellions, and which had drawn up the Montreal Annexation Manifesto, which sought closer economic ties and subsequent development opportunities under US influence.

1854 Canadian-American Reciprocity Treaty (Elgin-Marcy Treaty)

The treaty develops from the annexation attempts described above, covering British-US trade broadly, and assures economic cooperation between the Province of Canada (particularly its resources) and the USA (particularly its markets). It is in operation until 1866 when it is defeated by long-antagonistic protectionist groups in the US which manage to leverage concern about implicit British support of the Confederate states.

James Douglas Serves as First Governor of British Columbia, 1858–64

James Douglas is appointed first Governor of the new British colony of British Columbia. Governor Douglas' mother, Martha Ann Ritchie, who was born in Guyana (Demarara), is Creole of mixed Black and white ancestry; his wife, Lady Amelia Connolly Douglas, is Métis, of Cree and French-Irish background.

First Governmentally Sanctioned Settlement of African Americans in Western Canada, 1858

An estimated 600 to 800 African Americans migrate from California to Vancouver Island and Salt Spring Island, to escape discriminatory US laws preventing them from owning property and requiring them to wear badges. The group is granted settlement rights by James Douglas.

1860s Annexation Petitions

British confidence in the future of the western provinces of British North America is low, with many agreeing with American predictions that Canada would ultimately join the US. This becomes particularly pronounced after the US purchase of Alaska, with views evenly divided in British Columbia over whether they should accept annexation. Ultimately, they opt for confederacy with Canada, but petitions in 1867 (to Queen Victoria) and 1869 (to Ulysses S. Grant) attempt to steer a different course.

1866 Annexation Bill

A bill calling for the annexation of British North America is put before Congress on 2 July 1866, but it never comes to a ratifying vote.

Fenian Raids on Upper Canada, 1866 and 1870–1

Militias fighting against British colonial power in Ireland invade Upper Canada as a means of attacking British colonial policy. The actions help motivate the Canadian colonies to Confederate for self-protection.

Canadian Independence from Great Britain, 1867

The Dominion of Canada obtains independence from Great Britain, bringing the three colonies of Canada, Nova Scotia and New Brunswick into a single Confederation that will use the old British North America Act as the basis for many of its laws. The first Prime Minister, Sir John A. Macdonald, pushes for the westward expansion of a national railroad, in part to guard against US expansionism.

Alaska Purchase, 1867

Russia sells Alaska to the USA, precipitating a UK–Canada–USA disagreement about the coastal boundary of the territory.

British Columbia Joins Confederation, 1871

Following Manitoba's formation and membership of the Dominion, and membership of the newly acquired Northwest Territories in 1870, British Columbia joins the Canadian confederation, effectively putting an end to the concerted annexation attempts of the 1860s.

Battle of The Greasy Grass/Little Big Horn, 1876

Sitting Bull and his followers decamp from the territory of the USA into Canada, following their defeat of the US 7th Cavalry under the command of General George Custer during the Great Sioux War. The move is one of numerous Indigenous uses of the so-called 'Medicine Line' as a means of evading or countering nation state power structures.

Prosper Bender's Treatise on Annexation, 1883

In an 1883 article in the *North American Review*, Canadian author Prosper Bender pontificates about the unwieldy costs of the transcontinental railroad promised by John A. Macdonald and asserts the inevitability of favourable annexation by the US.

Canada and the Canadian Question, 1891

Picking up on Bender's theme, Goldwin Smith predicts the inevitability of annexation and urges Canadians to welcome it. Like Bender's, his views do not appear to be popular.

Convention of 1892

By a convention in 1892 the boundary line is laid down through the islands in Passamoquoddy Bay and a provision is made for a joint survey of the Alaskan boundary from Portland Canal to the 141st meridian (International Boundary Commission).

Sir John Thompson's Anti-annexation Speech, 1893

Attempting to turn back what appeared to be a tide of enthusiasm for annexation driven by the Continental Union Association, Prime Minister Thompson delivers a speech on Canadian nationalism and British loyalty.

The Alaska Tribunal Award, 1898

With the Klondike gold rush in 1898, the Alaskan boundary becomes a problematic issue. By mutual agreement, in 1899 a provisional boundary is laid down above the head of Lynn Canal and across the Chilkoot and White Passes. In 1903 a convention between the two countries results in the creation of the Alaska Boundary Tribunal to resolve the Southeast Alaska boundary question.

In 1905 a short section of the south-east Alaska boundary, undefined by the Award, and subsequently agreed upon by the Commissioners, is formally accepted by both countries in an exchange of notes (International Boundary Commission).

Many Canadian observers at the time feel the process has been unfair, and there are accusations that the US has bribed the British Commissioner. The dispute marks an early moment in which Canadians begin to define their national interests in opposition to those of the UK.

The Americanization of the World, 1901

London newspaper editor W. T. Stead muses in the above book on the inevitability of Canadian annexation by the US. In fact, public feeling will pull in the opposite direction after gold is discovered in the Yukon, with calls for annexation of parts of Alaska through revision of the original map of the boundary line between the Russian Empire and the US. Arbitration is sought.

Boundary Resolution, 1903

In response to the above demands, the Chief Justice of Britain sides with the US and the boundary map is resolved in favour of the American claims.

Survey of Alaska–Canada Border Begins, 1904

This work is finally completed in 1914. Sections of the sea border remain unresolved, where the USA insists that it falls 20 km south of the line of the land border. This line cuts across Dixon Entrance, a particularly resource-rich stretch of sea between Alaska and the Queen Charlotte Islands (renamed as Haida Gwaii in the 2010 Haida Gwaii Reconciliation Act).

The Boundary Treaty, 1908

In 1908, a treaty is signed which provides for the more complete demarcation of the boundary from the Atlantic to the Pacific and the preparation of accurate modern charts throughout. Although the land sections of the boundary had been marked by monuments, mounds or rock cairns, the water boundary has hitherto been marked on the charts prepared by former Commissioners only as a curved line through the various rivers and lakes on its course, and it has not been shown at all on the chart of the St. Croix River. In the treaty of 1908, a provision is made to suitably mark the water boundary by buoys, monuments and ranges and in such other ways as the Commissioners deem fitting. The terms of the treaty are to be carried out on each of the various sections of the boundary under the direction of two Commissioners, one to be appointed by each country. For the St. Lawrence River and Great Lakes section, however, the work is undertaken by the International Waterways Commission (now defunct), which has a membership of three Commissioners from each country.

Treaty of 1910

By a treaty in 1910, the boundary is defined through Passamaquoddy Bay to a point in the middle of Grand Manan Channel.

Canada Enters the First World War as part of the British Empire, 1914

Canada declares war on Germany and Austro-Hungary as part of the British Empire. The United States remains neutral until 1917.

Levi General – Deskaheh – Attempts to Speak before the League of Nations, 1923–4

Although not a border issue specifically, the border plays a role in the movements of Six Nations of the Grand River Chief Deskaheh in the early 1920s, as he traverses it numerous times in his dealings with attorney George P. Decker, and in his ultimate failure to cross it as he spent his final days on the Tuscarora Reservation in upper New York State. His is also the first use of a Haudenosaunee passport in 1921. Seeking League of Nations intervention in disputes between the Haudenosaunee, Canada, and Great Britain, Deskaheh and Decker travelled to Geneva in 1923, where Deskaheh conducts a series of lectures throughout Switzerland, although he does not succeed in his ambition to speak before the League of Nations. Returning to the US he lives out his final months in Rochester, NY, with Chief Clinton Rickard on the Tuscarora Reservation.

Indian Defense League, 1925–6

As he is dying, Deskaheh calls for his medicine man from Six Nations. As the man does not speak English, he falls foul of the USA's new Immigration Law (1924) that prevents non-English speakers from entering the country. On his deathbed, Deskaheh is reported to have told Rickard to 'fight for the line'. The latter establishes the Indian Defense League (IDL) to advance the right to unrestricted Indigenous travel across the Canada–US border. A statue of Rickard stands in Niagara Falls State Park. The IDL has held annual free border-crossing rallies at the Niagara Falls crossing since 1928.

Treaty of 1925

The 1925 Treaty makes minor adjustments to the boundary line at Grand Manan Channel, at the north-westernmost point of Lake of the Woods, and on the 49th parallel, where the boundary is changed from a slightly curved line between monuments to a series of straight lines. In this treaty, a provision is made for the continued maintenance of the international boundary by the Commissioners appointed under the Treaty of 1908, and by their successors. One of its responsibilities is maintenance of the Peace Arch, which was built on the exact line between the two nations, in Washington State in the United States and British Columbia in Canada. On the US side, the monument reads 'Children of a Common Mother', and on the Canadian side 'Brethren Dwelling together in Unity' (International Boundary Commission).

Trail Smelter Controversy Begins, 1927

Pollution from the smelter in Trail, eastern British Columbia, reaches Washington state, precipitating a cross-border environmental complaint eventually resolved in 1941.

Aird Royal Commission Formed to Study Broadcasting in Canada and the Ku Klux Klan Influences the Saskatchewan Election, 1929

Prime Minister Mackenzie King's government forms the commission which will eventually develop rules on Canadian content and broadcast protection (1933) administered by the CRTC. Separately the same year, the Ku Klux Klan, which had appeared in Canada in 1921, brought down the Saskatchewan provincial government having gained roughly 25,000 members in the province. After an embezzlement trial in 1927, it severed all ties with the American Klan, and emphasised its purpose to keep Canada British (Pitsula).

Opening of The Ambassador Bridge between Detroit, Michigan and Windsor, Ontario, 1929

The bridge is still the largest single conduit of Canada–US trade, and the busiest single border crossing. It carries approximately 25 per cent of Canada–US trade each year (Detroit Historical Society).

The Border Patrol Placed Under Authority of Two Directors, 1932

One director was located in El Paso, Texas, the other in Detroit. The majority of the Border Patrol at this time was placed on the Canada–US border, where liquor smuggling was a priority.

Also in this year, the peace garden on the border between North Dakota and Manitoba is established.

Auto Workers Reach Across the Border: Oshawa, Ontario, 1937

Having established a local chapter of the American Federation of Labor, Trades and Labor Congress (AFL, TLC) at the General Motors plant in Oshawa, Ontario in 1928, workers stage walkouts in February 1937 in response to pay cuts and increases in assembly targets. Workers contact the United Auto Workers (UAW) in Detroit, Michigan, and a local chapter of UAW is formed. Further strikes in April lead to a resolution in which GM accedes to an eight-hour day, a wage increase and improved working conditions.

Canada Declares War on Germany, 1939

Canada declares war in support of the United Kingdom. The United States remains neutral until the attack on Pearl Harbor in 1941.

St Pierre and Miquelon Liberated by General Charles de Gaulle, 1941

Vice Admiral Émile Henry Muselier liberates two tiny islands in the Gulf of St. Lawrence from nominal Vichy French control, on the orders of General Charles de Gaulle. The action, launched from Halifax, Nova Scotia, is largely symbolic, but is carried out against the wishes of the US State Department, which is attempting to maintain US neutrality. The islands are vestige territories, retained after French defeat by the British.

Alaska Highway Construction and Canadian Governmental Jurisdiction, 1942–6

The US begins building a highway to Alaska, much of which necessarily runs through Canada. The highway is eventually turned over to Canadian jurisdiction.

Newfoundland Joins the Confederacy as Tenth Province, 1949

Not a border event per se, this nevertheless comes after much activity by the Economic Union Party in pursuit of annexation by the US.

Korean War, 1950–3

Canada and the US send military forces (roughly 26,000 and 36,000 respectively) to fight for the UN in the Korean War.

Canada Council Created, 1957

The Canada Council, a federal body for the promotion of Canadian culture, is formed on the recommendation of the Massey Commission (formally titled The Royal Commission on National Development in the Arts, Letters and Sciences).

St. Lawrence Seaway Opens, 1959

After decades of negotiation, the joint US–Canada project, the St. Lawrence Seaway, is completed and opened.

Columbia River Treaty Signed, 1961

The Columbia River Treaty codifies water rights and use in the Columbia River, a major source of American water and energy production.

Merchant–Heeney Commission, 1964

Prime Minister Pearson and President Johnson form the Merchant–Heeney commission to study Canadian–American relations.

Vietnam War Draft Resisters Head to Canada, 1965

From 1965, Canada becomes the haven of choice for American draft resisters and deserters. After May 1969 the Canadian authorities no longer allow immigration officials to ask the military status of American immigrants. During this same period, some 30,000 Canadians volunteer for the American military.

Mohawk Arrests at the International Border, 1968

In December 1968, Canadian police arrested forty-one Mohawk protestors who had blocked the Seaway International Bridge in protest against failures to uphold the Jay Treaty.

US and North Vietnam Sign a Peace Agreement, 1973

Canada serves on the International Commission of Control and Supervision, ensuring the treaty is respected. Canada also contributes peacekeeping forces.

Mohawk Occupation of Moss Lake Camp for Girls, 1974–5

On 13 May 1974, a large group of Mohawks from both the US and Canada take over the disused 612-acre camp in the Adirondack Mountains in New York, renaming it Ganienkeh.

American Diplomats Rescued by Canadian Embassy in Tehran, 1979–81

Known as the 'Canadian Caper', the rescue of six US diplomats from Tehran involves the Canadian government, the CIA and the British Embassy. Islamist students seeking the return and trial of the US-backed Shah after the Iranian Revolution enter the US embassy on 4 November 1979 and take most of its personnel hostage. The six – four men and two women – avoid capture and are sheltered by the British mission and Canadian diplomats before spending the remainder of their ordeal split between Canadian immigration officer John Sheardown's home, the official residence of Canadian Ambassador Ken Taylor and his wife, and the houses of Swedish Ambassador Kaj Sundberg and Swedish Consul Cecilia Lithander. In January 1980, using Canadian passports and forged entry documents, and disguised as a film crew, the diplomats accompanied by two CIA operatives are smuggled through the Mehrabad airport and flown to Zurich. The remaining hostages in Iran are held until 1981. The Canadians involved in the rescue are appointed to the Order of Canada. One British official involved is given honorary membership of the order, while Canadian Ambassador Ken Taylor is awarded the Congressional Gold Medal by the US.

Annexation Movements and the 1st Quebec Referendum, 1980s

The 1980s annexation arguments are led by the Unionist Party in Saskatchewan and Parti 51 in Quebec. Both seek provincial annexation with the US, but both were short-lived. Separately in Quebec, the Sovereignty Association referendum for secession from Canada, pushed by Parti Quebec, is defeated by 59.56 per cent to 40.44 per cent.

Indigenous Protest at the Canada–US Border, 1986–2013

According to the Indigenous Borderlands and Border Rites project, there have been regular protests, ceremonies and celebrations at a number of border-crossing sites including the Rainbow Bridge, Niagara Falls, the North Channel Bridge at Massena, the Seaway International Bridge and the Sault Ste. Marie International Bridge since 1986, in addition to the annual gathering at the Rainbow Bridge organised by the Indian Defense League. In 2009, protests formed among Mohawk against the arming of border guards on Cornwall Island, part of Akwesasne territory.

Free Trade Agreement (FTA) Takes Effect, 1989

After six years of negotiation, the Canada–US Free Trade Agreement comes into force.

The Oka Crisis, 1990

Mohawk communities and activists protest the proposed building of a golf course on an ancestral burial ground at Oka, Quebec. They are joined by activists and warriors from other Indigenous groups across Canada and the US. At its peak, 600 armed Mohawk warriors face officers of the Sûreté du Québec and the Royal 22nd Regiment of the Canadian Armed Forces.

North American Free Trade Agreement (NAFTA) Takes Effect, 1994

The trilateral trade agreement between the US, Canada and Mexico supersedes the FTA.

Operation Gatekeeper, 1 October 1994

Under Bill Clinton's administration, Operation Gatekeeper launches with additional funds allocated to Border Patrol in an effort to seal off the section of the Mexico–US border near San Diego. Although not directly related to the Canada–US border, it saw a major increase in the funding of the Border Patrol nationally.

September 11 Attacks, 2001

In the aftermath of terrorist attacks on the United States, Canada offers support for Americans stranded abroad, and agrees to strengthened joint border security measures. Much emphasis was placed on the Canada–US border as an 'easy' entry point for potential terrorists (to both Canada and the US).

USA PATRIOT Act, October 2001

The Act *Uniting and Strengthening America by Providing Appropriate Tools Required to Intercept and Obstruct Terrorism* was enacted in direct response to the 9/11 attacks. It saw the strengthening of surveillance, greater efficiency in interagency communications, and higher penalties for terrorist acts. It allows for the indefinite detention without trial of immigrants. It effectively tripled the number of Border Patrol, customs service, and Immigration and Naturalization Service (INS) personnel along the Canada–US border.

NEXUS and FAST, 2002

Established as a pilot project at the Port Huron-Sarnia border crossing in 2000, NEXUS is formally launched in 2002, enabling fast-track border screening between the US and Canada and the US and Mexico (for Mexican holders of Viajero Confiable status). The Free and Safe Trade (FAST) process launches at the same time.

Safe Third Country Agreement, 2004

Entered into force in December 2004, the Safe Third Country Agreement (STCA) is a treaty that was signed two years earlier between Canada and the USA. Under the agreement, persons seeking refugee status from outside North America must stake their claim in the first of the two countries in which they arrive, unless they meet an exception under the STCA.

REAL ID Act, 2005

Among other measures, the REAL ID Act establishes new federal standards for state-issued drivers' licences and ID cards, funds some pilot projects into border security, and waives laws that prevent the erection of physical barriers at border sites.

Western Hemisphere Travel Initiative, 2007

The USA introduces the WHTI, which insists that all travellers must show a valid passport, or other approved ID when entering the US from anywhere in the Western Hemisphere. For Canadians this means a passport, provincial driving licence, or FAST or NEXUS card.

Beyond the Border Program Established, 2011

Canada and the US develop a joint border security programme with increased use of technology and surveillance as a means of facilitating trade while controlling the movement of people.

Idle No More, 2013

Indigenous grassroots movement Idle No More's many cross-border impacts include border-site activity. On 16 January 2013, for instance, as part of a national day of action, protestors gather near the Ambassador Bridge in Windsor, Ontario and slow down traffic heading towards the border for several hours. Given the importance of this crossing, the disruption was significant.

The Grandmothers Statement, 2015

Coming out of the Wabanaki Confederacy Conference, this declaration comprises a series of statements pertaining to the revitalisation of the Confederacy's Lodge – a 'living constitution and decision-making structure of the Confederacy'. Given the composition of the Confederacy, which is made up of the five nations of Mi'kmaq, Maliseet, Passamaquoddy, Abenaki and Penobscot, this is a necessarily cross-border arrangement. The declaration, significantly in this context, includes a commitment to 'establish decolonized maps of our traditional territories'.

Revival of Parti 51, 2016

Hans Mercier revived the annexationist Parti 51, arguing that Quebec could become a US state. They secured 0.03 per cent of the popular vote in the 2018 Quebec provincial election.

Refugee Movement to Canada, 2017

As a result of stricter US policies regarding refugee and asylum claims, immigrants begin walking across the Canada–US border. The first groups of immigrants arrive in winter, and many are severely injured by frostbite and exposure. This becomes known as the 'border-crossing crisis'.

Tariff Imposition and NAFTA Renegotiation, 2018–19

In March 2018 the United States levies tariffs of up to 25 per cent on numerous Canadian products, with a special focus on aluminium and steel products, using an executive order under the auspices of national security. Canada responds with retaliatory tariffs on American products. The tariffs are removed as part of a joint renegotiation of the North American Free Trade Agreement in May 2019.

Border Protests and Blockades in Support of Wet'suwet'en, 16 and 17 February, 2020

On 16 February 2020, hundreds of protestors hold a protest at the Rainbow International Bridge crossing in Niagara Falls in support of the Wet'suwet'en hereditary chiefs and their opposition to Coastal GasLight's pipeline construction across unceded lands in British Columbia. The following day, protesters actively blockade the Thousand Islands crossing near Kingston, Ontario.

Softwood Lumber Tariffs, 1982–2020

Softwood lumber disputes have rumbled on since the early 1980s when the US lumber industry press for tariffs to be applied to cheaper Canadian imports. In 1982, 'Lumber I' ends with the US Department of Commerce (DoC) finding that Canadian lumber did not put US producers at a disadvantage. In 1986, 'Lumber II' is initiated when the US Coalition for Fair Lumber Imports petitions the Department of Commerce again. This time their case is successful, and a 15 per cent import duty is imposed on Canadian lumber. 'Lumber III' begins in 1991 with Canada announcing its withdrawal from the Memorandum of Understanding drawn up under 'Lumber II'. The DoC resolved in 1992 to impose a countervailing duty of 6.51 per cent. A binational panel set up under the terms of the Canada–USA FTA agreement reviews the outcome and found the decision lacking in substantiating evidence of a subsidy on the Canadian side. In 1996, the Softwood Lumber Agreement ended this phase of the dispute with a five-year trade agreement. 'Lumber IV' begins in 2001 when the Softwood Lumber Agreement runs out. In 2002, the DoC imposes a combined duty of 27.22 per cent. By 2003, 15,000 Canadian lumber workers have been laid off and the

WTO has become involved – ultimately finding in Canada's favour. 'Lumber IV' eventually resulted in a new softwood lumber agreement, which expired in 2015, reigniting the dispute. In 2017, the Trump administration announces average tariffs of 24 per cent on Canadian lumber, challenged by Canada under NAFTA and escalated once again to the WTO in 2018. In August 2020, the WTO rules that the US incorrectly determined that Canada was improperly subsidising lumber.

COVID-19, 2020–21

In March, Canada and the USA move to restrict all non-essential travel across the international border in order to limit the spread of the novel coronavirus.

Challenge to the Safe Third Country Agreement, 2020

In July 2020, a Canadian Federal Court declares the STCA invalid, arguing that its compulsion that asylum seekers who arrive in the USA and then seek to enter Canada should return to the USA to file their claim contravenes their human rights. The ruling determines that current immigration practices under the Trump administration mean that the USA does not qualify as a 'safe' country, thus violating Canada's Charter of Rights.

Colville Confederated Tribes Recognised by Canadian High Court, 2021

On Friday 23 April 2021, the Canadian High Court recognised the Colville Confederated Tribes in Washington State as successors to the Sinixt, thus acknowledging their constitutionally protected rights to hunt in the traditional territories of the Sinixt in British Columbia. The case ended a dispute that dates back to 1955, when the Sinixt were pushed across the border into Washington and subsequently declared extinct (Cecco).

AntiVax Protests, February 2022

Anti-vaccination protesters, the so-called 'freedom convoy', briefly shut down three major border-crossing points at the Ambassador

Bridge, Ontario; Emerson, Manitoba; and Coutts, Alberta in February 2022.

Bibliography

Canada, Indigenous and Northern Affairs. Treaty of Albany, 1701. https://www.aadnc-aand c.gc.ca/eng/1314977704533/1314977734895.

Cecco, Leyland. '"An indescribable moment": Indigenous Nation in US has Right to Lands in Canada, Court Rules'. 2021. Accessed 25 April 2021. https://www.theguardian.com/world/2021/apr/25/indigenous-people-canada-sinixt-us-border-hunting-rights?fbclid=IwAR1Etg5nflSzFe_n 68Q9ucX2XJkPmXnVKfzCI6VwFtOkOc1ckOpRDLmzQjM

Detroit Historical Society. 'Ambassador Bridge'. 2018. Accessed 8 February 2020. https://detroithistorical.org/learn/encyclopedia-of-detroit/ambassador-bridge

International Boundary Commission. 2015. http://www.internationalboundarycommission.org/en/

Pitsula, James M. *Keeping Canada British: The Ku Klux Klan in 1920s Saskatchewan.* Vancouver: University of British Columbia Press, 2014.

Author Biographies

Pierre-Alexandre Beylier is an Associate Professor at Université Grenoble-Alpes/ILCEA4, specialising in North American studies. In 2013, he completed a PhD at Université Paris 3-Sorbonne Nouvelle entitled 'The Canada/US Border Since 9/11: Continuity and Change'. His book, *Canada/Etats-Unis: les Enjeux d'une Frontière*, was published in May 2016.

Victor Konrad is Adjunct Research Professor at Carleton University in Ottawa. He has devoted his career to higher education advancement and development between these neighbouring countries. His research is centred on the transfer of culture across borders, and he has published extensively about Native American encounters with Europeans, cultural landscape transitions, and Canada–US borderlands. Professor Konrad has taught at universities in the United States and Canada, and from 1980 to 1990 he served as Director of the Canadian-American Center at the University of Maine.

Chris LaLonde is Professor at SUNY Oswego in the Department of Cinema and Screen Studies. He is author of *William Faulkner and the Rites of Passage* (1996) and *Grave Concerns, Trickster Turns: The Novels of Louis Owens* (2002) as well as numerous essays on Anishinaabeg writing.

Tanis MacDonald is the author of *Straggle: Adventures in Walking While Female* (2022), *The Daughter's Way: Canadian Women's Paternal Elegies* (2012: finalist for the Gabrielle Roy Prize in Canadian literary criticism), and four books of poetry, the latest of which is *Mobile* (2018). Her work on poetry, publics, and the elegy has appeared in the collections *Public Poetics*, *The Oxford Handbook of Canadian Literature*, *Material Cultures in Canada*, and *Canadian Literature and Cultural Memory*, and in the journals

Literature and Philosophy, *Studies in Canadian Literature*, *Atlantis*, *Canadian Literature*, and *Canadian Poetry*. She is Professor in the Department of English and Film Studies at Wilfrid Laurier University in Waterloo, Ontario, Canada.

Vincent Manzerolle is an Assistant Professor in the Department of Communication, Media and Film at the University of Windsor, Ontario, Canada. His teaching and research focuses on the history, political economy and theory of media. He has published on a range of topics including credit technologies, consumer databases, apps, wireless connectivity, and mobile payment systems, and he is a co-editor of *The Audience Commodity in a Digital Age*. His monograph, *Ubiquitous Connectivity and Virtual Workplace: Everything, Everywhere, All the Time*, was published in December 2022.

Jeffrey Orr is Associate Professor of Digital Communication at the University of the Fraser Valley in British Columbia, Canada. His research interests include visual rhetoric, border studies, and microrhetorical communication. His current research examines the rhetoric of governmental health communication, and public rhetoric pertaining to border policy on the Arctic.

Gillian Roberts is Professor of Contemporary Literature and Culture in the Department of American and Canadian Studies at the University of Nottingham in the UK. She is the author of *Race, Nation and Cultural Power in Film Adaptation* (2023), *Discrepant Parallels: Cultural Implications of the Canada–US Border* (2015), *Prizing Literature: The Celebration and Circulation of National Culture* (2011), editor of *Reading between the Borderlines: Cultural Production and Consumption across the 49th Parallel* (2018), and co-editor (with David Stirrup) of *Parallel Encounters: Culture at the Canada–US Border* (2013). She was Co-Investigator (with David Stirrup) of the Culture and the Canada–US Border international research network, funded by the Leverhulme Trust (2012–15).

David Stirrup is Professor of American Literature and Indigenous Studies at the University of York, UK. He is the author of *Visuality and Visual Aesthetics in Contemporary Anishinaabe Writing* (2020) and *Louise Erdrich* (2010), and co-editor of *Tribal Fantasies: Native Americans in the European Imaginary* (2012, with James Mackay),

Parallel Encounters: Culture at the Canada–US Border (2013, with Gillian Roberts) and *Enduring Critical Poses: Beyond Nation and History* (2021, with Gordon Henry, Jr and Margaret Noodin). He is Co-Principal Investigator of The Métis: A Global Indigenous People, funded by the AHRC (2023–5, with Chris Andersen); Indigenous Knowledges: A Digital Residency Exchange and Best Practices Pilot, funded by the AHRC-NEH (2022–3, with Jennifer Jenkins); Beyond the Spectacle: Native North American Presence in Britain, funded by the AHRC (2017–21, with Jacqueline Fear-Segal); and of the Culture and the Canada–US Border international research network, funded by the Leverhulme Trust (2012–15, with Gillian Roberts). He is a founding editor of the open access journal of contemporary Indigenous literature, *Transmotion*.

Index

49th parallel, 5, 9, 169, 201
9/11, 2–3, 18, 91, 105, 175–8, 184, 189, 204, 236

activism, 164, 180–1
affect 30, 33, 35, 41, 43–4, 45, 46, 161, 162, 164, 168
Afroperipheral, 163–4
Alaska, 3–4, 12, 218, 225, 226, 227, 228, 232
Alemán, Jesse, 175–7
Anishinaabe, 5, 114, 115, 116–20, 122, 126, 139, 140, 147, 219, 223
Anzaldúa, Gloria, 5–7, 114, 134, 136, 138, 141–2, 148
ArriveCan, 196
Atwood, Margaret, 33

biosecurity, 14, 16
Black
  border crossing, 174, 209
  citizenship, 168
  diaspora, 158, 206
  history, 17, 19, 159, 161–3, 165–7, 170, 175, 189
  -ness, 46, 206
  owned, 52, 159
  Pacific, 158
  poetry, 164
Blackfoot/Blackfeet, 218
'borderization' see Mbembe, Achille
borderlands and borderland practice, 1–6, 8, 53, 54, 86, 114, 115, 118, 123, 125, 137, 141, 143, 145–6, 176, 199, 201, 202, 203–4, 207, 217, 234
Border Media, 54, 56–7, 59, 63
border policing, 3, 9, 15, 17, 94, 184, 142, 149–50, 231, 234, 235, 236; see also Canadian Border Security Agency
Border Security: Canada's Front Line (television show), 29, 202
  state control of, 31
border theory, 1–2, 6–7, 9, 19, 132–5, 137–41, 143, 145, 148–9, 195–6, 197–8, 200–1, 204–6
British Columbia, 3, 19, 161–62, 165, 169–70, 174, 175, 177, 180, 222, 225, 226, 230, 238, 239
Bruyneel, Kevin, 5, 7, 133, 145–7, 149, 208; see also third space of sovereignty

Can-pass, 20, 196
Canadian Border Security Agency (CBSA)
  organisational identity and, 33–6, 196
  public awareness of, 31–2
  see also border policing
Christie, Stuart, 7, 144, 145; see also plural sovereignty
circulation, 53–6, 60, 62, 63–4, 65–6, 68, 136, 203
citizenship, 2, 6, 17, 32, 42, 89–90, 103–4, 118–19, 131–2, 133,

144, 146, 147, 159–64, 167–9,
  175–6, 180, 201, 206–7
Coast Salish, 177, 180, 188; see also
  Skwxwú7mesh
Code, Lorraine, 176, 177
colonialism, 12, 65, 119, 139–40,
  146, 175, 186, 189, 205; see
  also settler colonialism
continental liberty, 115, 117–19,
  123, 124–5, 139, 205
COVID-19, 11, 53, 196

Dawson City, 3
DeLanda, Manuel, 65
Derrida, Jacques, 175, 183, 185,
  187, 188–9
  hauntology, 164, 174, 206
  inheritor, 175, 187
  revenant, 183, 185, 188
  see also spectrality
Detroit, 12, 18, 52, 57–9, 61–2, 65,
  67–8, 72–3
Durham Peters, John, 62–3
Douglas, James, 165–6, 225

Foucault, Michel, 10–12, 14, 38
Fraser, Fil, 165
fur trade, 5, 17, 63, 66, 123–4, 216,
  218
frontier, 3, 14, 33, 57, 65, 87–8, 90,
  115, 136, 137, 139, 146, 203

ghosts, 179, 185, 186, 188–9
Gothic, 175, 181

Haudenosaunee, 142, 145, 147, 149,
  216, 217, 218, 219, 220, 229
hybridity, 1, 6, 135, 138, 140, 141,
  143, 145, 162, 195, 206

imperialism, 13, 179, 189
Indigenous
  artists and writers, 119, 133, 134
  legal and political struggles, 7,
  133, 137–8, 141, 208–9, 221,
222, 223, 226, 230, 234, 235,
  237
border crossing, 5–6, 15, 18, 132,
  142–6, 147, 148, 149, 204–5,
  206, 209
land and land claims, 3, 4, 12, 16,
  87, 88, 146, 175, 176–7, 179,
  180, 181, 183, 189, 201
(Literary) Studies, 6–7, 133, 135,
  136, 139, 142, 147, 149
nations, 4
people and settlers, 57, 87, 133,
  145, 149, 179, 183, 188, 201,
  216, 218–19
see also Anishinaabe; Coast Salish;
  Métis; Mohawk; Skwxwú7mesh;
  sovereignty
infrastructure, 3, 9–10, 11, 13, 15,
  17–18, 31–2, 52, 54–7, 59,
  61–6, 69, 72–3, 93, 203
Innis, Harold, 12, 59–61, 63–4, 67,
  73–4

Jay Treaty, the, 6, 15, 58, 66, 132,
  145, 221, 222, 223
Johnson, E. Pauline see Tekahionwake

Laine, Jussi P., 198, 207
Lake of the Woods, 16, 123, 125,
  126, 219, 222, 224, 230
liminal, liminality, 15, 62, 114, 116,
  135–6, 146, 159, 183, 198, 199,
  203, 204, 206–7
logistical media, 62, 71–2
logistics, 61–3, 71
London, Jack, 3, 14

Mbembe, Achille, 54, 55, 161, 202
Medicine Line, the, 4, 7, 17, 132,
  134, 218, 226
mereotopology, 198
Métis, 134, 165, 177, 225
Mexico–US border, the, 1–3, 6–8, 18,
  83, 85–6, 94–6, 98, 103, 133,
  176, 183, 195, 203, 235

Mignolo, Walter, 114, 205, 206
migration, 17, 18, 30, 33, 67, 85, 94, 119, 120, 124, 160, 161–2, 166–8, 170, 183
Mohawk, 5, 131, 148, 179, 180–1, 204, 208, 217, 219, 220, 233, 234, 235

Nail, Thomas, 6, 197
national identity formation, 39–40
nationalism
    formal and vernacular 8, 13, 30, 32, 33, 34, 42–3, 45–7, 176, 179, 202, 227
    inter-Indigenous-nationalism, 139
    literary nationalism, 139, 140, 149
    transnationalism, 135, 139, 197
natural reason, 115, 117–18, 120–1, 125–6, 139, 205
Nexus program, 16, 41, 236
Northwest Angle, 4, 9, 222

ontological security, 13–15, 16
Other, 14, 177, 186, 189, 199

pandemic *see* COVID-19
Point Roberts, 4, 9
Pratt, Mary Louise, 114, 144

racism, 30, 166
    Blackface, 186
recognition, 6, 132, 143, 149, 188, 219

Sault Ste Marie, 5, 234
Schimanski, Johan, 16, 200–1
security theatre
    as game show, 39–42
    as confession, 41–2
    as reality television 31, 42
settler colonialism, 12, 119
Simpson, Audra, 131–2, 134, 135, 141, 142, 145, 148, 149, 204, 208; *see also* nested sovereignty

Simpson, LeAnne Betasamosake, 147, 148; *see also sui generis* sovereignty
Skwxwú7mesh (Squamish), 180
Soja, Edward, 207
sovereignty, 19, 115, 117–19, 125, 132, 133, 138, 143, 148–9, 161, 176–7, 180, 181, 188, 197, 207–8, 222
    nested, 145, 208; *see also* Simpson, Audra
    overlapping, 144; *see also* Taylor, Christopher
    plural, 144; *see also* Christie, Stuart
    sui generis 146–7; *see also* Simpson, LeAnne Betasamosake
    third space of, 2, 5, 7, 145, 146, 147, 149, 208; *see also* Bruyneel, Kevin
space-time, 54, 60, 66, 71, 203
spectrality, 19, 175, 183, 187, 189, 207, 208–9
survivance, 18, 115, 117, 118, 120, 124–6, 138, 146, 205

Taylor, Christopher, 140, 144, 148; *see also* overlapping sovereignty
Tekahionwake, 179–81
    Legends of Vancouver, 179–80
territoriality, 119, 147, 198, 208
trickster, 115, 116, 117, 121–2, 126, 136, 138–41, 146, 149, 206

Vancouver, 11, 19, 29, 35, 43, 45, 100, 168, 174, 177, 178, 179, 181, 184–5, 186, 188, 225

Warroad, 126
White Earth Reservation, 116, 119, 121, 122, 123, 206
Windsor, 12, 18, 52, 57–9, 61–2, 65, 67–8, 72–3

Yukon, 3–4, 169, 228